Programming Chrome Apps

Marc Rochkind

Beijing · Cambridge · Farnham · Köln · Sebastopol · Tokyo

Programming Chrome Apps

by Marc Rochkind

Printed in the United States of America.

Published by O'Reilly Media, Inc., 1005 Gravenstein Highway North, Sebastopol, CA 95472.

O'Reilly books may be purchased for educational, business, or sales promotional use. Online editions are also available for most titles (*http://safaribooksonline.com*). For more information, contact our corporate/institutional sales department: 800-998-9938 or *corporate@oreilly.com*.

Editors: Brian MacDonald and Rachel Roumeliotis	**Indexer:** WordCo Indexing Services, Inc.
Production Editor: Matthew Hacker	**Cover Designer:** Ellie Volckhausen
Copyeditor: Bob Russell, Octal Publishing, Inc.	**Interior Designer:** David Futato
Proofreader: Eileen Cohen	**Illustrator:** Rebecca Demarest

January 2015:   First Edition

Revision History for the First Edition:

2014-12-12:   First release

See *http://oreilly.com/catalog/errata.csp?isbn=9781491904282* for release details.

ISBN: 978-1-491-90428-2

[LSI]

To Valerie, Gillian, and Claire

Table of Contents

Preface

Almost nobody reads past the first sentence or two of a preface, so I'll say the most important thing right away: *this book is about programming Chrome Apps, not Chrome Extensions or web apps in general.*

Still here? There's some more important stuff to know, so please continue.

Chapter 1 explains in detail what a Chrome App is, but briefly, its relationship to Chrome is the same as a Windows app to Windows, or a Mac app to OS X: an app that you install on the platform and that makes use of application program interfaces (APIs) unique to that platform. This would be obvious but for the fact that the platform in this case, Chrome, is better known as a web browser and most of the "apps" that you run on it are really just fancy web pages. I'm thinking of Gmail, Facebook, Amazon, and a zillion others. Hence the confusion.

Why consider programming a Chrome App at all? Here are two good reasons:

- They're portable across all of the major operating systems: Windows, Mac OS X, Linux, Chrome OS (for Chromebooks and Chromeboxes), and, with some restrictions, even Android and iOS.

- Although web apps are equally as portable, they can't access the local computer as Chrome Apps can. The most important example of this is that Chrome Apps can access the computer's filesystem, just as native apps can.

I'm unable to think of any other platform that offers these two advantages.

With the good comes the not-so-good. Here are the chief disadvantages of Chrome Apps:

- On desktop operating systems, they run only under Chrome (although they can have their own launch icon and they appear to run standalone).

- Although the Chrome API is extensive and growing, it isn't even close to encapsulating every native API.

A disclaimer: I'm not with Google, never have been, don't even know anyone who works on Chrome at Google, and Google didn't authorize this book. So, even though you won't get any inside info in this book, you will get an entirely objective viewpoint. If I think something is screwed up, I'll let you know.

What You Should Already Know

In the world of web-programming books, this one's fairly advanced, as I assume you already know JavaScript, HTML, CSS, and your way around the Document Object Model (DOM), which is a JavaScript object that represents the HTML elements of a web page. That said, my use of those technologies is fairly basic, so if you're rusty or don't mind jumping off a metaphorical cliff, you can read up on what I'm assuming you know as you encounter it.

Some popular technologies sometimes used to write Chrome Apps, such as jQuery and the AngularJS framework, aren't covered in this book, because they aren't specific to Chrome Apps and because they would obscure the example code. That code might be clearer to those who know these tools, but it would greatly inconvenience everyone else. Rather, I've tried to write the examples in the simplest possible way, using plain, unadulterated JavaScript. Another point is that cross-browser portability, an important benefit of these technologies ordinarily, is irrelevant when you're writing a Chrome App.

Why I Wrote This Book

I first wrote a Chrome App—then called a "Packaged App"—a few years ago when they were first released by Google. At that time, they were an offshoot of Chrome Extensions, and the documentation had the terminology for Apps and Extensions throughly confused. I got my app running, but it was obvious that apps for Chrome had a long way to go.

By late 2013, things had been cleaned up a lot. They were now called Chrome Apps, there were a lot more APIs, and the documentation was better, though still not well edited.

Meanwhile, Samsung had introduced a $250 Chromebook. I bought one and realized that for most of what I did when I wasn't downstairs in my office, it was just as good as my MacBook Air. I wasn't the only one to feel this way: today, Chromebooks are at or near the top of Amazon's laptop best-seller list.

So, here's the book I wish I'd had when I started with Chrome Apps. Now that it's in your hands, you can start way ahead of where I was.

Navigating This Book

At this point most prefaces describe what's in each chapter, but I've always thought that was silly because the same information is in the Table of Contents. I will say this much: read all of Chapter 1 carefully, even if you're in the habit of skipping the first chapter of any programming book, because that's where I explain how Chrome Apps are different from other things you run in a browser and, most important, their limitations relative to ordinary web pages. After that, I've written the rest to be read sequentially because later chapters build on earlier ones, but you can certainly skip around if you want.

There's lots of code in this book, but I usually explain it in small bites so that you can more easily digest it. That might make it hard for you to see what's going on in the app as a whole, so, as I go through an app, keep its code open in a text editor as a reference. See the section "Using Code Examples" on page xii a bit later in this Preface for information on how to get the code.

Online Resources

I'll refer to URLs for documentation throughout this book, but the most important one is Google's official Chrome App site at *developer.chrome.com/apps*. You'll want to look around that site right away, and you'll likely keep going back to it as you read this book.

Conventions Used in This Book

The following typographical conventions are used in this book:

Italic
: Indicates new terms, URLs, email addresses, filenames, and file extensions.

`Constant width`
: Used for program listings, as well as within paragraphs to refer to program elements such as variable or function names, databases, data types, environment variables, statements, and keywords.

 This element signifies a general note.

Using Code Examples

You can download supplemental material (code examples, exercises, and so on) at *https://github.com/oreillymedia/programming_chrome_apps*.

This book is here to help you get your job done. In general, if example code is offered with this book, you may use it in your programs and documentation. You do not need to contact us for permission unless you're reproducing a significant portion of the code. For example, writing a program that uses several chunks of code from this book does not require permission. Selling or distributing a CD-ROM of examples from O'Reilly books does require permission. Answering a question by citing this book and quoting example code does not require permission. Incorporating a significant amount of example code from this book into your product's documentation does require permission.

We appreciate, but do not require, attribution. An attribution usually includes the title, author, publisher, and ISBN. For example: "*Programming Chrome Apps* by Marc Rochkind (O'Reilly). Copyright 2015 Marc Rochkind, 978-1-491-90428-2."

If you feel your use of code examples falls outside fair use or the permission given above, feel free to contact us at *permissions@oreilly.com*.

Safari® Books Online

Safari Books Online is an on-demand digital library that delivers expert content in both book and video form from the world's leading authors in technology and business.

Technology professionals, software developers, web designers, and business and creative professionals use Safari Books Online as their primary resource for research, problem solving, learning, and certification training.

Safari Books Online offers a range of product mixes and pricing programs for organizations, government agencies, and individuals. Subscribers have access to thousands of books, training videos, and prepublication manuscripts in one fully searchable database from publishers like O'Reilly Media, Prentice Hall Professional, Addison-Wesley Professional, Microsoft Press, Sams, Que, Peachpit Press, Focal Press, Cisco Press, John Wiley & Sons, Syngress, Morgan Kaufmann, IBM Redbooks, Packt, Adobe Press, FT Press, Apress, Manning, New Riders, McGraw-Hill, Jones & Bartlett, Course Technology, and dozens more. For more information about Safari Books Online, please visit us online.

How to Contact Us

Please address comments and questions concerning this book to the publisher:

O'Reilly Media, Inc.
1005 Gravenstein Highway North
Sebastopol, CA 95472
800-998-9938 (in the United States or Canada)
707-829-0515 (international or local)
707-829-0104 (fax)

We have a web page for this book, where we list errata, examples, and any additional information. You can access this page at *http://bit.ly/programming_chrome_apps*.

To comment or ask technical questions about this book, send email to *bookquestions@oreilly.com*.

For more information about our books, courses, conferences, and news, see our website at *http://www.oreilly.com*.

Find us on Facebook: *http://facebook.com/oreilly*

Follow us on Twitter: *http://twitter.com/oreillymedia*

Watch us on YouTube: *http://www.youtube.com/oreillymedia*

Acknowledgments

I first met Tim O'Reilly in the late 1980s, after my book *Advanced UNIX Programming* had been out for a couple of years. He seemed to be publishing on all the hot Unix topics of the day. I went on to write three more books but never managed to do one with Tim's company. After decades of wishing I had an animal of my own, it's finally happened: I'm a crested screamer! Thanks, Tim, for all you've done for programmers over the years.

I'd also like to thank my editor, Brian MacDonald, for all of his astute comments; Heather Scherer, the project manager; and the technical reviewers, who helped greatly in improving the book. Thanks, too, go to Bob Russell, a terrific copyeditor, whose suggestions make the book seem like it was written by a better writer than me.

CHAPTER 1

Your First Chrome App

In this chapter, I'll take you step by step through building your first, simple Chrome App. I'll explain the key differences between a Chrome App and an ordinary web app of the sort with which you may already be familiar. I'll tell you how to run your app, how to use the new Chrome Dev Editor, and how to publish it to the Chrome Web Store.

From Web Apps to Chrome Apps

To build this first Chrome App, let's begin with something you already know how to build: a simple web app that converts meters to feet, as shown in Figure 1-1. To use the app, you enter an amount of meters in the first field and then click the Convert button. The app then displays the equivalent amount in feet in the second field.

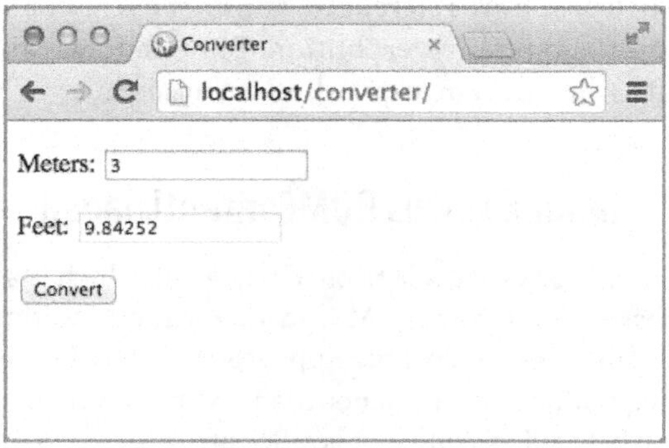

Figure 1-1. Converter web app running in Chrome

Like all web apps, the user interface for our sample app is built from an HTML file, (*index.html*), which you can see in the following:

```
<!DOCTYPE html>
<html lang="en">
<head>
    <meta charset="utf-8" />
    <title>Converter</title>
    <script src="converter.js"></script>
</head>
<body>
    <p>
        <label for="meters">Meters:</label>
        <input type="text" id="meters">
    </p><p>
        <label for="feet">Feet:</label>
        <input type="text" id="feet" readonly>
    </p><p>
        <button id="convert">Convert</button>
    </p>
</body>
</html>
```

The <script> tag brings in the following JavaScript, which is in the file *converter.js*:

```
window.onload = function () {
    document.querySelector("#convert").addEventListener("click",
        function () {
            var meters = document.querySelector("#meters");
            var feet = document.querySelector("#feet");
            feet.value = meters.value * 3.28084;
        }
    );
};
```

The code executes in the window.onload event handler to ensure that all of the HTML elements are loaded before they're referenced. Another event handler is set up to do the actual work when you click the Convert button. Both handlers are passed anonymous functions that execute when the corresponding event fires.

---

onload versus DOMContentLoaded

An alternative to the onload event is DOMContentLoaded, which is a little better for web pages because it fires as soon as the DOM is loaded without waiting for things such as images and styles. But, because all Chrome App resources must be local, the performance difference is inconsequential, and I prefer onload because I want to know that the entire interface is complete before I execute any JavaScript.

Use any text editor you like for these two files and all other source files you'll need. It's convenient to use an editor that can group files in a folder together, but that's not essential.

Two more small files turn this web app into a Chrome App. The first, *manifest.json*, identifies the web app as a Chrome App. The manifest is coded in JavaScript Object Notation (JSON) to define values for at least four required properties, like this:

```
{
    "app": {
        "background": {
            "scripts": [ "background.js" ]
        }
    },
    "manifest_version": 2,
    "name": "Converter",
    "version": "1.0.0"
}
```

Here are the properties:

app.background
: The name of the background script. This property is what identifies this app as a Chrome App, not something else such as an Extension.

manifest_version
: This is always 2, indicating that the app will use the second and newest version of the Chrome application programming interface (API).

name
: The name of the app.

version
: The version of the app, set to anything you like, as long as it's one to four dot-separated integers.

 Unlike the more relaxed rules for JavaScript, JSON requires that you enclose all keys in double-quotes.

The script file referenced from the manifest, *background.js*, is where execution begins. In contrast, processing for a web app begins with the HTML file. In practice, the JavaScript in a background script only sets up application-wide event handlers, leaving the bulk of the processing to the JavaScript referenced from the HTML file (*converter.js*, in this case).

The most important application-wide event is the chrome.app.runtime.onLaunched event, fired when the application launches. When that happens, an application usually wants to create a window in which to run the HTML file, like this, in *background.js*:

```
chrome.app.runtime.onLaunched.addListener(
    function () {
        chrome.app.window.create('index.html');
    }
);
```

There are a few other events that you might set up handlers for in your background script, such as `chrome.runtime.onInstalled` and `chrome.runtime.onSuspend`; I'll discuss those when we actually need them.

Keep in mind that, unlike other JavaScript files in your app, the background script can be unloaded by Chrome when it's inactive and then reloaded (executed from the top) when it becomes active again. As a result, it's important to do nothing there other than to add event listeners. Technically, the background script runs an *event page*, which can be unloaded, not a *background page*, which stays loaded. Chrome Apps can never have background pages, even though the `background` property is what appears in the manifest and the file is usually named *background.js*.

Chrome Apps don't need any kind of linker or packaging utility. You just put these four files (*index.html, converter.js, manifest.json*, and *background.js*) in a folder called, for example, *converter*, and you have a Chrome App.

If you'd like, you can use CSS for styling, and you can put it in any of the usual places: in the HTML file or in separate CSS files. Just remember that they need to be present in the app folder; you cannot download them from a website. You can also have several JavaScript files if you want, each referenced from a `<script>` tag in the HTML file. Again, make sure that all resources are local—inside the app folder.

Running a Chrome App

Here's what you do to run your Chrome App:

1. In Chrome, open the Extensions page, in either of two ways: you can access it by using the Window menu or the Chrome customization menu (the icon at the upper right of the Chrome window) or, in the address bar, you can type `chrome://exten sions`. ("Extensions" is somewhat of a misnomer, because the page is used for Chrome Apps as well as Extensions.)

2. Ensure that the "Developer mode" checkbox is checked.

3. Click the "Load unpacked extension" button and then select the Chrome App's folder.

4. After the app installs, click the Launch link, as shown in Figure 1-2.

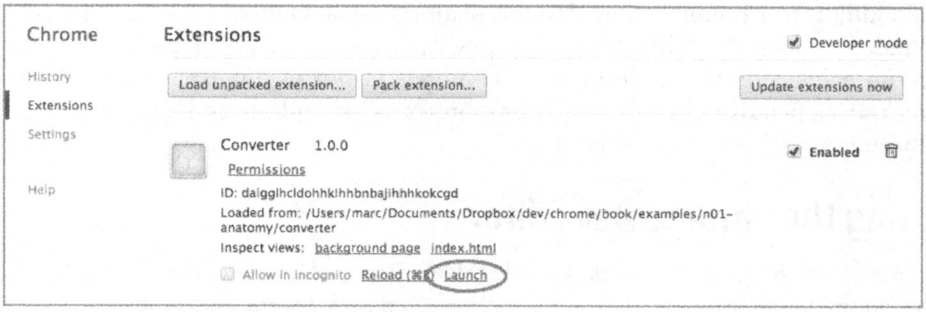

Figure 1-2. Converter Chrome App installed in Chrome

When the app launches, the `chrome.app.runtime.onLaunched` event is fired, its handler executes, a window is created, and you'll see the app running in its own window, as depicted in Figure 1-3.

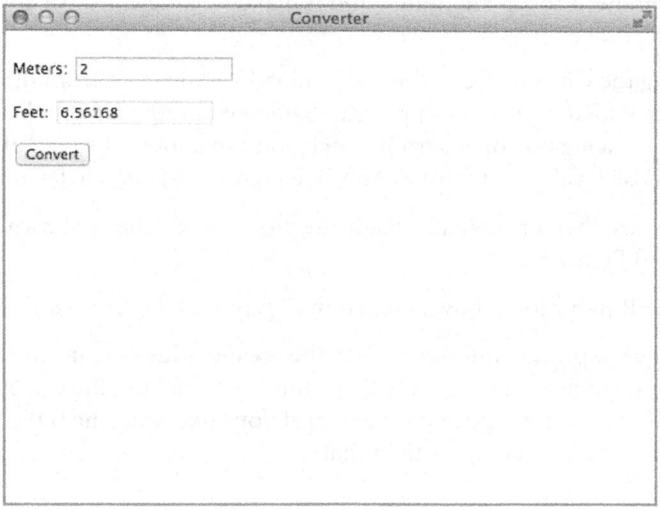

Figure 1-3. Converter Chrome App running

An app running in its own window is nifty, but there's a lot more to Chrome Apps besides that. Unlike web apps downloaded from a server, Chrome Apps have access to special APIs that can access files anywhere on the computer, carry out automatic file synchronization, access hardware (for example, audio, USB, and Bluetooth), and much more. That's what this book is about!

In addition to running on the desktop platforms that support Chrome (Mac OS X, Windows, Linux, and ChromeOS), Chrome Apps can use a technology called Cordova to run natively on the Android and iOS mobile platforms. I'll explain how Cordova works in Appendix D. (There are Chrome browsers for Android and iOS, but as of now, Chrome Apps don't run on them.)

Using the Chrome Dev Editor

As I was finishing up this book, Google released a developer preview of an integrated development enviroment (IDE) for Chrome called the Chrome Dev Editor. In addition to handling Chrome Apps written in JavaScript (what this book covers), you can also use the Dart language (a Google successor to JavaScript) and develop web apps in either language (along with HTML and CSS, of course).

Although the text editor built in to the Chrome Dev Editor is pretty minimal compared to what you're probably using, it does make testing easier by avoiding the need to load unpacked extensions from the Extensions page, it makes uploading to the Chrome Web Store easier (no need to zip anything), and it makes testing Cordova apps *much* easier (see Appendix D).

To begin using the Chrome Dev Editor, download and install it from the Chrome Web Store as you would any Chrome App. Next, launch it and then, from the menu, choose New Project. A dialog box opens from which you can choose the type of app you want to create. Choose JavaScript Chrome App (see Figure 1-4) and click Create.

The app's files are then created automatically, three of which are shown in Figure 1-5, Figure 1-6, and Figure 1-7.

Next, click the Run button (shown circled in Figure 1-7). Figure 1-8 shows the results.

To develop your app, you edit and modify the created files as you want, although you might prefer to switch to your favorite text editor for that. I use the Chrome Dev Editor only for building the initial app and for testing; I don't like using the IDE's built-in editor for anything much more complex than that.

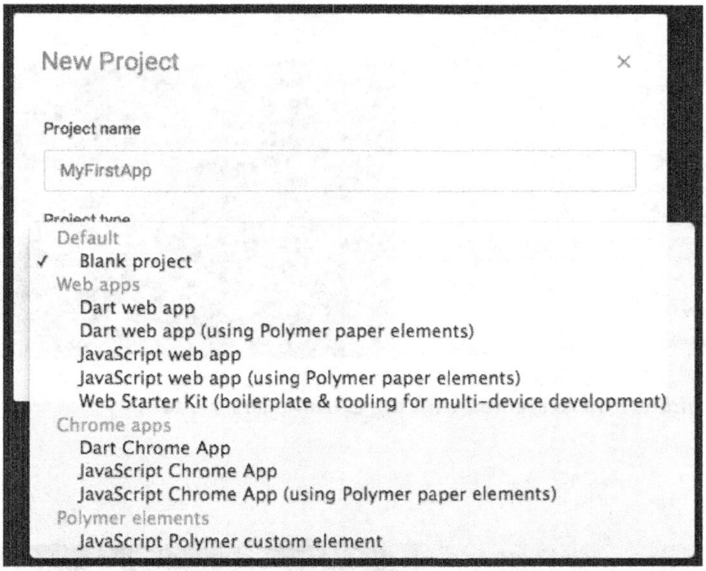

Figure 1-4. *Creating a new app with the Chrome Dev Editor*

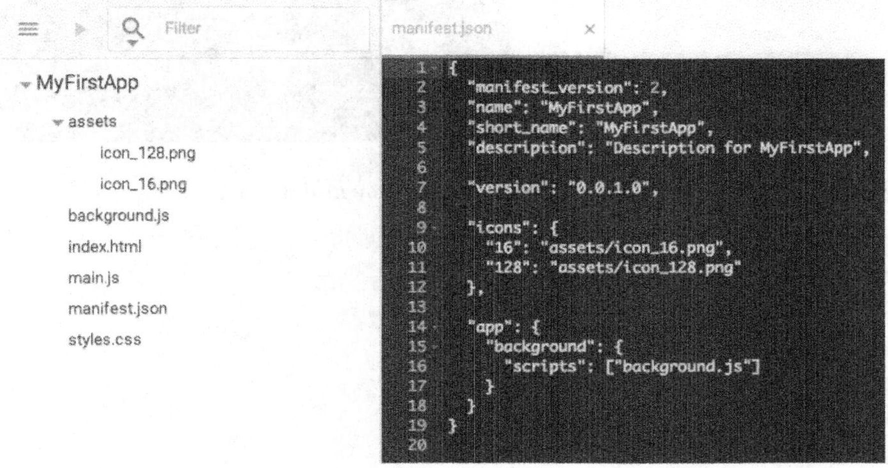

Figure 1-5. *manifest.json as created with the Chrome Dev Editor*

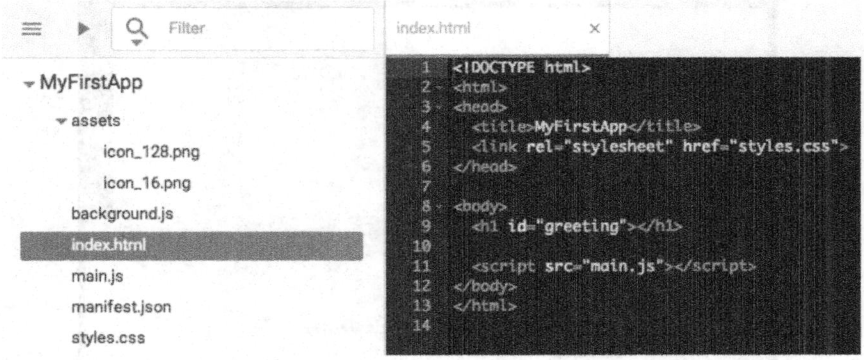

Figure 1-6. index.html as created with the Chrome Dev Editor

Figure 1-7. main.js as created with the Chrome Dev Editor

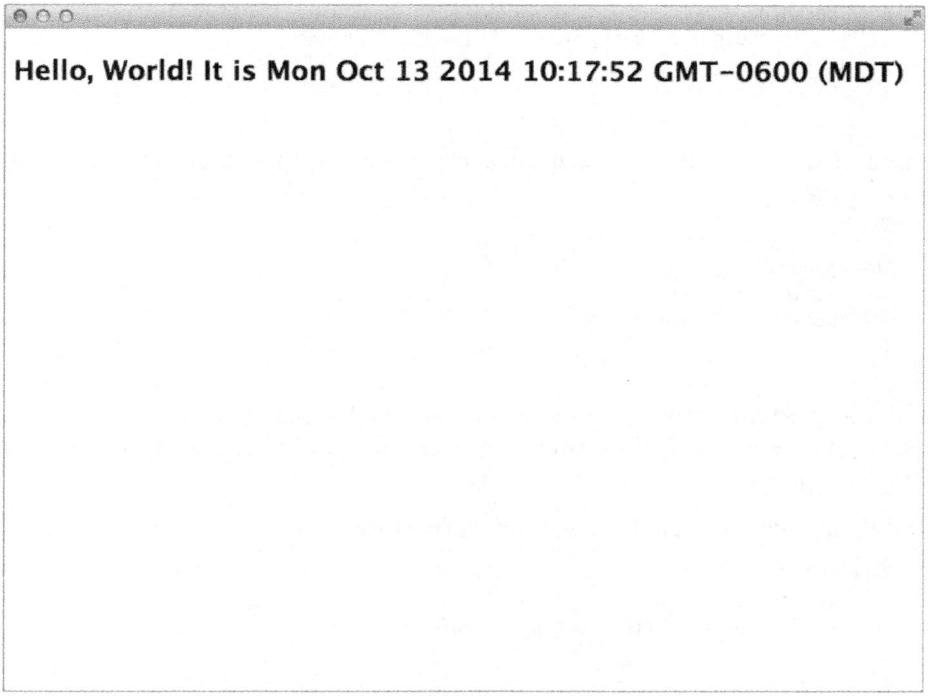

Hello, World! It is Mon Oct 13 2014 10:17:52 GMT−0600 (MDT)

Figure 1-8. Running the app created with the Chrome Dev Editor

Differences Among Chrome Apps, Chrome Extensions, and Hosted Apps

There are two other kinds of executables that run on Chrome but aren't the same as Chrome Apps and aren't covered by this book:

Chrome Extensions
These modify or extend the operation of the Chrome browser. Extensions also have access to special APIs, but they're generally different from Chrome App APIs.

Hosted Apps
These are just web-page URLs packaged up so that they can be uploaded to the Chrome Web Store. There are no special APIs for them.

The *manifest.json* file determines what kind of executable you have. As we've seen, Chrome Apps always have an `app.background.scripts` property in their *manifest.json* file, like this:

```
...
"app": {
```

```
    "background": {
        "scripts": [ "background.js" ]
    }
}
....
```

Chrome Extensions have a `background.scripts` property (`background` at the top level), as in the following:

```
...
"background": {
    "scripts": [ "eventpage.js" ],
    "persistent": false
}
....
```

(If the `persistent` property is omitted or `true`, the Extension has a background page instead of an event page; this distinction is absent from Chrome Apps, which always have event pages.)

Hosted Apps have an `app.launch` property, like this:

```
"app": {
    "launch": {
        "web_url": "http://basepath.com/"
    }
}
```

In the interest of being thorough with my description: Chrome Apps used to be called "Packaged Apps," a term still erroneously used by some people. Packaged Apps worked differently and had a different *manifest.json* format, and they're no longer supported by Chrome. Their manifest had an `app.launch.local_path` property:

```
"app": {
    "launch": {
        "local_path": "main.html"
    }
}
```

If you have old code with a manifest like this, you need to convert it to a Chrome App with the `manifest_version` property set to 2.

Again, in the interest of being thorough: there are also web apps with no *manifest.json* file at all that aren't installed into Chrome; they run when their URL is requested by a browser. These are just web pages that might run some JavaScript to give them an app-like user interface. There are zillions of these: Gmail, Amazon, Facebook, and so on. The web app that started this chapter is one of these, too.

Chrome App Restrictions

In return for running in its own window and getting access to the Chrome APIs, Chrome Apps have to live with some restrictions, mostly for security. After all, if an app is able to access hardware devices and any of the user's files, it had better play by some very strict rules, officially called the Content Security Policy (CSP). Let's take a look at these rules:

- There can be no JavaScript in any HTML files—not in a `<script>` element, and not as an attribute, like this:

    ```
    <button onclick='go();'>Go</button>
    ```

    Instead, you put any JavaScript in its own file (or files) and attach event listeners with JavaScript, as we saw in the Converter example.

- No navigation can appear in the HTML file, such as:

    ```
    <a href='page1.html'>Next Page</a>
    ```

    or:

    ```
    <form action="process_form.php" method="POST">
    ```

    You can still use forms, but all processing must be done in JavaScript via an event listener attached to a submit button. Instead of using multiple HTML pages to show various parts of the user interface, you must modify the document object model (DOM) in JavaScript. This is why apps such as Chrome Apps are sometimes called *single-page apps*.

- No on-the-fly compiling of strings to JavaScript with `eval`, `setTimeout`, `setInterval`, or `new Function` is allowed. In practice, even if you don't do these things, libraries you might want to use do, which makes finding libraries that work with Chrome Apps challenging. (`setTimeout` and `setInterval` with function callbacks are allowed.)

    This restriction prevents Cross-Site Scripting (XSS) attacks, in which JavaScript is injected into HTML.

- Access to external resources is restricted. For example, it's illegal to do this:

    ```
    <img src='http://basepath.com/images/shahn.jpg'>
    ```

    To access an external image, you must retrieve it as a blob from JavaScript, construct a blob URL, and show that in an image element. (You can see an example in Chapter 3.)

    If the image is inside the app folder, you are allowed to reference it locally, so you can treat any static images shipped with your app normally:

    ```
    <img src='logo.png'>
    ```

- None of the built-in dialogs, such as `alert` or `confirm`, can be used. Instead, you can pop up your own modal dialog, as I'll show in Appendix A. If you just want to display something for debugging, you can use `console.log` to write to the console.

- You cannot use cookies. Because cookies are local data sent to the server with HTTP requests, they're meaningless in Chrome Apps. Instead, there are several other ways to keep local data (see Chapter 3).

- You cannot use embedded processing plug-ins, such as Flash, Silverlight, or ActiveX.

- You cannot use a Web SQL database, which is nonstandard but is implemented in Chrome for non–Chrome-App pages. For Chrome Apps, there's a non-SQL IndexedDB API (Chapter 3).

Even though these restrictions might seem to be burdensome, they're mostly not a problem if you stop thinking of Chrome Apps as web apps and think of them instead as local, installed apps that can access the web. This is exactly the same mindset that Mac, Windows, and Linux programmers have had for years.

Although there's no way to test the theory, it's probably true that it's easier for someone who never heard of the web to learn to program Chrome Apps than it is for anyone familiar with developing for the web. But it's likely that if you're reading this book, you're in the latter group. So, programming Chrome Apps will be confusing at first, and you'll keep bumping into the restrictions (with mysterious error messages on the console), but after a while you'll catch on.

More on the Manifest

The *manifest.json* file for the Converter app used just the four required properties, but there are lots more properties, only a few of which you're likely to use unless you're doing something pretty exotic. Many of them aren't even documented.

There are three recommended properties (according to Google):

`default_locale`
A subdirectory of the *locales* directory (in the app folder) that contains the default strings. There's more on this in Chapter 6, in "Internationalization and Localization" on page 207.

`description`
A plain text string (no HTML) that describes the app. In a homage to mainframe line printers of 50 years ago, the length is limited to 132 characters. (OK, I'm kidding about the homage, but not the strange limit.)

`icons`

> One or more icons; you need only one for running on Chrome (as opposed to Cordova for mobile platforms).

There's no need for an icon during development, but you'll want one when you publish your app. Your icon should be 128 × 128 pixels; it will be resized as necessary by Chrome. Several image formats are supported, but PNG icons work best because they support transparency.

You can draw an icon using almost any graphics program. If you don't have one, you can download Gliffy Diagrams, a free Chrome App available from the Chrome Web Store.

Suppose that you have an icon file named `icon-128.png`. You would need to code the `icon` property in the manifest like this:

```
"icons": {
    "128": "icon-128.png"
}
```

Note that `"128"` is a string, like all JSON keys, not a number.

Although any 128 × 128 icon will work according to the Chrome API documentation, for the Chrome Web Store there are additional recommendations (e.g., margins) which you can read about in "Supplying Images" on the Chrome developer site (*http://bit.ly/supplying_images*).

The most important optional property is `permissions`, which I discuss in the next section. I'll explain any others you might want to use in conjunction with the API calls that they affect.

Permissions

Most of the Chrome APIs that are available only to Chrome Apps require a specific permission to be listed in the `permissions` property in the manifest. This is so the user can be prompted to agree to the permission when the app is installed from the Chrome Web Store. For example, Figure 1-9 shows what I saw when I tried to install UberConference:

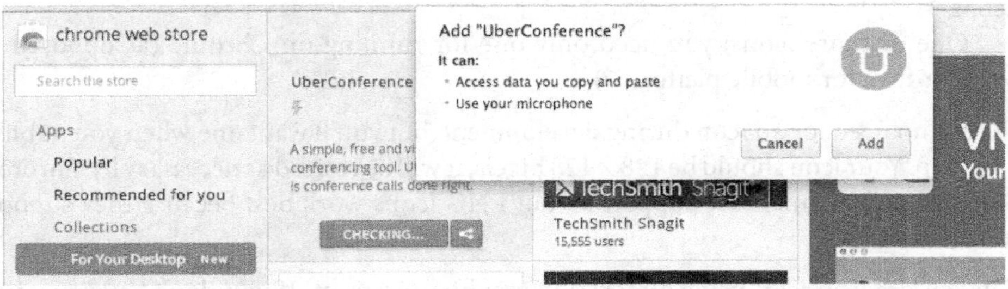

Figure 1-9. A permission-request dialog box

The dialog box included "Access data you copy and paste" because UberConference listed the `clipboardRead` and `clipboardWrite` permissions, and "Use your microphone" came from the `audio` permission, which was requested in the manifest, something like this:

```
"permissions": [
    "clipboardRead",
    "clipboardWrite",
    "audio"
]
```

You can read through the list of permissions on the Chrome developer site (*http://bit.ly/ declare_permissions*). I'll introduce specific permissions as we proceed, along with the APIs that need them.

Debugging Chrome Apps

Suppose that you have a bug, such as in the following example where `feet` is misspelled on the last line of the `click` event handler (`"use strict"` makes that a detectable error):

```
"use strict";
window.onload = function () {
    document.querySelector("#convert").addEventListener("click",
        function () {
            var meters = document.querySelector("#meters");
            var feet = document.querySelector("#feet");
            feat.value = meters.value * 3.28084;
        }
    );
};
```

When you click the button, the Developer Tools debugger shows you exactly where and what the problem is. Figure 1-10 shows that in this case, it's a `ReferenceError`, which you can see in the panel on the right.

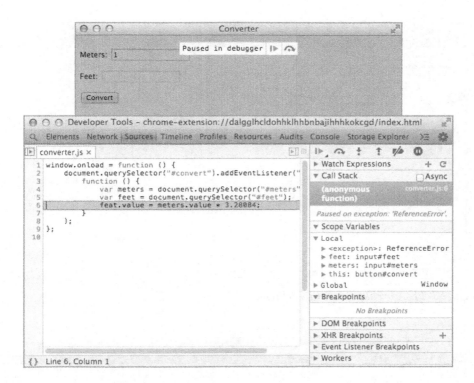

Figure 1-10. The Developer Tools debugger gives the location of a bug

You can also set breakpoints by clicking on the line number in the margin, as shown in Figure 1-11. Then, when you click the button, execution pauses, as shown in Figure 1-12.

As with most debuggers, you can use the Developer Tools debugger to single-step, go into and out of functions, inspect variables, and so forth. You can read more and even watch some videos at *developer.chrome.com/devtools*.

An even more useful Developer Tools tab is the Console. Here, you can see error messages generated by Chrome and your own debugging output that you write with the console API. For more documentation on this, go to the Console API Reference (*http://bit.ly/console_api*).

The call I use the most is `console.log` to write messages to the log, as demonstrated in Figure 1-13, which I got by adding one line:

```
var meters = document.querySelector("#meters");
console.log(meters);
var feet = document.querySelector("#feet");
feet.value = meters.value * 3.28084;
```

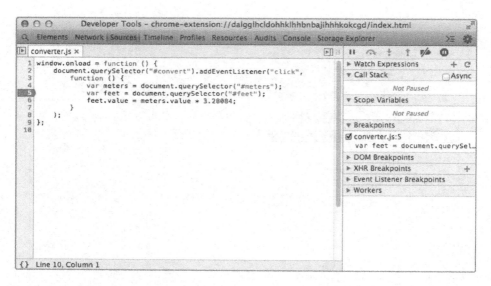

Figure 1-11. A breakpoint set in debugger

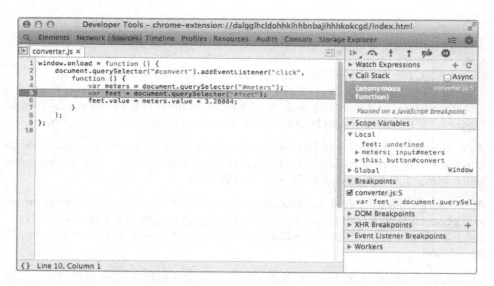

Figure 1-12. App paused at the breakpoint

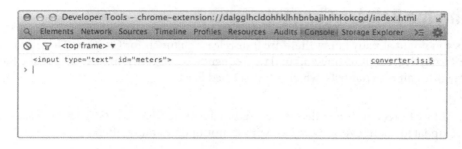

Figure 1-13. Value displayed as HTML

If you want to see the JavaScript object (see Figure 1-14), use `console.dir` instead:

```
var meters = document.querySelector("#meters");
console.dir(meters);
var feet = document.querySelector("#feet");
feet.value = meters.value * 3.28084;
```

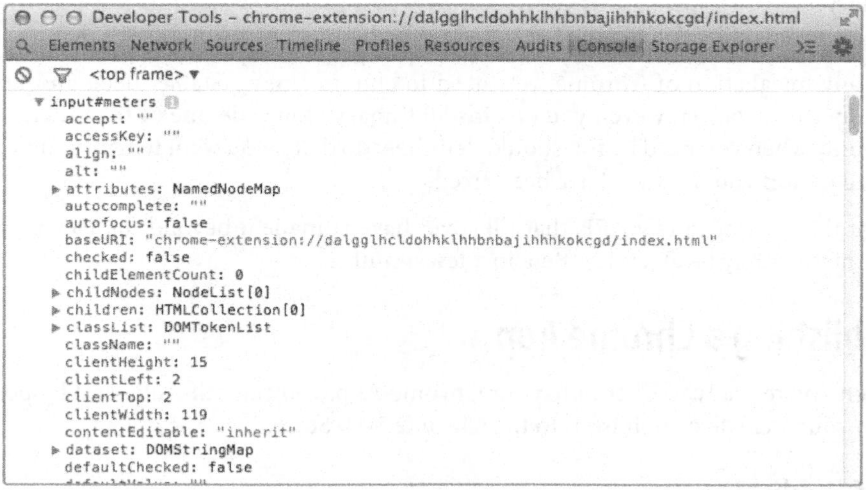

Figure 1-14. Value displayed as JavaScript object

There are additional console API calls for assertions, error logging, and getting a stack trace, which you can read about in the Console API Reference (*https://develop er.chrome.com/devtools/docs/console-api*).

Chrome Release Channels

As you might already know, there are four release channels for Chrome. These provide differing degrees of testing and update frequency. As releases mature, they make their way through the channels, which are described here:

Stable
> Most tested, and intended to be used by most nondevelopers. These releases are updated about every six weeks, with minor updates more often.

Beta
> A release due to become stable as soon as it's fully tested, subjected to field testing as a beta, and had some remaining bugs fixed. That takes about a month. Major updates occur about every six weeks, with minor updates oftener.

Dev
> More buggy than beta. These are updated once or twice a week, with no lag for major versions.

Canary
> Updated daily. You get the latest code, whether it works or not.

For any installation of Chrome, you need to choose among Stable, Beta, and Dev. (I usually run Beta.) However, you can install Canary alongside one of the others, to be run only when you need it. You should definitely do that if you want to try out new APIs or see if bugs you discover have been fixed.

As of this writing, a few APIs that I'll cover haven't made it beyond the Dev channel, but they'll surely be at least in Beta in a few months.

Publishing a Chrome App

When you're ready to distribute your Chrome App, you can self-publish it by posting it on your website or publish it to the Chrome Web Store.

Self-Publishing

To self-publish your Chrome App, you first need to pack it into a form of ZIP file called a CRX file (filename ending with *.crx*), which you do by clicking the "Pack extension" button on the Chrome Extensions page (make sure "Developer mode" is checked). Then, you copy that CRX file to your website and put a link to it somewhere so that your users can download it.

There's no "Load packed extension" button to go with "Load unpacked extension," which you use during development. Instead, the user must find the downloaded CRX file by using the Mac Finder, Windows Explorer, Chrome OS Files app, or whatever Linux equivalent he or she is using, and drag it to the Chrome Extensions page. A dialog box should then display, asking the user to confirm that he or she wants to install it.

Note that on ChromeOS, the file can't be on the Google Drive; the user must place it in the *Downloads* directory or on an external device (hard drive, USB stick, or SD card).

The installation instructions are somewhat tricky, so you might find that self-publishing is much less convenient than using the Chrome Web Store.

Publishing on the Chrome Web Store

Unlike Apple, which has a fairly rigorous, arbitrary, and slow (measured in weeks) approval process for its store, Google doesn't seem to care what's put into its store, and it makes new and updated apps available within hours. You can even upload apps that are restricted to a group of testers. When I signed up, there was a one-time fee of $5 to use the store (Apple charges about $100 per year).

You need a ZIP file of the app's folder (ending with *.zip*), not a CRX file. And, be aware that you can't just change the filename of a CRX file to end with *.zip*, because it's not exactly a ZIP file. You have to zip the folder by using whatever your operating system's file browser (Finder, Windows Explorer, Chrome OS Files app, and so on) provides or by using a separate ZIP utility.

To begin, go to the Chrome Developer Dashboard (*http://bit.ly/developer_dashboard*), sign in with your Google account (if you're not already signed in), and pay the fee. Next, click the "Add new item" button and upload your app. You'll then be presented with a form where you enter a detailed description; the app's icon (the same file that's referenced by the manifest, in most cases); some screenshots; some promotional tile images; your website URL; the regions where you want the app distributed; the pricing (if it isn't free); the language; whether it's "mature content"; and whether it's for all users, only people with the link, or just trusted testers, possibly including members of a Google Group that you own or manage. I won't go into the details of all these fields; Google has lots of documentation and advice to which you can refer.

After your app is in the store, anyone you've allowed to access it can install it right from the store, without dealing with the Extensions page at all.

The Chrome Dev Editor automates the job of zipping and uploading your app, although you still have to fill out the submission form the usual way. From the menu, just choose Publish to Chrome Web Store.

Chapter Summary

In this chapter we explored how to build a minimal Chrome App; identified its principal parts such as the *manifest.json* file; and saw how to run it, debug it, and publish it.

Now you're ready to start exploring the Chrome APIs, many of which are available only to Chrome Apps.

CHAPTER 2

Local Files, Sync Files, and External Files

The subject of this chapter and that of Chapter 3 is storage outside of an app's memory that persists from launch to launch. Chrome Apps can access seven types of storage (see Table 2-1), which offer the following three kinds of data structures:

files
> Named files organized by a hierarchy of directories

KVP
> Key-value pairs, which are a collection of keys and their values

indexed KVP objects
> Key-value pairs organized into objects that are indexed for speedy access

Some storage is *sandboxed*, which means that it's accessible only to the app, determined by the app ID, and kept separately for each user, determined by his or her Google account. Storage might also be synchronized (*synced*, for short, which we'll use throughout this chapter and elsewhere in the book), which means that it's automatically copied to multiple computers to keep them consistent.

As Table 2-1 shows, Local Files and IndexedDB are standard APIs available to any web page, whereas the others are only for Chrome Apps.[1] There is a standard API for Local Storage, as well, but it's not available to Chrome Apps, and the Chrome API variant is better anyway. Some browsers, including Chrome, implement a Web SQL Database API, but it's not available to Chrome Apps either.

We explore the first three types of storage in this chapter, Chapter 3 discusses the three KVP storage types, and Chapter 5 looks at Media Galleries.

---

1. Some are available to Extensions, but my focus is on Chrome Apps.

Table 2-1. Storage available to Chrome Apps

Storage	Structure	Sandboxed?	Sync?	Chrome Apps only?
Local Files	file	yes	no	no
Sync Files	file	yes	yes	yes
External Files	file	no	no	yes
Local Storage	KVP	yes	no	yes
Sync Storage	KVP	yes	yes	yes
IndexedDB	indexed KVP objects	yes	no	no
Media Galleries	file	no	no	yes

The file-structured storage types provide different APIs for getting at files, but after you access a file, they use the same API for reading, writing, truncating, and seeking via a `FileEntry` object. That common API is discussed in the next section.

We'll start out with a simple note-taking example—let's call it the Note app to make it easy on ourselves—using Local Files. Then, we'll enhance it to use Sync Files. Finally, we'll turn it into a simple text editor by modifying it to use External Files. Chapter 3 continues the example by adding options for colors that are stored in Local Storage and then Sync Storage. It's best to read this and the next chapters sequentially so that you can follow the example code.

Local Files

Local files have many of the features you'd expect: hierarchical directories, random access, and reading and writing. What they don't have is any way to access them outside of a single app's sandbox. They're tied to an app ID and user and hidden very deeply in the computer's filesystem.

To give you an idea of how hidden, the example file that I use for demonstration in this chapter is stored on my computer here:

/Users/marc/Library/Application Support/Google/Chrome/ Default/Storage/ext/ jncbmmfnahjgnlehenndimadigaignfl/ def/File System/primary/p/00/00000001

The name I gave it, *note.txt* is nowhere to be found. That's because it's inside a Google LevelDB database, also stashed in an obscure place. So, a local file isn't meant to be seen by anything outside the app that created it. That limitation aside, we can still build a note-taking app that saves its text in a local file and then retrieves it again when it's relaunched.

 Occasionally, you need to know an app's ID. To find it, go to the Extensions page and look in the app's section, as illustrated in Figure 2-1.

Storage–Local   1.0.0   ☑ Enabled   🗑
    Permissions   Not from
    ID: fdigabifhligdjlmnkhaadijffmjocal   Chrome Web
    Inspect views: background page index.html   Store.
    ☐ Allow in Incognito

Figure 2-1. Getting an ID for an app

Local files were introduced by the World Wide Web Consortium (W3C) as part of its HTML5 development, and they're available to all Chrome web pages, not just Chrome Apps. The file API that they use is also used with the Chrome-App-only APIs, so it's important that you understand how to use it. I'll explain the basics here—everything we'll need to work with the apps in this book. For more detailed information on this, read *Using the HTML5 Filesystem API* by Eric Bidelman (O'Reilly).

To use local files, you proceed in steps, and there are more steps than you'd think would be needed. First, you get a filesystem, then a directory entry, then a file entry, then a file writer, then a blob, and, finally, you write the blob. As we build the Note app, I'll break down the steps into separate functions so that you can follow what's going on. Otherwise, the cascade of callbacks would be impenetrable.

The Note app is pretty simple, as you can see in Figure 2-2. There's a text area in which you can type and a Save button that you click to save your work. When you launch the app, what you've previously saved appears in the text area.

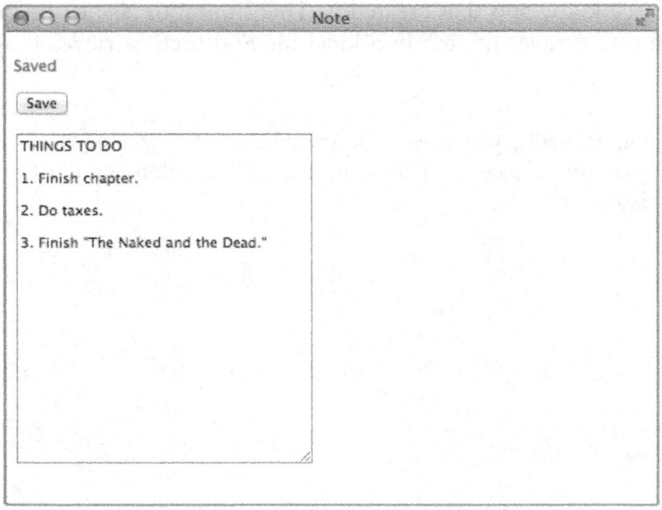

Figure 2-2. Our Note app after saving

The app's *background.js* file is exactly the same as the one for the Converter app we created in Chapter 1, and its manifest is almost the same, except for a permission that I'll describe shortly. The *index.html* is about what you'd expect:

```
<!DOCTYPE html>
<html lang="en">
<head>
    <meta charset="utf-8" />
    <title>Note</title>
    <script src="note.js"></script>
</head>
<body>
    <p id="message"> </p>
    <button id="save">Save</button>
    <p><textarea id="textarea" cols="30" rows="20"></textarea></p>
</body>
</html>
```

FileSystem and DirectoryEntry

An app can't just begin manipulating files without a formal introduction. It must first request a filesystem and a space allocation with a call to requestFileSystem:

```
requestFileSystem(type, size, successCallback, errorCallback)
```

type is either PERSISTENT, which means that the data you write stays until you delete it, or TEMPORARY, which means that the browser can delete the data if it wants to, like a cache. The W3C standard doesn't say how long a browser is obligated to keep temporary storage, but you can assume it will stay around at least as long as the app is running.

The idea behind the `size` argument is that the user might be asked to approve that amount of space. However, Chrome Apps never do that. Instead, my testing indicates that you need to request the `unlimitedStorage` permission in the manifest, like this:

```
{
    "app": {
        "background": {
            "scripts": [ "background.js" ]
        }
    },
    "manifest_version": 2,
    "name": "Note",
    "version": "1.0.0",
    "permissions": [
        "unlimitedStorage"
    ]
}
```

I've seen some documentation that suggests the user has to agree to this permission when the app is installed, but I've never seen that with an actual app.

Chrome OS calls this API `webkitRequestFileSystem`, whereas Cordova (an Android/iOS platform for Chrome Apps, which is discussed in Appendix D) calls it `requestFileSystem`, so it's best to figure out which it is and call that one. You can see this technique in the `onload` handler, which also sets up the Save button:

```
window.onload = function () {
    var requestFileSystem = window.webkitRequestFileSystem ||
        window.requestFileSystem;
    requestFileSystem(PERSISTENT, 0, haveFileSystem, errorHandler);
    document.querySelector("#save").addEventListener("click", save);
};
```

The `requestFileSystem` API is the first of many that we'll see that are *asynchronous*. This means that it returns right away, but with its actual work deferred until later. Because JavaScript is single-threaded, that can't happen until the `onload` handler returns, but when it actually happens is outside of the app's control. When the request is ready, the success callback `haveFileSystem` is called (we'll see it soon).

Using Asynchronous Calls Correctly

If you've used another programming language for which system calls are mostly synchronous, you might be tempted to request a filesystem like this:

```
var fs = requestFileSystem(PERSISTENT, 0); // wrong
```

If you do this in a Chrome App, you'll find that `fs` is `undefined`. Perhaps a more common mistake is to make the call correctly but assume that you can use the results right away:

```
var fileSystem;
requestFileSystem(PERSISTENT, 0,
    function (fs) {
        fileSystem = fs;
    }
);
fileSystem.root.getDirectory("Note", gotDirectory); // wrong
```

Any processing that needs the `FileSystem` must be deferred until the `requestFileSystem` success callback has been called (no need for the global):

```
requestFileSystem(PERSISTENT, 0,
    function (fs) {
        fs.root.getDirectory("Note", gotDirectory);
    }
);
```

The code in the Note app example is structured a bit differently, but you'll see that all processing that depends on the result of an asynchronous call is properly sequenced.

The error callback is `errorHandler`, which goes to considerable lengths to figure out where a useful error message might be. We'll use this error handler over and over; in the interest of brevity, I won't show the code each time we use it in an app, so here it is:

```
function errorHandler(e) {
    console.dir(e);
    var msg;
    if (e.target && e.target.error)
        e = e.target.error;
    if (e.message)
        msg = e.message;
    else if (e.name)
        msg = e.name;
    else if (e.code)
        msg = "Code " + e.code;
    else
        msg = e.toString();
    showMessage('Error: ' + msg);
}
```

Showing Transient Messages

We'll be calling `showMessage`—which is what the `errorHandler` calls—any time we need to display a message to the user, not only in the Note app, but throughout this book. We don't want messages to stay around forever, because after a while they're no longer meaningful. For example, the message "Saved" is fine just after a save, but when the user begins typing it's misleading. So, we use a timer to get rid of a message after five seconds:

```
var timeoutID;

function showMessage(msg, good) {
    console.log(msg);
    var messageElement = document.querySelector("#message");
    messageElement.style.color = good ? "green" : "red";
    messageElement.innerHTML = msg;
    if (timeoutID)
        clearTimeout(timeoutID);
    timeoutID = setTimeout(
        function () {
            messageElement.innerHTML = " ";
        },
        5000
    );
}
```

Recall that there was a <p> element with the ID message in *index.html*. We clear the message by setting to a nonbreaking space (rather than an empty string) so that the vertical layout in the window won't change as messages come and go.

Curly Braces

In his terrific book *JavaScript: The Good Parts* (O'Reilly), Douglas Crockford suggests using curly braces for all if statements, even when the body is a single statement. Following those recommendations, the errorHandler function would be coded like this:

```
function errorHandler(e) {
    console.dir(e);
    var msg;
    if (e.target && e.target.error) {
        e = e.target.error;
    }
    if (e.message) {
        msg = e.message;
    }
    else if (e.name) {
        msg = e.name;
    }
    else if (e.code) {
        msg = "Code " + e.code;
    }
    else {
        msg = e.toString();
    }
    showMessage('Error: ' + msg);
}
```

As you've noticed, I don't follow Crockford's curly-brace advice, mostly because I don't like the added clutter. But Crockford is probably right, and I'm a bad example.

Getting DirectoryEntrys

Getting back to the requestFileSystem call in the onload handler, the haveFileSystem function receives the requested filesystem:

```
var directoryEntry;

function haveFileSystem(fs) {
    fs.root.getDirectory("Note",
        {
            create: true,
            exclusive: false
        },
        function (de) {
            directoryEntry = de;
            read();
        },
        errorHandler
    );
}
```

Here we get a DirectoryEntry for the directory to hold the note:

```
getDirectory(path, options, successCallback, errorCallback)
```

The path can have multiple levels, but any parent directories in it must already exist. The options argument can have two optional Boolean keys. The first, create, means that the directory is created if necessary; if create is missing or false, the call fails if the directory isn't there. If the second option, exclusive, is true, creation fails if the directory already exists. If neither option is true, the call succeeds only if the directory exists. Most commonly, you specify create: true when you want to create the directory if needed, which is what we did here, and no options if the directory must already exist. (It's meaningless for both create and exclusive to be true.)

There's no concept of getting a DirectoryEntry for reading or writing; it can always do both.

You can also remove a directory and all its contents, across multiple levels:

```
removeRecursively(successCallback, errorCallback)
```

You can read the contents of a directory by using the createReader method, but I won't go into the details.

Looking back at the success callback, we save the DirectoryEntry for later use and call read to read the note and display it in the text area. We'll see read itself soon.

Getting FileEntrys and Creating FileWriters

Given a `DirectoryEntry`, you can also get a `FileEntry` by using the call:

```
getFile(path, options, successCallback, errorCallback)
```

This call is much like `getDirectory`, except that the success callback gets a `FileEntry`. Because there are a couple places in the Note app where we'll need a `FileEntry`, there's a function to get one:

```
var fileEntry;
var fileWriter;

function getFileEntry(callback) {
    if (fileWriter)
        callback();
    else if (directoryEntry) {
        directoryEntry.getFile('note.txt',
            {
                create: true,
                exclusive: false
            },
            function (fe) {
                fileEntry = fe;
                fileEntry.createWriter(
                    function (fw) {
                        fileWriter = fw;
                        callback();
                    },
                    errorHandler
                );
            },
            errorHandler
        );
    }
}
```

The only file this app needs is *note.txt* in the directory we already have an entry for, *Note*. If `getFile` succeeds, we save the `FileEntry` it got in the global `fileEntry` and go on to create a `FileWriter` by using the call:

```
createWriter(successCallback, errorCallback)
```

By now, you're getting into the swing of things, so you've probably already guessed that the `FileWriter` is passed to the success callback—and you're right! We save it in the global `fileWriter`. Then, with both the `FileEntry` and a `FileWriter` saved, we call the callback. Note that the `errorHandler` we saw earlier is used for the error callbacks.

Writing a File with the FileWriter API

The `FileWriter` methods are:

```
write(data);
truncate(size);
seek(offset);
```

You write a `Blob` by using `write`, always at the current position, which you can query (but not change) by referencing the read-only `position` property. To change it, you call `seek`, which is the only one of the three methods that's synchronous, because all it does is set a property. Another property is `length`, and you can change that by using the `truncate` method.

Blobs

A JavaScript `Blob` represents raw data constructed from an `Array` of parts, each of which can be, among other things, a string or a `Blob`, as shown in the following example:

```
var blob = new Blob(["Here's a string."], {type: 'text/plain'});
```

Note that the first argument is an `Array`, not a plain string.

A `File` object, which is what you get when you read a `FileEntry`, is a subclass of `Blob`. Think of a `File` as the data in a file, not the file itself as it exists on the filesystem.

There are various methods and properties of a `Blob` and a `File` that you might need at some point, but I won't go into them here, because all we need for the Note app is the constructor. You can read all about them in a good JavaScript book such as *JavaScript: The Definitive Guide* by David Flanagan (O'Reilly). Or, you can go to the entry for `Blob` on the Mozilla Developer Network (*http://bit.ly/blob_mdn*).

If a file exists, setting `create: true` when we get its `FileEntry` has no effect, unlike with most other operating systems, for which a "create" option truncates an existing file. With the `FileWriter` APIs, if you want to truncate the file, you must do it explicitly, and, because that's asynchronous, you have to ensure that truncation is complete before you write. That's what the `save` function (the Save button `click` handler) does:

```
function save() {
    getFileEntry(
        function() {
            fileWriter.onwrite = function(e) {
                fileWriter.onwrite = function(e) {
                    dirty = false;
                    showMessage("Saved", true);
                };
                var blob = new Blob([document.querySelector("#textarea").value],
                    {type: 'text/plain'});
                fileWriter.write(blob);
            };
            fileWriter.onerror = errorHandler;
```

```
            fileWriter.truncate(0);
        }
    );
}
```

The handler calls `getFileEntry`, which we just saw. When the callback is executed, we have a `FileWriter` (saved earlier in the global `fileWriter`), and we use the `FileWrit er` API to truncate the file and write the contents of the text area to it as a `Blob`. (Ignore the setting of the `dirty` flag for now; I'll explain it later in this chapter.)

It's very important that the `write` occur after the `truncate` has completed, which is how the `save` is coded. Don't do it this way:

```
fileWriter.truncate(0);
fileWriter.write(blob); // wrong -- truncate not completed
```

You might think that `truncate` is fast enough so that it's likely to complete before the `write` is issued, but the single-threadedness of JavaScript makes that impossible, because the `truncate` can't even begin until JavaScript execution returns to the system. For the same reason, in the `save` function, it doesn't matter whether you set the `onwrite` handler before or after you issue the `FileWriter` operation.

After you've written to a file, although it's very difficult to find it on your computer's filesystem, you can easily view it in the Developer Tools Resources tab, as shown in Figure 2-3.

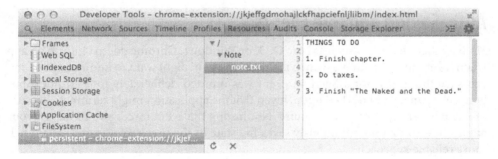

Figure 2-3. note.txt shown in Developer Tools

Reading a File

Now let's look at `read`, which was called from `haveFileSystem` after we got the `DirectoryEntry`:

```
function read() {
    getFileEntry(
        function() {
            if (fileEntry)
```

```
                fileEntry.file(haveFile, errorHandler);
        }
    );
}

function haveFile(file) {
    var reader = new FileReader();
    reader.onload = function() {
        document.querySelector("#textarea").value = reader.result;
    };
    reader.readAsText(file);
}
```

The `read` function calls `getFileEntry`, just as `save` did, but this time we call the `Fil` `eEntry` method `file` to get a `File` object (a subclass of a `Blob`), which is passed to the `haveFile` success callback. With the `File`, we create a `FileReader` object, call its `read` `AsText` message with the `File` as the argument, and then stick the result into the text area when it's available.

 It might seem strange that writing and reading are done completely differently: you get a `FileWriter` from the `FileEntry` when you want to write, but you get a `File` (a `Blob`) from the `FileEntry` when you want to read, and create the `FileReader` separately. You could argue that a `FileEntry` should deliver a `FileReader`, so reading is more like writing, but that's not the way they designed it.

Auto-Saving and Idle Events

Unlike other platforms, such as Mac OS X or Windows, Chrome doesn't inform an app when it's about to terminate, which is something you might want to know about so you can save the user's work. Such an event was omitted deliberately for Chrome Apps because it can never be relied upon, given that the application might terminate because of a computer crash or power failure. Not having the event forces you to design your application so that it continuously saves the state of the user's work, which is a much more reliable approach.

But first, before we can implement auto-saving, we have to know if the user changed anything. In the simple Note app, there's only the text area to worry about, and we can observe changes there by listening for four text-area events: `keypress`, `paste`, `cut`, and `change`. But, none of those four fires when the text is changed by pressing the Backspace or Delete keys, so you need to test for those actions explicitly by listening for a `key` `down` event and checking the `keyCode` property of the event against 8 and 46, the codes for backspace and delete. Upon any change, a global flag, `dirty`, is set:

```
var dirty = false;

function setupAutoSave() {
    var taElement = document.querySelector("#textarea");
    taElement.addEventListener("keypress", didChange);
    taElement.addEventListener("paste", didChange);
    taElement.addEventListener("cut", didChange);
    taElement.addEventListener("change", didChange);
    taElement.addEventListener("keydown", didChange);
}

function didChange(e) {
    if (e.type !== 'keydown' ||
      e.keyCode === 8 || e.keyCode === 46) // backspace or delete
        dirty = true;
}
```

Listening for a change event is insufficient by itself, because it only fires when the text area loses focus, and that might not happen for minutes, or even hours, which isn't safe.

We add a call to setupAutoSave to the end of the onload handler:

```
window.onload = function () {
    // ...
    setupAutoSave();
};
```

Now, the dirty flag indicates whether the text has been changed since the last save. Looking back at the code for the save function, that's why the flag was turned off with a successful save:

```
function save() {
    // ...
                fileWriter.onwrite = function(e) {
                    dirty = false;
                    showMessage("Saved", true);
                };
    // ...
}
```

There are a couple of ways to save automatically:

- Checking the dirty flag at regular intervals, such as every 15 seconds
- Checking the flag when the app becomes idle; that is, no user input for a defined interval

Waiting until the app is idle is a little better because there's no point saving while the user is actively typing. That's easy to implement with the chrome.idle API:

```
chrome.idle.setDetectionInterval(15);

chrome.idle.onStateChanged.addListener(
```

```
        function (state) {
            if (state === "idle" && dirty)
                save();
        }
    );
```

The StateChanged event fires when the idle state changes, testing it every 15 seconds (the minimum allowed). It can be active, idle, or locked. The locked state means that the screen is locked or the screensaver is activated. All we care about is idle, in which case save is called if the text area is dirty (modified since the last save).

Use of chrome.idle requires that we request idle permission; thus the permissions in *manifest.json* need to be changed to the following:

```
"permissions": [
    "unlimitedStorage",
    "idle"
]
```

We'll keep the Save button, although typically note-taking apps don't have one (for example, Google's Keep app doesn't).

Sync Files

A note-taking app that keeps its note hidden away on a single computer isn't really that useful. Modern note-takers sync their notes so that they're available on whatever device you're using and, as a bonus, automatically backed up. It's surprisingly easy to modify our Note app to sync; all we need to do is use the *Sync FileSystem*, available only to Chrome Apps.

How Syncing Works

The Sync FileSystem keeps a *local copy* of directories and files, and you code input and output (I/O) between the application and that local copy, just as you do for Local Files. In the background, a system task built into Chrome copies data back and forth between the local copy and a copy on Google Drive, called the *remote copy*. There might be a delay of a minute or so before this syncing occurs. If syncing isn't active, perhaps because the computer is offline, I/O between the app and the local copy proceeds normally, and syncing occurs sometime later, when the computer again has access to the Internet.

To show how the Sync FileSystem works, we'll modify the Note app so that it syncs. Anything typed or otherwise modified is written to the Sync FileSystem (a local copy, that is) and then synced with the remote copy on Google Drive. If the file is changed by another computer, an event is fired, alerting the app that the local copy changed and that the text area should be updated. Figure 2-4 illustrates our Note app running on two computers, showing the local copies of the *note.txt* file that contains the note, and the remote copy.

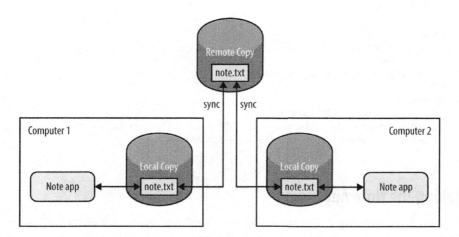

Figure 2-4. Two installations of Note synced to a shared remote copy

The local copy used by the Sync FileSystem isn't the same one used by Local Files. These are two separate sandboxes.

Figure 2-5 shows the new Note app running after some text has been typed.

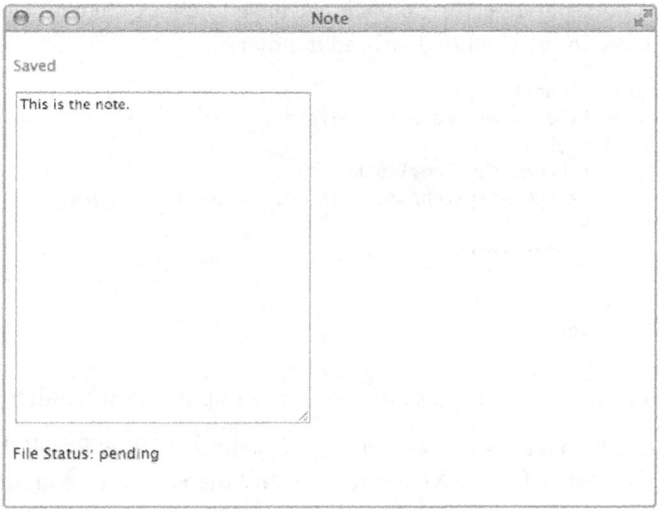

Figure 2-5. Note app showing file status after text has been typed

One thing that's new is the file status ("pending") at the bottom; this was put there by a function that we'll see as we go through the code. Here's the new *index.html*:

```
<!DOCTYPE html>
<html lang="en">
<head>
    <meta charset="utf-8" />
    <title>Note</title>
    <script src="note.js"></script>
</head>
<body>
    <p id="message"> </p>
    <p><textarea id="textarea" cols="30" rows="20"></textarea></p>
    <p>File Status: <span id="status"></span></p>
</body>
</html>
```

Making the Note App Sync

After we get a syncing FileSystem, how we deal with DirectoryEntry, FileEntry, FileWriter, and the other file objects is the same as before; therefore, we can retain most of the Note app code, and I won't repeat those functions that are exactly the same here.

You request a sync FileSystem by calling chrome.syncFileSystem.requestFileSystem, whose only argument is the callback:

```
chrome.syncFileSystem.requestFileSystem(callback)
```

Because there's no separate error callback, we have to check chrome.runtime.lastError, as you can see in the modified onload handler:

```
window.onload = function () {
    chrome.syncFileSystem.requestFileSystem(
        function (fs) {
            if (chrome.runtime.lastError)
                showMessage(chrome.runtime.lastError.message);
            else
                haveFileSystem(fs);
        }
    );
    setupAutoSave();
};
```

We've tossed out the Save button, so the code to set up its event handler is gone.

On success, we call haveFileSystem, which is exactly as before. Recall that its job is to get the DirectoryEntry for the *Note* directory and then call the read function.

What is changed is the getFileEntry function, which both read and save call. In the earlier version, we just created the file if it didn't exist, but now that we're syncing, we can't do that. Here's the problem: suppose that the syncing Note app is installed on a new computer. Initially, there's no *note.txt* file on that computer, but it's possible that after a few seconds the current version will be synced down from Google Drive. Meanwhile, if we had created the file, that would count as a change, and it's possible that the new empty file would overwrite the saved one.

So, for any call to read, if the file doesn't exist, we don't want to create it. However, for save, we do want to create a nonexistent file because we really do need to write it. We modify getFileEntry to take a first argument that indicates the value of the create option:

```
var fileEntry;
var fileWriter;

function getFileEntry(create, callback) {
    if (fileWriter)
        callback();
    else if (directoryEntry) {
        directoryEntry.getFile('note.txt',
            {
                create: create,
                exclusive: false
            },
            function (fe) {
                fileEntry = fe;
                fileEntry.createWriter(
                    function (fw) {
                        fileWriter = fw;
                        callback();
                    },
                    errorHandler
                );
            },
            function (e) {
                if (e.name === 'NotFoundError')
                    callback();
                else
                    errorHandler(e);
            }
        );
    }
}
```

With this change, if create is false, an error occurs if the file doesn't exist. Accordingly, we check for that particular error and just execute the callback in that case.

To see how the new getFileEntry is used, here's the modified read function (called from haveFileSystem, as before):

```
function read() {
    showFileStatus();
    getFileEntry(false,
        function() {
            if (fileEntry)
                fileEntry.file(haveFile, errorHandler);
```

```
        }
    );
}

function haveFile(file) {
    var reader = new FileReader();
    reader.onload = function() {
        document.querySelector("#textarea").value = reader.result;
    };
    reader.readAsText(file);
}
```

The call to `getFileEntry` now has a first argument of `false`. If the file doesn't exist, `fileEntry` is undefined, so the text area remains empty. If the file isn't on Google Drive either, empty is how the text area should remain, until the user types. We'll see soon what happens if the file is on Google Drive and is synced down later.

The call at the top to `showFileStatus` shows the file status; I'll get to that in a bit.

The `save` function operates exactly as it did for local files because the first argument to the new `getFileEntry` is `true`:

```
function save() {
    getFileEntry(true,
        function() {
            fileWriter.onwrite = function(e) {
                fileWriter.onwrite = function(e) {
                    dirty = false;
                    showMessage("Saved", true);
                };
                var blob = new Blob([document.querySelector("#textarea").value],
                    {type: 'text/plain'});
                fileWriter.write(blob);
            };
            fileWriter.onerror = errorHandler;
            fileWriter.truncate(0);
        }
    );
}
```

Now that there is no longer a Save button, `save` is called only from the `chrome.idle.on StateChanged` event handler.

Listening for the FileStatusChanged Event

The app needs to show the note if it has been synchronized down from Google Drive. To do that, it sets a listener for the `chrome.syncFileSystem.onFileStatusChanged` event:

```
chrome.syncFileSystem.onFileStatusChanged.addListener(
    function (detail) {
```

```
        if (detail.fileEntry.name === "note.txt") {
            showMessage(detail.fileEntry.name + " &bull; " +
                detail.direction + " &bull; " + detail.action +
                " &bull; " + detail.status, true);
            if (detail.direction === 'remote_to_local' &&
                detail.status === 'synced')
                    read();
            showFileStatus(detail.status);
        }
    }
);
```

When the event fires, it means that the background syncing has changed the file status, and the event handler is called with a `detail` object that has the following four properties:

fileEntry

> The `FileEntry` for the file whose status has changed. It has two interesting properties: `name`, which we're using in the example code, and `path`.

status

> One of `synced`, `pending`, or `conflicting`. A conflict occurs if two or more local copies on different devices have been changed. By default, that won't occur, because the last writer prevails. However, you can call `chrome.syncFileSystem.setCon flictResolutionPolicy` to set the policy to `manual`, in which case conflicts won't be resolved automatically. The default is `last_write_win`, and that's what you'll almost always want.

action

> Set if the `status` is `synced`; one of `added`, `updated`, or `deleted`.

direction

> Either `local_to_remote` or `remote_to_local`.

In the code, all four properties are used to display a status message by using `showMes sage`, and the file status is shown by `showFileStatus`, which we'll see in a moment. For example, after I typed on my Mac, the message in Figure 2-6 appeared after a few seconds.

Figure 2-7 shows the Note app running on my Windows computer after I typed a bit more text.

You can see that local changes were copied up to the remote (Google Drive), which were then copied down. All of this was entirely automatic. The application only knew about the change to the remote copy from the event that was fired.

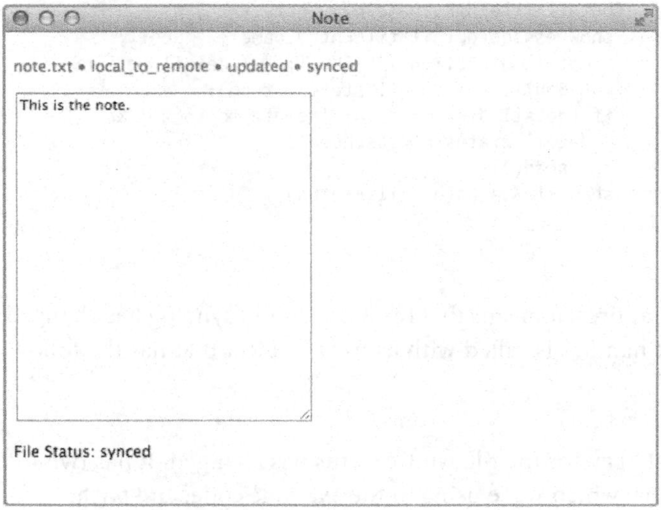

Figure 2-6. *The Note app after local-to-remote sync*

Figure 2-7. *The Note app after remote-to-local sync*

Going back to the event handler, the purpose of the following code is to show the note if it was just copied from Google Drive:

```
if (detail.direction === 'remote_to_local' &&
    detail.status === 'synced')
        read();
```

That's what causes all instances of the app to show the same text after syncing. If the file didn't exist when the app was first started, causing read to do nothing back then, when the event fires the file will exist and the call to read will display it in the text area.

We don't care to do anything when a local_to_remote event occurs, other than to show the status on the screen. Because the text being synced is already in the text area, it doesn't have to be updated.

Showing File Status

The showFileStatus function updates the status shown at the bottom of the window. It uses the chrome.syncFileSystem.getFileStatus API to get the status if none was passed in. If there's no FileEntry because no local copy yet exists, the notation "no local copy" is displayed:

```
function showFileStatus(status) {
    var statusElement = document.querySelector("#status");
    if (status)
        statusElement.innerHTML = status;
    else
        getFileEntry(false,
            function() {
                if (fileEntry)
                    chrome.syncFileSystem.getFileStatus(fileEntry,
                        function (status) {
                            statusElement.innerHTML = status;
                        }
                    );
                else
                    statusElement.innerHTML = "no local copy";
            }
        );
}
```

There's also a call to showFileStatus added to the end of showMessage. This causes the status to display whenever a message (such as "Saved") is shown:

```
function showMessage(msg, good) {
    // ...
    showFileStatus();
}
```

Finding Remote Copies on Google Drive

If you browse your directories on Google Drive, you won't find the remote copies. However, if you really want to see them, you can open up your Google Drive in a browser window and click the All Items link at the left, as illustrated in Figure 2-8.

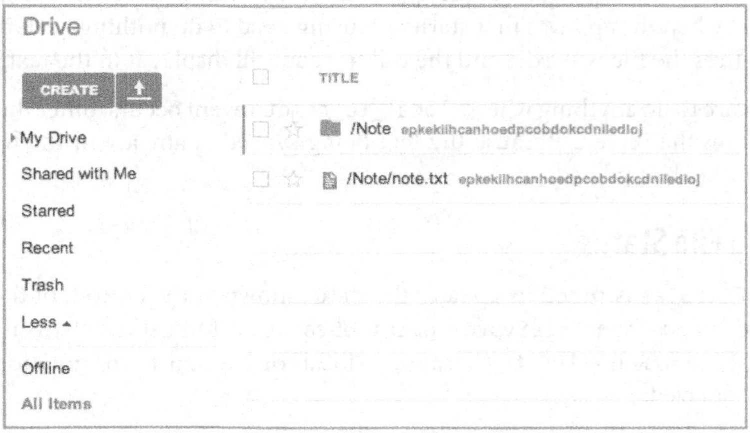

Figure 2-8. Sync directory and file on Google Drive

It's undocumented what happens if you make changes directly on Google Drive—they might not be synced—so don't do it. File access should be only through the Sync File-System APIs.

External Files

Local Files are of limited use because its infeasible to find them on the local filesystem and, even if you could find them, how and where they're stored isn't documented and probably will change at some point. That limits such files to data completely internal to the application, which is useless for applications such as text editors or image viewers. Sync Files have their uses, of course, but they also are captives of the app's sandbox.

However, because Chrome Apps run with much tighter security than ordinary web apps, they can use an API that provides access to any user-visible directory or file on the computer, with only one restriction: the user must explicitly choose the file or the directory it's in, via file-open or file-save dialogs, the same ones you see on native apps. (Media files are an exception; see "The mediaGalleries API" on page 173 for an alternative way to access them.)

External Files use the same file API as Local Files and Sync Files, except for two differences:

- You use `chrome.fileSystem.chooseEntry` to show a file-open/save dialog that provides a `FileEntry` object. When you have one of those, you manipulate it the usual way, as we've been doing.

- You don't have to request a filesystem, because `chrome.fileSystem.chooseEntry` knows what filesystem to use.

A Simple Editor

Figure 2-9 shows the Simple Editor example app that I'll use to illustrate the use of the `chrome.fileSystem` API:

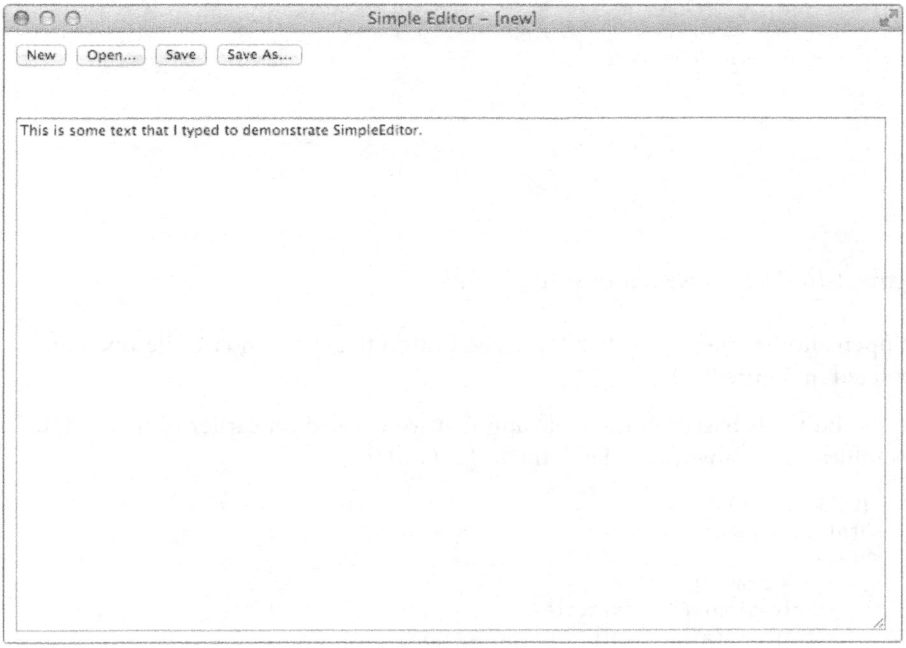

Figure 2-9. The Simple Editor app

After typing some text into the text area and clicking the Save button, a standard save-file dialog opens, as shown in Figure 2-10.

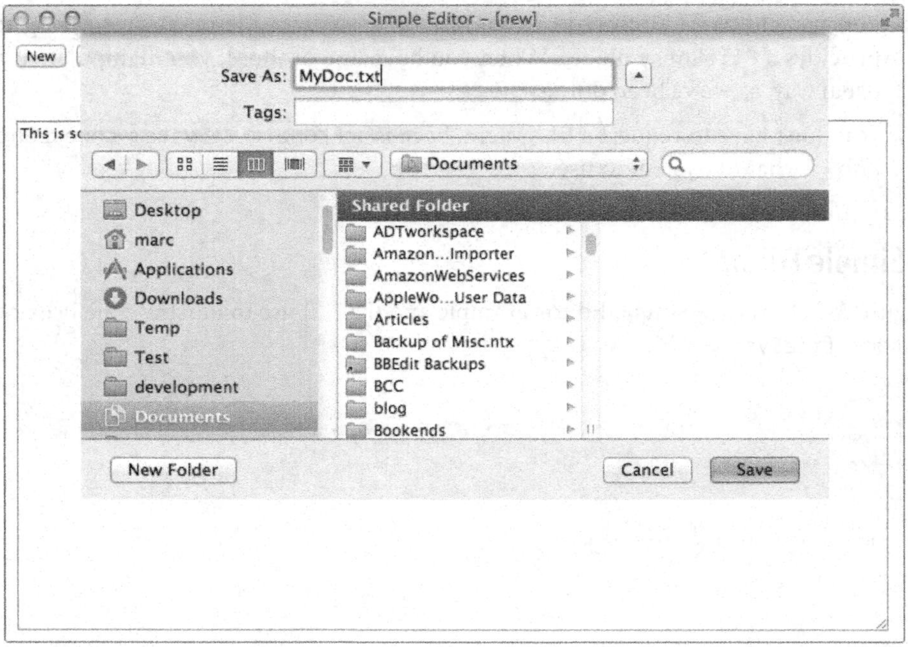

Figure 2-10. The Simple Editor save-file dialog

To open another file, I can click the Open button to get a standard file-open dialog, as depicted in Figure 2-11.

Simple Editor is based on the Note app that we worked on earlier in this chapter and resembles it in many ways. Here's the *index.html* file:

```
<!DOCTYPE html>
<html lang="en">
<head>
    <meta charset="utf-8" />
    <title>SimpleEditor</title>
    <script src="lib/Dialogs.js"></script>
    <script src="SimpleEditor.js"></script>
</head>
<body>
    <button id="new">New</button>
    <button id="open">Open...</button>
    <button id="save">Save</button>
    <button id="saveas">Save As...</button>
    <p id="message"> </p>
    <textarea id="textarea" cols="60" rows="20" style='outline: none;'></textarea>
</body>
</html>
```

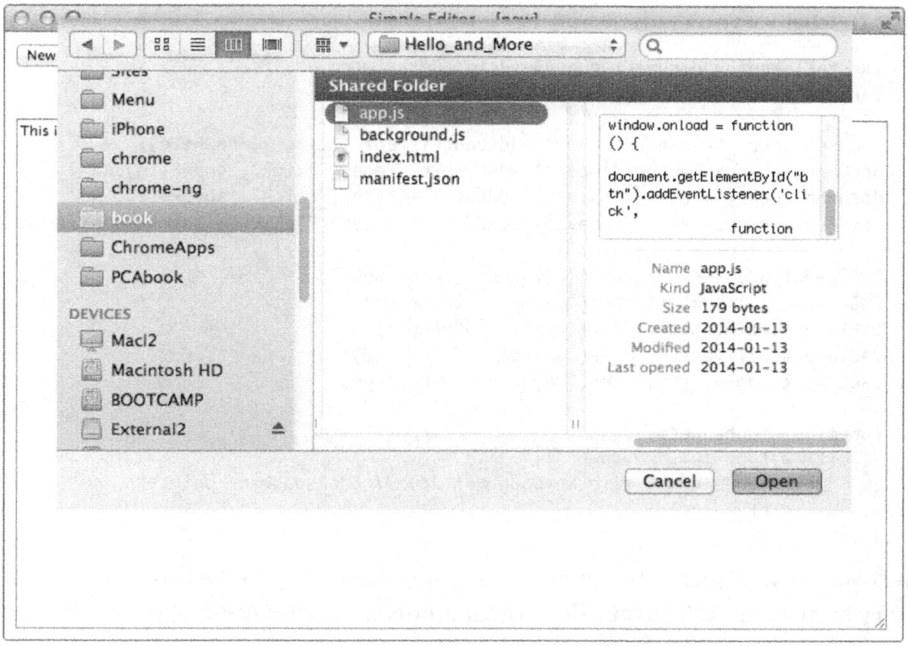

Figure 2-11. The Simple Editor open-file dialog

Note that the *Dialogs.js* file (see Appendix A) is included so that the Simple Editor app can pop up a modal dialog, as we'll see a little later.

Is a Text Area the Right Choice?

A text area is fine for the examples in this book, but it falls well short of what you need for a real text editor. You'll likely want find-and-replace, syntax highlighting, line numbers, automatic indent and outdent, and much more. The open source, embeddable code editor Ace (*ace.c9.io*) is a better choice, and it works well in Chrome Apps. It's what the Chrome Dev Editor uses.

All of the JavaScript is in the `window.onload` handler; this ensures that all of the elements defined in the HTML have been created:

```
window.onload = function () {
    // ... entire app goes here ...
};
```

Setting up handlers for the buttons and for reacting to changes in the text area is very close to what we've already seen:

```
var taElement = document.querySelector("#textarea");
var dirty = false;

document.querySelector("#new").addEventListener("click", newFile);
document.querySelector("#open").addEventListener("click", openFile);
document.querySelector("#save").addEventListener("click", saveFile);
document.querySelector("#saveas").addEventListener("click", saveFileAs);

taElement.addEventListener("keypress", didChange);
taElement.addEventListener("paste", didChange);
taElement.addEventListener("cut", didChange);
taElement.addEventListener("change", didChange);
taElement.addEventListener("keydown", didChange);

function didChange(e) {
    if (e.type !== 'keydown' ||
      e.keyCode === 8 || e.keyCode === 46) // backspace or delete
        dirty = true;
}
```

The `newFile` and `openFile` functions store new contents into the text area, so it's necessary to first check the `dirty` flag, which is done by `dirtyCheck`:

```
function dirtyCheck(callback) {
    if (dirty)
        Dialogs.confirm('Discard changes?', 'Discard', 'Keep', callback);
    else
        callback();
}
```

If dirty is set, the user is asked whether what's been typed should be discarded (Figure 2-12).

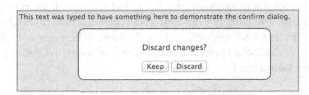

Figure 2-12. The confirm dialog asking the user whether changes can be discarded

See Appendix A for how `Dialogs.confirm` is used. If the user chooses to discard the text, or if the flag is unset, the callback is called. If `dirty` is set but the user wants to keep the text, the callback isn't called. That's what's done in `newFile`, the New button's event handler:

```
function newFile() {
    dirtyCheck(
        function() {
            fileEntry = null;
            taElement.value = "";
            taElement.focus();
            dirty = false;
            document.title = 'Simple Editor - [new]';
        }
    );
}
```

If it's OK to clear the text area, the `dirty` flag is turned off and the document name is reset.

Choosing Files and Directories

Here is the API for choosing a file:

```
chrome.fileSystem.chooseEntry(options, callback)
```

`option` has a `type` property with one of the following three values:

openFile

> Get a `FileEntry` for an existing file.

saveFile

> Get a `FileEntry` for a file to be written.

openDirectory

> Get a `DirectoryEntry`.

The option you pick interacts with the permissions in the manifest. You need at least `fileSystem` permission, which allows you to open a file for reading and nothing else:

```
"permissions": [
    "fileSystem"
]
```

If you add `write`, you can also save a file, and any file opened is available for both reading and writing, which is what Simple Editor needs:

```
"permissions": [
    {
        "fileSystem": [
            "write"
        ]
    }
]
```

If you add the `directory` permission, you can use the `openDirectory` option. To enable writing, you must also have asked for `write` permission, like this:

```
    "permissions": [
        {
            "fileSystem": [
                "directory",
                "write"
            ]
        }
    ]
```

If `chrome.fileSystem.chooseEntry` isn't canceled by the user, the callback is called with a `FileEntry` as an argument, and you can use any of the methods that we saw earlier in this chapter, just as with Local Files and Sync Files.

Now, the `openFile` function—the Open button's event handler—should be understandable, especially as we've already seen how a `FileEntry` is manipulated:

```
var fileEntry;

function openFile() {
    dirtyCheck(
        function() {
            chrome.fileSystem.chooseEntry(
                {
                    type: 'openFile'
                },
                function (fe) {
                    if (fe) {
                        fileEntry = fe;
                        fe.file(
                            function (file) {
                                var reader = new FileReader();
                                reader.onloadend = function(e) {
                                    taElement.value = this.result;
                                    taElement.focus();
                                    dirty = false;
                                    showMessage('Opened OK', true);
                                    document.title = 'Simple Editor - ' + fe.name;
                                };
                                reader.readAsText(file);
                            },
                            errorHandler
                        );
                    }
                }
            );
        }
    );
}
```

There are two things to note here: we save the `FileEntry` in a global variable, and the `dirty` flag is turned off.

The saveFile function also calls chrome.fileSystem.chooseEntry but with a different option:

```
function saveFile() {
    if (fileEntry)
        save();
    else
        chrome.fileSystem.chooseEntry(
            {
                type: 'saveFile'
            },
            function (fe) {
                if (fe) {
                    fileEntry = fe;
                    save();
                    document.title = 'Simple Editor - ' + fe.name;
                }
            }
        );
}
```

Keep in mind that if the global fileEntry is set, the file to be saved is the same one that was opened, so we just save without prompting the user for a filename.

The actual work of saving is done by save—the Save button's event handler—which is almost identical to the one in the Note app:

```
function save() {
    fileEntry.createWriter(
        function(fileWriter) {
            fileWriter.onerror = errorHandler;
            fileWriter.onwrite = function(e) {
                fileWriter.onwrite = function(e) {
                    showMessage('Saved OK', true);
                    dirty = false;
                    taElement.focus();
                };
                var blob = new Blob([taElement.value],
                  {type: 'text/plain'});
                fileWriter.write(blob);
            };
            fileWriter.truncate(0);
        },
        errorHandler
    );
}
```

Observe that once more we turn off the dirty flag.

Given the way saveFile is constructed, saveFileAs (the "Save As" button's event handler), can piggyback on it by just killing fileEntry first:

```
function saveFileAs() {
    fileEntry = null;
    saveFile();
}
```

The `showMessage` and `errorHandler` functions are almost identical to those we've already seen, so I'm not going to show them again.

Adding Backup by Using Retained File Entries

Suppose that you want to add a backup feature to Simple Editor so that it automatically keeps a second copy when a file is saved. The obvious way to do that is for the user to choose a backup directory, and then the app can create as many files as you want in that directory.

However, it's inconvenient for the user to choose the backup directory every time the app is launched. That should be done just once, when the app is used for the first time, or maybe on rare occasions when the user wants to change it.

To accommodate this, the `chrome.fileSystem` API has *retained file entries* that can be saved and reused without having to create them fresh each time with `chrome.fileSystem.chooseEntry`. The rule that the user must have chosen the directory is still obeyed, just maybe sometime in the distant past.

A good place to save the retained entry is in local storage, along with other app preferences. We'll see the local-storage API in the next chapter; for now we'll use two higher-level functions whose code we'll defer showing until then:

```
setParams(x);

getParams(x, callback);
```

For `setParams`, the argument is an object that's saved in local storage, like this:

```
setParams({ BackupFolderID: entryID });
```

For `getParams`, the argument is a key whose value is wanted, or an array of such keys, and the retrieved keys and their values are passed as an object to the callback function, like this:

```
getParams("BackupFolderID",
    function (items) {
        // do something with items.BackupFolderID
    }
);
```

To see how all this works in practice, we'll modify Simple Editor to back up any saved files. I'll show only the new stuff, as most of the app won't change.

Figure 2-13 shows Simple Editor after the backup has been set with a standard directory-choosing dialog. (We'll see how shortly.) The chosen backup path is momentarily displayed.

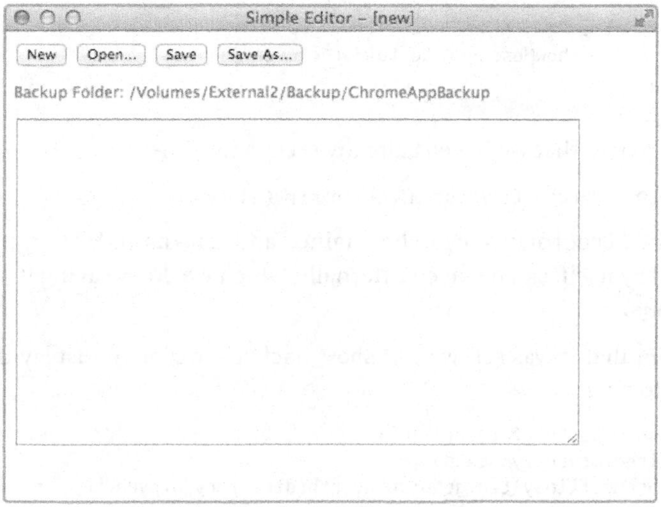

Figure 2-13. Simple Editor after setting the backup directory

In the manifest, we need `directory` and `retainEntries` permissions for the `fileSys tem`. We also need `storage` permission so that we can save the `DirectoryEntry` for backups in local storage with `setParams` and `getParams`:

```
"permissions": [
    {
        "fileSystem": [
            "write",
            "directory",
            "retainEntries"
        ]
    },
    "storage"
]
```

Here's a function, `setBackup`, to set the backup (we'll see where it's called later):

```
var directoryEntryBackup;

function setBackup() {
    chrome.fileSystem.chooseEntry({
            type: 'openDirectory'
        },
        function (entry) {
```

```
                    if (entry) {
                        directoryEntryBackup = entry;
                        var entryID = chrome.fileSystem.retainEntry(entry);
                        setParams({ BackupFolderID: entryID });
                        show_backup_folder();
                    }
                    else
                        showMessage("No folder chosen");
                });
        }
```

The only thing here that we haven't already seen is this line:

```
        var entryID = chrome.fileSystem.retainEntry(entry);
```

This causes the `DirectoryEntry` to be retained and returns an ID to it that, unlike the `DirectoryEntry` itself, can be saved externally, which we do by saving it in local storage with `setParams`.

Just to confirm that it was set, we call `show_backup_folder` to display the path to the backup directory:

```
        function show_backup_folder() {
            if (directoryEntryBackup)
                chrome.fileSystem.getDisplayPath(directoryEntryBackup,
                    function (path) {
                        showMessage('Backup Folder: ' + path, true);
                    });
            else
                showMessage('No backup folder');
        }
```

We use the `chrome.fileSystem.getDisplayPath` API call to get a displayable path.

To take advantage of the backup directory, we have to change the `save` function to save the file twice: once where the user wanted to save it, and once to the backup directory. The `saveToEntry` function handles the actual saving, given a `FileEntry` and a callback to be called when the file is saved:

```
        function saveToEntry(fe, callback) {
            fe.createWriter(
                function(fileWriter) {
                    fileWriter.onerror = errorHandler;
                    fileWriter.onwrite = function(e) {
                        fileWriter.onwrite = function(e) {
                            callback();
                        };
                        var blob = new Blob([taElement.value],
                          {type: 'text/plain'});
                        fileWriter.write(blob);
                    };
                    fileWriter.truncate(0);
                },
```

```
            errorHandler
    );
}
```

Now, we can implement the double save easily by calling `saveToEntry` twice (look in the middle for the second call):

```
function save() {
    saveToEntry(fileEntry,
        function () {
            dirty = false;
            taElement.focus();
            if (directoryEntryBackup)
                directoryEntryBackup.getFile(fileEntry.name,
                    {
                        create: true,
                        exclusive: false
                    },
                    function (fe) {
                        saveToEntry(fe,
                            function () {
                                showMessage('Saved/Backedup OK', true);
                            }
                        );
                    },
                    errorHandler
                );
            else
                showMessage('Saved/OK (no backup)', true);
        }
    );
}
```

It's not an error if the user never set a backup directory, but we do want to indicate that no backup was saved, which we do by displaying the message. Also, we don't bother keeping the `FileEntry` for the backup around, as we did for the primary file, but just get a fresh one each time.

So, that all works, but the entire point of a retained entry is that the user doesn't have to set it each time the app launches. Because the ID is in local storage, all we need to do is add this code, which executes on every launch:

```
getParams("BackupFolderID",
    function (items) {
        if (chrome.runtime.lastError)
            showMessage('Unable to get backup folder ID. (' +
                chrome.runtime.lastError.message + ')');
        else if (items && items.BackupFolderID)
            chrome.fileSystem.restoreEntry(items.BackupFolderID,
                function (entry) {
                    directoryEntryBackup = entry;
                    show_backup_folder();
```

```
                }
            );
        else
            setBackup();
    }
);
```

Note the call to `chrome.fileSystem.restoreEntry` to get a `DirectoryEntry` back from the stored ID. If there's no backup directory set, `setBackup` (which you just saw) is called to set it. This happens when the app is first launched; subsequent launches find that it's already set.

One toy-like limitation of this example is that there's no directory tree in the backup directory, so files of the same name but in different directories will overwrite one another. What it takes to fix this defect is to use the complete path of the `FileEntry` to create all of the needed intermediate directories before saving the backup, a task I leave to you.

Here's another limitation: there's not only no auto-save, but there's not even a warning when the app exits. That's not really a good design—it's better to use the method that we used in the Note app to save automatically. Because it's a text editor, users probably expect Save and Save As buttons, so you might want to retain those.

We're not finished with our editor. In Chapter 3, we'll add options to set the text colors as well as a button with which the user can change the backup directory.

Chapter Summary

In this chapter, we discussed how to use Local Files, Sync Files, and External Files using HTML5 APIs and APIs unique to Chrome Apps. Our exploration continues in Chapter 3 with the key-value-pair APIs.

Local Storage, Sync Storage, and IndexedDB

This chapter covers three more storage types first introduced in Table 2-1 in Chapter 2: Local Storage, Sync Storage, and the IndexedDB database. All three store key-value pairs (KVPs), not files.

We'll be extending the Simple Editor app from Chapter 2, using Local and Sync Storage. Then, I'll introduce a mailing-list app to demonstrate what you can do with IndexedDB.

Local and Sync Storage

Many browsers, including Chrome, support `localStorage`, which is similar to persistent cookies in that it stores KVPs. The main difference is that `localStorage` has greater capacity and isn't passed to the server along with HTTP requests. Similarly, `session Storage` is similar to session cookies in that it lasts only as long as the current session.

However, Chrome Apps can't use `localStorage`. Instead, there's a Chrome API, `chrome.storage.local`, that's better: it can store JavaScript objects (`localStorage` is limited to strings) and, like most Chrome APIs, it operates asynchronously, allowing the app to be more responsive. What's more, there's a variant, `chrome.storage.sync`, with the same API, which is automatically synchronized between computers running the same app, similar to the way that Sync Files are synchronized.

 As is specified in Chapter 2, you need `storage` permission in your manifest to use the `chrome.storage` APIs.

Chrome Apps can use `sessionStorage`, but there's no reason to do so. Because a Chrome App HTML page can't be refreshed and can't navigate to another page in the same window, there's no concept of session, and any global variables you define within your JavaScript will persist for as long as the window is open. (In case you were wondering, cookies don't work in Chrome Apps, which is no loss.)

`chrome.storage.local` persists even if the app is reinstalled, as long as its ID is the same. The ID is important also for `chrome.storage.sync`, because this is what ties together the same app installed on multiple computers. You can think of the ID as identifying the storage. This means that the storage is really *local*, not only to your computer, but also to the app ID; there's no way to share it between apps.

Setting and Getting Local Storage

You set values in local storage by using `chrome.storage.local.set`:

```
chrome.storage.local.set(items, callback)
```

There's a single callback. An error occurred if it's called with `chrome.runtime.lastError` defined; otherwise, setting succeeded. The `items` argument is an object whose keys are set to the corresponding values in local storage. Other keys already there are unaffected.

To retrieve one or more keys from local storage, you call `chrome.storage.local.get`:

```
chrome.storage.local.get(x, callback)
```

The argument is the key to retrieve, or an array of keys to retrieve, or `null` to retrieve the entire contents of local storage (for this app). Here, too, the callback is for an error if `chrome.runtime.lastError` is defined.

To see what you can expect to store and get back, consider this example:

```
var obj = {
    k_array: [ 1, 2, 3, 4, "five", { number: "six" } ],
    k_date: new Date(),
    k_function: function () { return 123; },
    k_object: { k2_key1: "one", k2_key2: "two" },
    k_regex: /abc/,
    k_string: "string value"
};
chrome.storage.local.set(obj,
    function () {
        chrome.storage.local.get(null,
            function (items) {
                if (chrome.runtime.lastError)
                    console.log(chrome.runtime.lastError);
                else
                    console.dir(items);
            }
```

```
        );
    }
);
```

Note the argument of `null` to the `get` function, called from the `set` callback.

The console is shown in Figure 3-1.

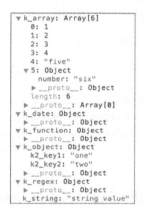

Figure 3-1. A console showing local storage objects

You can see that strings and numbers are stored without problem, and so are arrays and objects that ultimately store strings and numbers, but dates, functions, and regular expressions aren't handled. The workaround is to store dates and regular expressions as strings. However, there's no purpose in storing functions in local storage, so they don't need a workaround.

Local storage is best for small amounts of data, say a megabyte or two at most. It's ideal for recording app preferences, as we're about to see. For larger amounts of data, files or IndexedDB are better.

Implementing setParams and getParams

The examples in Chapter 2 need to use local storage to store the backup directory's entry ID, which is done through two wrapper functions, `setParams` and `getParams`, whose code we can now show:

```
function setParams(x, wantSync) {
    var storageArea = wantSync ? chrome.storage.sync : chrome.storage.local;
    storageArea.set(x,
        function () {
            if (chrome.runtime.lastError)
                console.log(chrome.runtime.lastError);
        }
```

```
            );
        }

        function getParams(x, callback, wantSync) {
            var storageArea = wantSync ? chrome.storage.sync : chrome.storage.local;
            storageArea.get(x,
                function (items) {
                    if (chrome.runtime.lastError)
                        console.log(chrome.runtime.lastError);
                    else
                        callback(items);
                }
            );
        }
```

As we'll see, the local and sync storage APIs are the same, except for the storage area object they operate on, so you can set an optional wantSync to true for sync storage. In Chapter 2, when these functions are first used, the argument is omitted, so the entry ID is stored in local storage, which is what is needed for the entry ID, because it's inherently local.

Adding Color Options to the Simple Editor App

To further show how you can use local storage to store and retrieve KVPs, we'll modify Simple Editor to provide options for setting the text-area background and foreground colors. Figure 3-2 shows the new Options button, and Figure 3-3 shows the dialog that opens when you click it and select new colors. Figure 3-4 shows the new colors after you dismiss the dialog.

Let's look only at the changes to implement the color options. First, there's another line of HTML in *index.html* for the Options button:

```
...
<button id="saveas">Save As...</button>
<button id="options" style='float: right;'>Options...</button>
<p id="message"> </p>
<textarea id="textarea" cols="60" rows="20" style='outline: none;'></textarea>
...
```

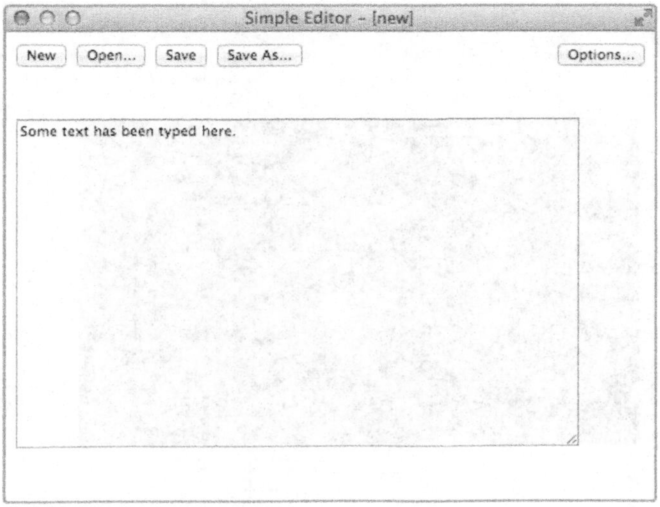

Figure 3-2. Simple Editor with default colors

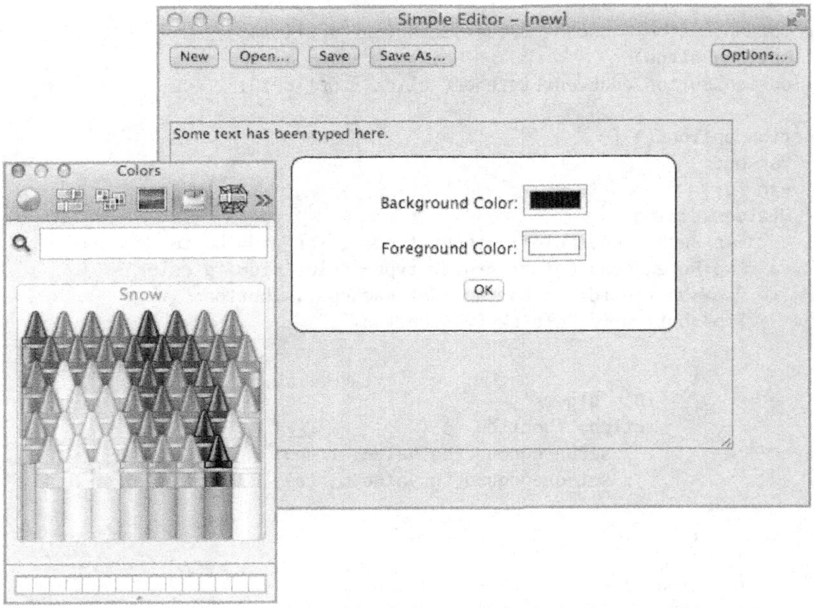

Figure 3-3. The color-choosing dialog with color picker

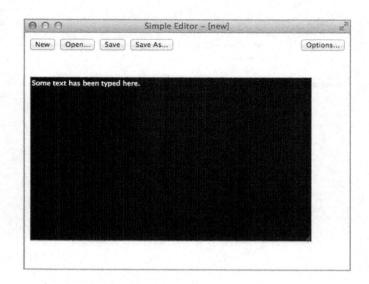

Figure 3-4. Simple Editor with new colors applied

The event handler is set for the Options button like so:

```
var optionsButton = document.querySelector("#options");
if (optionsButton)
    optionsButton.addEventListener("click", options);

function options() {
    var bg;
    var fg;
    Dialogs.dialog(
        "<p>Background Color: <input type='color' id='bg-color'>" +
        "<p>Foreground Color: <input type='color' id='fg-color'>" +
        "<p><button id='setbackup'>Set Backup...</button>" +
        "<p><button id='dlg-ok'>OK</button>",
        [
            {
                id: 'dlg-ok',
                action: function () {
                    setBackground(bg.value, true);
                    setForeground(fg.value, true);
                }
            }
        ],
        function () {
            bg = document.querySelector('#bg-color');
            fg = document.querySelector('#fg-color');
            var bgcolor = taElement.style["background-color"];
            var fgcolor = taElement.style["color"];
            if (bgcolor && fgcolor) {
```

```
            bg.value = rgb2hex(bgcolor);
            fg.value = rgb2hex(fgcolor);
        }
        else {
            bg.value = "#ffffff";
            fg.value = "#000000";
        }
        document.querySelector("#setbackup").addEventListener("click",
          setBackup);
    }
  );
}
```

The complicated call to `Dialogs.dialog` is explained in detail in Appendix A, but, briefly, here's how you would set up this dialog:

- Supply HTML for the dialog, consisting of two color pickers, a button to set the backup directory (in case we want to change it), and an OK button.

- Supply an action for the OK button to call `setBackground` and `setForeground` to set the colors from the color-picker values. Actions here also dismiss the dialog.

- Supply an initialization function that sets the initial state of the color pickers to whatever the current text area styles are. (See "About rgb2hex" on page 61 for what that function does.) The function also sets the event handler for the Set Backup button, which is the identical `setBackup` function that you can see in "Adding Backup by Using Retained File Entries" on page 50.

Note that the action for the Set Backup button isn't set in the action argument, where the OK button's action is, because we don't want the dialog dismissed when the backup is set.

About rgb2hex

When a color style is retrieved, it's in the form `rgb(R,G,B)`, where the components span a range of 0–255. However, the color picker (`<input type="color">` element) requires that it be initialized using the form `#rrggbb`, where the components are in hex. The function `rgb2hex` makes the conversion, as shown here:

```
function rgb2hex(rgb) {
    var components = rgb.match(/^rgb\((\d+),\s*(\d+),\s*(\d+)\)$/);
    function hex(x) {
        return ("0" + parseInt(x).toString(16)).slice(-2);
    }
    return "#" + hex(components[1]) + hex(components[2]) + hex(components[3]);
}
```

Here are the two functions called when you click the OK button in the dialog:

```
function setBackground(color, wantSave) {
    if (color) {
        document.querySelector("#textarea").style["background-color"] = color;
        if (wantSave)
            setParams({ background: color }, wantSync);
    }
}

function setForeground(color, wantSave) {
    if (color) {
        document.querySelector("#textarea").style["color"] = color;
        if (wantSave)
            setParams({ foreground: color }, wantSync);
    }
}
```

The wantSync global is set to false, so we'll be using local storage:

```
var wantSync = false;
```

Later, we'll be using sync storage, and all we'll have to do to get it is set the global to true.

To use either storage area, you must request storage permission in the *manifest.json* file (see also Chapter 2):

```
"permissions": [
    {
        "fileSystem": [
            "write",
            "directory",
            "retainEntries"
        ]
    },
    "storage"
]
```

The setForeground and setBackground functions change the colors in the window immediately and also, if the second argument is true, set the colors in local storage.

When the app is launched, we want to set the text area from whatever colors were saved in local storage:

```
getParams(["foreground", "background"],
    function (items) {
        if (chrome.runtime.lastError)
            console.log(chrome.runtime.lastError);
        else {
            setForeground(items.foreground);
            setBackground(items.background);
        }
    },
```

```
        wantSync
    );
```

Observe how the first line passes an array of two keys to `getParams` and onto the `get` method. If the function succeeds, it sets the foreground and background from those colors. The second argument to `setForeground` and `setBackground` is omitted; there's no need to set local storage, because that's where the colors just came from.

With these changes, Simple Editor sets its colors from local storage when it's first launched. If colors are changed via the Options dialog, they're saved back into local storage.

Sync Storage

Now, we'll change Simple Editor to work with sync storage, instead of local storage. By doing so, all installations of the app by a user will share options. Conveniently, we need to change only one line:

```
    var wantSync = true;
```

If you review the code, you'll see that only the colors are saved in sync storage, not the backup directory entry ID.

Sync storage behaves identically to local storage, except that Chrome synchronizes changes to the storage if the app is installed on more than one computer. If you disable syncing in Chrome settings, however, the two storage areas operate identically.

When a change is made to sync storage, that change is very quickly—within a second or two—reflected in the storage area accessed by every installation of the app. The next time the app is launched, it will retrieve the new colors.

If you want to make the app more responsive by informing it when the colors are changed, you can install the following handler for the `chrome.storage.onChanged` event:

```
chrome.storage.onChanged.addListener(
    function(changes, areaName) {
        if (areaName === "sync") {
            if (changes.foreground)
                setForeground(changes.foreground.newValue);
            if (changes.background)
                setBackground(changes.background.newValue);
        }
    }
);
```

Here, we care only about changes when the `areaName` argument to the callback is sync. (Another possible value is `local`, which doesn't apply to sync storage. A third value, `managed`, is documented but doesn't appear to apply to Chrome Apps.) The changes argument is an object indicating what changed. Each key is associated with an object with two properties: newValue, which is what we want, and oldValue, which does not concern us.

To see the syncing, you need to install the app on two computers. Because the IDs need to be the same, it won't do to move the source code over to the second computer and intall it with the "Load unpacked extension" button on the Extensions window. Instead, click the "Pack extension" button to create a *.crx* file and install that on both computers, guaranteeing that the ID will be the same. Or, upload the app to the Chrome Web Store and install it on both computers from there. (See "Publishing a Chrome App" on page 18.)

Note that only the color options are synced, not the text being edited, which is what the syncing version of the Note app did in Chapter 1. Simple Editor edits files local to a computer.

Removing Items and Clearing Storage

Two other APIs that you'll sometimes need are remove, for removing a key from local or sync storage, and clear, for clearing all keys:

```
chrome.storage.local.remove(x, callback)
chrome.storage.sync.remove(x, callback)

chrome.storage.local.clear(callback)
chrome.storage.sync.clear(callback)
```

In the callbacks, chrome.runtime.lastError defined means there was an error. The argument to remove, like the argument to get, can be a key or an array of keys, but it cannot be null.

IndexedDB

As Table 2-1 in Chapter 2 indicates, IndexedDB is sandboxed, so any data you store there is imprisoned in a single app. You can't do any of the common things that are done with a database, such as share it between apps or manage it with a database utility. Think of IndexedDB as being neither more nor less accessible than local files, over which its only advantage is that it stores indexed objects instead of flat data.

It would be nice if there were both Local IndexedDB and External IndexedDB, as there are with files, but that's not the case. Local is all you have.

I'll present two IndexedDB examples here:

- Some simple code sequences to do basic things, such as creating a database, adding objects, and retrieving an object.

- A complete app that maintains a mailing list, including import and export capabilities.

 In this book, I cover maybe half of the IndexedDB API, but enough so you'll get a thorough understanding of how to use it. You can read all the details at the entry for IndexedDB on the Mozilla Developer Network (*http://bit.ly/indexeddb_mdn*).

IndexedDB Objects and Method Chaining

IndexedDB is implemented in terms of API objects, such as `IDBFactory`, `IDBData base`, `IDBObjectStore`, `IDBIndex`, `IDBCursor`, and `IDBTransaction`. For example, to find an object by its key, you begin with an `IDBDatabase`, from which you get an `IDB Transaction`, from which you get an `IDBObjectStore`, from which you get an `IDBIndex` whose `get` method gives you the object with that key. Fortunately, the IndexedDB API implements method chaining, so the code to find an object isn't so bad:

```
db
.transaction("mailing-list")
.objectStore("mailing-list")
.index("name-index")
.get("Jones")
```

Opening a Database

You begin with `indexedDB`, which is an `IDBFactory` object from which you can request a particular version of a database. With conventional SQL databases, you execute so-called data manipulation language (DML) statements to create tables, indexes, views, and so on. IndexedDB has nothing like that, because any objects, with any keys, can be stored without advance notice.

Still, when a database is first created or when its design changes, you'd like the chance to at least construct some indexes. The way IndexedDB handles this is to introduce the idea of an *upgrade*. If you request a version that doesn't yet exist, the `onupgradenee ded` callback is called, giving you the chance to create needed objects. On subsequent requests for the same version, the upgrade callback isn't called, and you're just given access to the database.

For example, here's how to request a database and create an index called `name-index` when the database is new:

```
function openDatabase() {
    var request = indexedDB.open("db1", 1);
    request.onsuccess = function(event) {
        db = request.result;
```

```
          db.onerror = errorHandler;
          showMessage('Database opened', true);
      };
      request.onerror = errorHandler;
      request.onupgradeneeded = function(event) {
          var db = event.target.result;
          var store = db.createObjectStore("mailing-list", { autoIncrement: true });
          store.createIndex("name-index", "last", { unique: false });
      };
  }
```

The database is named db1 and we've requested version 1. Because that doesn't exist initially, the onupgradeneeded callback creates the object store and an index named name-index on the last key. If in the future the database is modified, perhaps by creating an additional index, the version would be changed to 2 and the onupgradeneeded callback would be changed as appropriate. If the version requested already exists, it's just opened, without calling the onupgradeneeded callback.

The showMessage and errorHandler functions are identical to what Simple Editor used (see "Local Files" on page 22).

In terms of conventional relational databases, you could think of an object store as a table, but it's not at all tabular, because each object in it could have different keys (columns, in relational database terms). Each object in an object store represents a *record*, and I'll often refer to an object stored in an IndexedDB database as a record. This is to distinguish it from all the other objects that JavaScript apps deal with.

Adding Objects in a Transaction

IndexedDB operations such as adding or retrieving an object occur in a *transaction*, represented by an IDBTransaction object. As with relational database transactions, a transaction is atomic—done in its entirety or not at all. Transactions are also independent, but inasmuch as IndexedDB databases are sandboxed and JavaScript is single-threaded, inconsistencies due to simultaneous updates aren't much of a problem, unless you access the database from Web Workers, which can run concurrently.

You get a transaction with the transaction method of an IDBDatabase object, like this, where we want a read/write transaction:

```
db
.transaction("mailing-list", "readwrite")
```

Then, from an IDBTransaction, you can get a reference to the IDBObjectStore:

```
db
.transaction("mailing-list", "readwrite")
.objectStore("mailing-list")
```

Given an IDBObjectStore, you can call the add method to add an object:

```
db
.transaction("mailing-list", "readwrite")
.objectStore("mailing-list")
.add(obj)
.onsuccess = function (event) {
    // adding succeeded
};
```

Putting that all together, here's code that adds three objects:

```
add({last: "Smith", first: "John"});
add({last: "Jones", first: "Mary"});
add({last: "Gonzalez", first: "Sharon"});

function add(obj) {
    db
    .transaction("mailing-list", "readwrite")
    .objectStore("mailing-list")
    .add(obj)
    .onsuccess = function (event) {
        console.log('added', obj);
    };
}
```

It's important to understand that aside from the last property, which is what the index is based on (see the call to createIndex in the openDatabase function that appears in the preceding section), no other property of the object has been introduced to the database. Indeed, any object stored in an IndexedDB database can have any properties. This is very much unlike a relational database, in which all columns must be part of a table's definition.

You can see these objects and the index on the Resources tab in Developer Tools (Figure 3-5 and Figure 3-6).

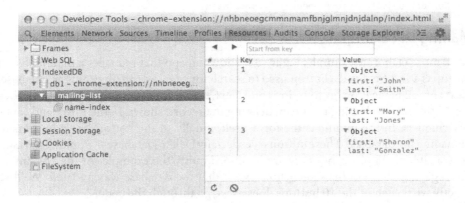

Figure 3-5. IndexedDB objects shown in Developer Tools

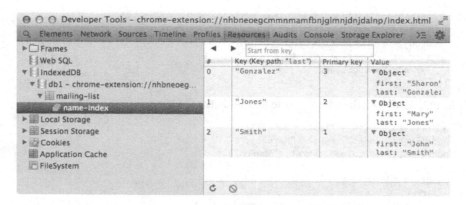

Figure 3-6. IndexedDB index shown in Developer Tools

Retrieving Objects by Using an Index

To retrieve an object by key using an index, you call the index method of the IDBOb
jectStore and then the get method of the IDBIndex:

```
db
.transaction("mailing-list")
.objectStore("mailing-list")
.index("name-index")
.get("Jones")
.onsuccess = function (event) {
    console.log("Found: ", event.target.result);
};
```

The console shows the following:

```
Found:  Object {last: "Jones", first: "Mary"}
```

Mailing List Example

For a more elaborate example, Figure 3-7 shows an app that manages a mailing list. At
the top is a text field and a button used to search for a record (an object in the database).
Next come 2 navigation buttons, Prev and Next, used to browse the database. Then there
are 3 buttons for clearing the form, deleting the record shown in the form, and saving
any changes. In the middle is the form itself. Finally, at the bottom are 4 buttons for
managing the database. These buttons—especially Delete Database—wouldn't normally
be available to all users, but they are here to simplify the example. At the bottom is a
message area that, in this screenshot, shows that the database was updated. We'll see
exactly what each of the 10 buttons does as we go through the code.

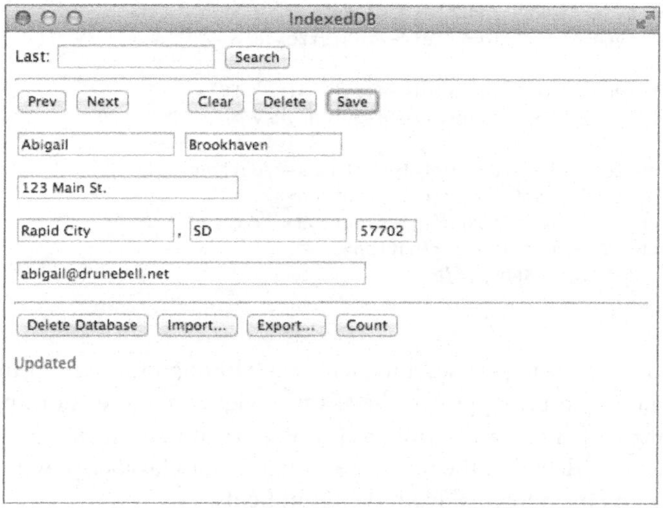

Figure 3-7. The Mailing List app using IndexedDB

Handling Forms

Here's the *index.html* file that defines the user interface:

```html
<!DOCTYPE html>
<html lang="en">
<head>
    <meta charset="utf-8" />
    <title>IndexedDB</title>
    <script src="lib/Dialogs.js"></script>
    <script src="IndexedDB.js"></script>
</head>
<body>
    <label for="search">Last:</label>
    <input type="text" id="search-key">
    <button id="search">Search</button>
    <hr>
    <button id="prev">Prev</button>
    <button id="next">Next</button>
    <button id="clear" style='margin-left: 40px;'>Clear</button>
    <button id="delete">Delete</button>
    <button id="save">Save</button>
    <p>
    <input type="text" id="field-first">
    <input type="text" id="field-last">
    <p>
    <input type="text" id="field-street" size="30">
    <p>
    <input type="text" id="field-city">,
```

```
        <input type="text" id="field-state">
        <input type="text" id="field-zip" size="5">
        <p>
        <input type="text" id="field-email" size="50">
        <input type="hidden" id="field-primaryKey">
        <hr>
        <button id="delete_db">Delete Database</button>
        <button id="import">Import...</button>
        <button id="export">Export...</button>
        <button id="count">Count</button>
        <p id="message"> </p>
    </body>
    </html>
```

Notice that an `<input>` tag is used for each field, although they're not inside a `<form>` element. Because Chrome Apps can't have any navigation, there's nothing to be gained by using a `form` with a submit button, as is pointed out in "Chrome App Restrictions" on page 11. Getting data that the user types is handled in JavaScript with this function, which returns an object formed from the input fields:

```
function getForm() {
    return {
        last: document.querySelector("#field-last").value,
        first: document.querySelector("#field-first").value,
        street: document.querySelector("#field-street").value,
        city: document.querySelector("#field-city").value,
        state: document.querySelector("#field-state").value,
        zip: document.querySelector("#field-zip").value,
        email: document.querySelector("#field-email").value
    };
}
```

There are two ways that data can populate the form:

- Typed by the user as a new record
- Retrieved from the database and perhaps modified by the user

When the user clicks the Save button, we have to know which case applies, because adding a new record and updating an existing record are different. That's the purpose of the hidden field `field-primaryKey` at the bottom of the form. If a record is retrieved, it will hold the primary key (an integer). If the record is new, that field will be empty. To make this work, the function that populates the form must put the primary key there if one exists:

```
function fillForm(object, primaryKey) {
    if (!object)
        object = {};
    if (!primaryKey)
        primaryKey = 0;
    document.querySelector("#field-last").value = val(object.last);
```

```
        document.querySelector("#field-first").value = val(object.first);
        document.querySelector("#field-street").value = val(object.street);
        document.querySelector("#field-city").value = val(object.city);
        document.querySelector("#field-state").value = val(object.state);
        document.querySelector("#field-zip").value = val(object.zip);
        document.querySelector("#field-email").value = val(object.email);
        document.querySelector("#field-primaryKey").value = primaryKey;
    }

    function val(x) {
        return x ? x : "";
    }
```

When `fillForm` is called with no arguments, as it is when the form is to be cleared, we don't want "undefined" to appear in the form, so the `val` function ensures that undefined properties show as as empty fields. We can see a call like that in the handler for the Clear button:

```
    document.querySelector("#clear").addEventListener("click",
        function () {
            fillForm();
        }
    );
```

Later, when we see the code for the Search button, we'll see that the call is instead this:

```
    fillForm(cursor.value, cursor.primaryKey);
```

Adding and Updating Records

With the primary key in a hidden field in the form, if the record is modified, the app will know that it's an update rather than an addition. We can see that in the code for the Save button's handler:

```
    document.querySelector("#save").addEventListener("click",
        function () {
            var store = db
                .transaction("mailing-list", "readwrite")
                .objectStore("mailing-list");
            var object = getForm();
            var key = document.querySelector("#field-primaryKey").value;
            var primaryKey = key ? parseInt(key) : 0;
            if (primaryKey === 0) {
                store
                .add(object)
                .onsuccess = function (event) {
                    showMessage('Added', true);
                };
            }
            else {
                store
                .put(object, primaryKey)
```

```
            .onsuccess = function (event) {
                showMessage('Updated', true);
            };
        }
    }
);
```

The database has already been opened and the global db defined with the same openDa
tabase function that we saw earlier. An object representing the data in the form is
returned by the call to getForm. If the value of the field-primaryKey field is defined,
primaryKey is nonzero; otherwise, the record is new and it's zero. The call to par
seInt ensures that primaryKey is an integer, not a string.

If parseInt is zero, the add method of the IDBObjectStore in store is called to add a
new object to the database. Otherwise, put is called to update an existing record, identified by its primary key.

Deleting Records

The handler for the Delete button uses the delete method of IDBObjectStore:

```
document.querySelector("#delete").addEventListener("click",
    function () {
        var primaryKey =
          parseInt(document.querySelector("#field-primaryKey").value);
        if (primaryKey > 0) {
            db
            .transaction("mailing-list", "readwrite")
            .objectStore("mailing-list")
            .delete(primaryKey)
            .onsuccess = function (event) {
                fillForm();
                showMessage('Deleted', true);
            };
        }
    }
);
```

A user can delete a record showing in the form only if it was retrieved from the database,
as indicated by the field-primaryKey field being nonzero. If it's zero, no record was
retrieved, so there's nothing to delete. (An improvement would be to disable the Delete
button when it's ineffective.)

Counting Records

The Count button calls the IDBObjectStore method count to count the records:

```
document.querySelector("#count").addEventListener("click",
    function () {
        db
```

```
        .transaction("mailing-list")
        .objectStore("mailing-list")
        .count()
        .onsuccess = function (event) {
            Dialogs.alert(event.target.result + ' objects in database');
        };
    }
);
```

If you click that button, you see the result in Figure 3-8.

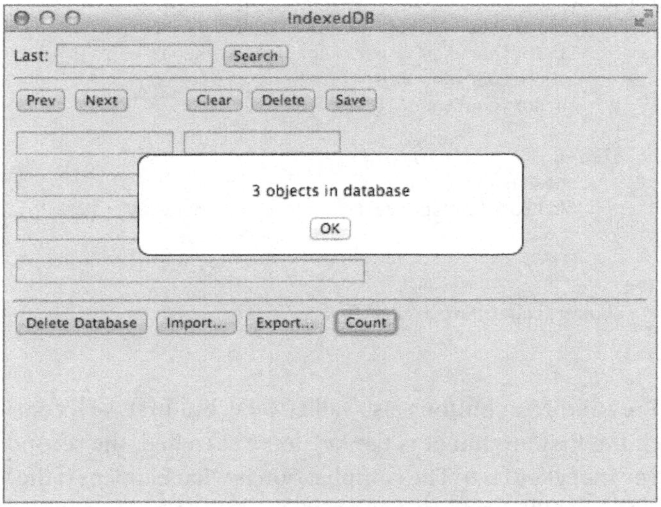

Figure 3-8. Result from clicking the Count button

Searching and Ranges

The Search button searches the database for the name the user typed in the Last field
(id="search-key"). If there's no exact match, it finds the next record in the index. This
involves a couple of new things, cursors and ranges, which I'll explain after you get a
chance to look at the code:

```
document.querySelector("#search").addEventListener("click",
    function () {
        fillForm();
        search(document.querySelector("#search-key").value, "next", 0);
    }
);

function search(key, dir, primaryKey) {
    primaryKey = parseInt(primaryKey);
    var range;
```

```
if (dir === "next")
    range = IDBKeyRange.lowerBound(key, false);
else
    range = IDBKeyRange.upperBound(key, false);
db
.transaction("mailing-list")
.objectStore("mailing-list")
.index("name-index")
.openCursor(range, dir)
.onsuccess = function (event) {
    var cursor = event.target.result;
    if (cursor) {
        if (primaryKey > 0) {
            if (primaryKey === cursor.primaryKey)
                primaryKey = 0;
            cursor.continue();
        }
        else {
            showMessage('');
            fillForm(cursor.value, cursor.primaryKey);
        }
    }
    else
        showMessage('Not found');
};
}
```

Actually, the Prev and Next buttons also call search, but first we'll consider the Search case, for which the first argument is the key to be searched, the second (dir) is next, and the third (primaryKey) is 0. The complication is what happens if the key isn't found, in which case we want the next key. For example, this makes it possible for a search for "Br" to find the first name that starts with "Br", perhaps "Brier."

To do that, instead of using the get method, which is what we saw in "Retrieving Objects by Using an Index" on page 68, we open a cursor on the IDBIndex object, which creates an IDBCursor object that's delivered to its onsuccess callback. With a cursor, you can go through records sequentially. Initially, the onsuccess callback for openCursor has the cursor (in event.target.result) set to the first record in the supplied range. However, if the continue method is called, the cursor moves to the next record in the range, and the onsuccess callback is called again. The cursor stays alive as long as you're in that callback. As soon as it returns—by falling off the end in this case—the cursor goes away.

However, for the Search button, primaryKey is 0, so continue isn't called, and in the else clause the message is cleared and fillForm is called to display the retrieved record, which is that to which the cursor is pointing.

If cursor is undefined, the call to openCursor found nothing in the range, and the message "Not found" is shown.

Now for an explanation of those ranges. The call to `IDBKeyRange.lowerBound` returns a range (an `IDBKeyRange` object) with a lower bound of key (what was typed in the search field). The second argument indicates whether the range should be open, which means that it excludes the key. Here, the key is included in the range so that an exact match will find the record with that last name.

Similarly, `IDBKeyRange.upperBound` returns a range with an upper bound of key.

Because the `dir` argument for the Search button is `next`, the range has an inclusive lower bound equal to the key. This means that the cursor that is opened begins there, with an exact match if there is one, and otherwise with the first record in the range.

I've only explained the part of `search` that the Search button uses, skipping the `primaryKey > 0` case. For the Next button, we have that case:

```
document.querySelector("#next").addEventListener("click",
    function () {
        search(document.querySelector("#field-last").value, "next",
            document.querySelector("#field-primaryKey").value);
    }
);
```

Observe that the first argument now is the last name from the form, not what was typed into the search field at the top of the window.

Here the `primaryKey` argument to `search` is the one from the form's hidden field, which has a nonzero value if that record was retrieved from the database. What the Next button should do is find the *next* record, not the one that's in the form, and that's what this code in the `search` function does:

```
if (primaryKey > 0) {
    if (primaryKey === cursor.primaryKey)
        primaryKey = 0;
    cursor.continue();
}
```

If `primaryKey !== cursor.primaryKey`, the record found is not the one in the form, so we call `continue` to get the next record, and that goes on until we do find the record in the form. Then, we set `primaryKey = 0` to stop after one more `continue`, taking the `else` case next time.

How could it happen that the record found is not the one in the form, when the search range included the last name from the form? Easy: two records have the same last name. The search will find the first one in the index, which might not be the one in the form, so we have to loop until the cursor is positioned on the correct record. *Then*, the next one is the one we want.

Handling the Prev button is similar, except the key is used to set the upper bound of the range, given that `dir` is not equal to `next`:

```
document.querySelector("#prev").addEventListener("click",
    function () {
        search(document.querySelector("#field-last").value, "prev",
            document.querySelector("#field-primaryKey").value);
    }
);
```

Let's recap how searching and navigation work:

1. The Search button finds the first record that matches what's typed into the search field, not necessarily an exact match.

2. The Next button finds the first record that's after the one appearing in the form (with the primary key set).

3. The Prev button finds the record that precedes the one in the form.

Deleting a Database

With most database applications, system-administrator operations such as deleting a database wouldn't be performed by application programs; rather, they would be done using a database utility that only administrators have permission to use. However, because IndexedDB databases are sandboxed, it isn't possible to create a separate utility, not even as a Chrome App, because its app ID wouldn't be the same as the one that owns the database. The same goes for importing and exporting the database: the app has to do it, or it can't be done.

That's why the Delete Database, Import, and Export buttons are there, although in a real app they might be tucked away in a menu, not right there on the main window. They might be password-protected, too.

But I'm in the Wild West (Colorado), so here's the code to delete a database:

```
document.querySelector("#delete_db").addEventListener("click", deleteDatabase);

function deleteDatabase() {
    console.log('d');
    Dialogs.confirm('Delete entire database?', 'Delete', 'Cancel',
        function () {
            fillForm();
            if (db) {
                db.close();
                db = null;
            }
            var request = indexedDB.deleteDatabase("db1");
            request.onsuccess = function() {
                openDatabase();
            };
            request.onerror = errorHandler;
        }
}
```

```
    );
}
```

The existing `IDBDatabase` object in db isn't used, because `deleteDatabase` is a method on the `IDBFactory` object `indexedDB`. After confirmation from the user, the form is cleared and the database is closed, just to be safe. (`db.close` is synchronous, so no callback is needed.) Then, `deleteDatabase` is called and, if it succeeds, the database is reopened so that the app can continue to be used. That is, the database is effectively cleared of data because a new one comes right back. (In your own IndexedDB app, you might want to do things differently.)

Importing Data

Again, importing is an operation that a separate database utility might do, if only such a thing were possible with IndexedDB in Chrome Apps. It works by opening an external file (see "External Files" on page 42) that contains data in JSON format, and then adding each record to the database. Here's the part that reads the file:

```
document.querySelector("#import").addEventListener("click", importData);

function importData() {
    chrome.fileSystem.chooseEntry(
        {
            type: 'openFile'
        },
        function (entry) {
            if (entry) {
                entry.file(
                    function (file) {
                        var reader = new FileReader();
                        reader.onloadend = function() {
                            var objects = JSON.parse(this.result);
                            loadData(objects);
                            showMessage('Opened OK', true);
                        };
                        reader.readAsText(file);
                    },
                    errorHandler
                );
            }
        }
    );
}
```

The JSON objects to be imported are passed to the `loadData` function, which adds them using the same methods that we saw earlier for the Add button:

```
function loadData(objects) {
    var transaction = db.transaction("mailing-list", "readwrite");
    transaction.oncomplete = function(event) {
```

```
        showMessage(objects.length + ' objects imported', true);
    };
    var store = transaction.objectStore("mailing-list");
    for (var x of objects)
        store.add(x);
}
```

Where does the JSON data to be imported come from? One place would be exported data, which comes in the next section. Or, you can get test data in JSON format from *generatedata.com*. It looks something like this:

```
[
    {
        "last": "Hart",
        "first": "Nero",
        "street": "467-6831 Aliquam Rd.",
        "city": "Bridgeport",
        "state": "CT",
        "zip": "36575",
        "email": "vulputate.nisi.sem@lectusconvallisest.co.uk"
    },
    {
        "last": "Keller",
        "first": "Simon",
        "street": "477-1645 Gravida Rd.",
        "city": "Kailua",
        "state": "HI",
        "zip": "48332",
        "email": "ante.ipsum.primis@Nullafacilisi.org"
    },
    ...
]
```

To protect the innocent, this data is fake (as you probably guessed from those ridiculous email addresses).

Exporting Data

Here's the first part of the code for the Export button:

```
document.querySelector("#export").addEventListener("click", exportData);

function exportData() {
    chrome.fileSystem.chooseEntry(
        {
            type: 'saveFile'
        },
        function (entry) {
            if (entry)
                saveToEntry(entry);
        }
    );
```

```
    }

function saveToEntry(entry) {
    entry.createWriter(
        function(fileWriter) {
            fileWriter.onerror = errorHandler;
            fileWriter.onwrite = function() {
                writeData(fileWriter);
            };
            fileWriter.truncate(0);
        },
        errorHandler
    );
}
```

After a `FileWriter` is created and the file is truncated, the actual writing is done by the
`writeData` function. We'll use a cursor to cycle through all the records in the database
and then use the `write` method of the `FileWriter` to write the record, like this:

```
function writeData(fileWriter) {
    var objects = [];
    db
    .transaction("mailing-list")
    .objectStore("mailing-list")
    .openCursor()
    .onsuccess = function (event) {
        var cursor = event.target.result;
        if (cursor) {
            fileWriter.onwrite = function () {
                cursor.continue(); // ouch!
            };
            fileWriter.onerror = errorHandler;
            fileWriter.write(cursor.value);
        }
        else
            writeObjects(fileWriter, objects);
    };
}
```

Because `openCursor` is called with no arguments, it begins with the first record in the
index. The function looks straightforward enough, but it won't work. Before I tell you
why, you might want to pause here and see if you can figure it out for yourself.

Give up? The problem is that, as I said earlier, the cursor is alive only within the `onsuc`
`cess` callback, and execution stays there when the `continue` method is called. However,
the call to `write` is asynchronous, so the `onsuccess` handler returns after it's called,
killing the cursor. In the `onwrite` callback the cursor is no longer defined. The JavaScript
`cursor` variable is still defined, because of function closure; it's just that the object it
points to is no longer in working order.

This is a real screwup, for sure. The `FileWriter` APIs aren't to blame. I think the fault lies with the way cursors are designed. But there's nothing to be done about it, so the way to export with a cursor is to add all the records to a giant object representing the entire database and then, when the cursor is no longer needed, write the entire thing at once. That's what this code does:

```
function writeData(fileWriter) {
    var objects = [];
    db
    .transaction("mailing-list")
    .objectStore("mailing-list")
    .openCursor()
    .onsuccess = function (event) {
        var cursor = event.target.result;
        if (cursor) {
            objects.push(cursor.value);
            cursor.continue();
        }
        else
            writeObjects(fileWriter, objects);
    };
}

function writeObjects(fileWriter, objects) {
    fileWriter.onwrite = function () {
        showMessage(objects.length + ' objects exported', true);
    };
    fileWriter.onerror = errorHandler;
    fileWriter.write(new Blob([JSON.stringify(objects)]));
}
```

Because in this example the primary keys are integers, another way to export would be to retrieve the records one-by-one via the primary key, iterating from 1 until no more objects exist. It's tricky to figure out what the maximum primary key is, because, as a result of deletions, it's not the same as the object count. But, if you can get past that, it would be possible to write the records one-by-one, instead of accumulating thousands of them in a huge object.

Chapter Summary

In this chapter, we described the key-value-pair APIs: Local Storage, Sync Storage, and IndexedDB, which completes the list of storage methods introduced at the beginning of Chapter 2. The one remaining storage topic, media galleries, we'll defer to Chapter 5.

CHAPTER 4

Networking and Messaging

This chapter is mostly concerned with communication between Chrome App clients and servers on the Internet, using both APIs unique to Chrome Apps and APIs that are part of HTML5, such as WebSockets. I also discuss communication between windows in the same app as well as between apps on the same computer. We also explore notifications that an app can pop up at the top of the screen to alert the user.

The first section, which looks at the Socket API, is highly technical and perhaps not of interest to many readers, but it's one of the most important Chrome APIs, so I cover it in detail. However, if you want to go directly to the APIs you're likely to actually use, you can skip that section and start with "The XMLHttpRequest API" on page 94.

Socket API

The Internet communicates by using TCP/IP, the initials of its two most important protocols: Transmission Control Protocol and Internet Protocol. These were developed from research sponsored by the United States government that began in the 1960s. The TCP/IP standard was eventually adopted by the Department of Defense in 1982. A year or so later, an API implementing TCP/IP was released by the University of California in version 4.2BSD (Berkeley Software Distribution) of Unix, and that API came to be called BSD Sockets.

It's not much of an exaggeration to call BSD Sockets the API of the Internet. Nearly all web servers, browsers, email systems, FTP clients and servers, and everything else that talks to the Internet is based on BSD Sockets. That makes BSD Sockets probably the most important and universally implemented API there is.

The BSD Sockets API is today the principal networking API on essentially all general-purpose operating systems, including Windows and Unix-like systems such as OS X and Linux. Other platforms built on Unix-like systems, such as iOS, Android, and Chrome OS, generally wrap the BSD Sockets API with one better suited to their programming environment, and we'll see the details of how Chrome does that later in this chapter.

How BSD Sockets Works

Although the C-language BSD Sockets API isn't used directly by Chrome Apps, it's informative to sketch how it works. The first thing to note is that it's synchronous, as were almost all of the Unix system calls at the time it was designed.

A server creates a socket by using `socket` and then calls `bind` to bind it to a name that can be accessed by clients, such as *api.openweathermap.org* or *23.21.124.185*. Then, it calls `listen` to indicate that it's ready to accept connections from clients, and `accept` to wait until a client connects. The server's thread that issued the `accept` is blocked (it's synchronous) and can't execute until an error occurs or somebody connects.

The client calls `socket` to create a socket. It then calls `connect` to connect to a name that some server is listening on (e.g., *api.openweathermap.org*). While it's waiting, the thread is blocked. When `connect` returns, the client has what in Unix is called a *file descriptor*, open for reading and writing on the socket, and it can use the conventional Unix-style `read` and `write` system calls to communicate with the server.

On the server, when the client connects, the `accept` call returns with a file descriptor for the server's use, open to another socket (not the one the server passed to `accept`), one just for that client. Then, the server must both service the client and issue another blocking `accept`. This requires tricky programming that I won't go into, because it's a Unix issue.

The sockets API is only for connecting client and server; what they say to each other after they're connected is up to them. In practice, various data protocols have been defined, such as HTTP (Hypertext Transfer Protocol) for the web, FTP (File Transfer Protocol), WebSockets, or one of the email protocols such as SMTP (Simple Mail Transfer Protocol) or IMAP (Internet Message Access Protocol). In an example that I'll present shortly, we'll see what HTTP data actually looks like.

Chrome Socket API

For two reasons, the BSD Sockets API isn't a good match for Chrome Apps: first, BSD Sockets is synchronous (`accept` and `connect` block until something happens), and second, it's a C-language interface. Thus, the Chrome Socket API is a thin layer on top of BSD Sockets that's designed specifically for JavaScript programs. (Don't confuse the Chrome Socket API with HTML5 WebSockets, discussed in "WebSockets" on page 109.)

There are three Chrome Socket APIs:

- `chrome.sockets.tcpServer` for implementing servers.

- `chrome.sockets.tcp` for implementing clients.
- `chrome.sockets.udp`, an alternative to TCP that uses packets instead of connections. This is very rarely used compared to TCP, and therefore not discussed in this book.

 Even though it's strange to think of developing a server as a Chrome App, it's possible, and it's good to know that the APIs are there if you ever need them. More commonly, of course, Chrome Apps are clients, so I'll present just `chrome.sockets.tcp`, and you can investigate the server APIs when and if you need them. Having said that, you'll rarely even be using `chrome.sockets.tcp`, because there are higher-level APIs that are much easier to use, such as `XMLHttpRequest` and WebSockets, which I'll get to later in this chapter.

To use the socket API, you need to add a `socket` section to the *manifest.json* file. It's not a permission but a section in its own right where you specify the host and port to which you want to connect:

```
{
    "app": {
        "background": {
            "scripts": [ "background.js" ]
        }
    },
    ...
    "sockets": {
        "tcp": {
            "connect": "api.openweathermap.org:80"
        }
    }
}
```

A client starts by creating a socket:

```
chrome.sockets.tcp.create(properties, callback)
```

The `properties` are for unusual situations and normally can be empty. The `callback` is called when the socket is created; it's passed a `createInfo` object with one important property, `socketId`, which identifies the socket. For example, this code displays the socket ID 3 on the console:

```
chrome.sockets.tcp.create({},
    function (createInfo) {
        console.log(createInfo.socketId);
    }
);
```

After you create the socket, the next step is to connect to a host and port:

```
chrome.sockets.tcp.connect(socketId, address, port, callback)
```

If `chrome.runtime.lastError` is defined when the callback is called, an error occurred; otherwise, the client has connected:

```
chrome.sockets.tcp.create({},
    function (createInfo) {
        console.log(createInfo.socketId);
        chrome.sockets.tcp.connect(createInfo.socketId,
            "api.openweathermap.org", 80,
            function (result) {
                if (chrome.runtime.lastError)
                    console.log(chrome.runtime.lastError.message);
                else {
                    console.log(result);
                }
            }
        );
    }
);
```

There isn't any interesting `result`, just a zero to indicate that all is well.

After the connection is made, the client can send data to the server. Because *api.open-weathermap.org* is an HTTP server, you must talk to it in HTTP, which means sending a `GET` request, which looks something like this:

```
GET /data/2.1/find/name?units=imperial&q=Chicago HTTP/1.1\r\n
Host: api.openweathermap.org\r\n
\r\n
```

Each line is terminated by a carriage return/newline combination (denoted by \r\n), and the request must end with a blank line. The path and query string are defined by the folks at *openweathermap.org* in their API specification for using their weather map service, which we'll be using for a few example apps. In JavaScript, you'd write the request like this:

```
var req = "GET /data/2.1/find/name?units=imperial&q=Chicago HTTP/1.1\r\n" +
    "Host: api.openweathermap.org\r\n\r\n";
```

But, you can't just send a plain string—it must be a JavaScript `ArrayBuffer`. Using the relatively new `TextEncoder` API, here's a function to do the conversion:

```
function str2ab(str) {
    var encoder = new TextEncoder('utf-8');
    return encoder.encode(str).buffer;
}
```

The reverse function, which we'll need later, is the following:

```
function ab2str(ab) {
    var dataView = new DataView(ab);
    var decoder = new TextDecoder('utf-8');
```

```
        return decoder.decode(dataView);
    }
```

The API `chrome.sockets.tcp.send` does the sending after the connection has been made:

```
chrome.sockets.tcp.send(socketId, arrayBufferData, callback)
```

Now, we can do a little HTTP by sending the GET request to *api.openweathermap.org*:

```
var req = "GET /data/2.1/find/name?units=imperial&q=Chicago HTTP/1.1\r\n" +
    "Host: api.openweathermap.org\r\n\r\n";

chrome.sockets.tcp.create({},
    function (createInfo) {
        console.log(createInfo.socketId);
        chrome.sockets.tcp.connect(createInfo.socketId,
            "api.openweathermap.org", 80,
            function (result) {
                if (chrome.runtime.lastError)
                    console.log(chrome.runtime.lastError.message);
                else {
                    console.log(result);
                    chrome.sockets.tcp.send(createInfo.socketId,
                        str2ab(req),
                        function (sendInfo) {
                            console.log(sendInfo);
                        }
                    );
                }
            }
        );
    }
);
```

The `sendInfo` on the console should display as `{bytesSent: 42, resultCode: 0}`.

The request has been sent, but we didn't set up a handler to receive anything back. We do that by using `chrome.sockets.tcp.onReceive.addListener`, whose callback function gets an `info` object with one property: `data`. It's an `ArrayBuffer`, so we use `ab2str` to convert it to text:

```
chrome.sockets.tcp.onReceive.addListener(
    function (info) {
        if (info.data)
            console.log(ab2str(info.data));
    }
);
```

With the `onReceive` handler in place, we can rerun the sending code, and the entire HTML of the response—the weather in Chicago—appears on the console, as shown in Example 4-1.

Example 4-1. Response from GET request

```
HTTP/1.1 200 OK
Server: nginx
Date: Wed, 19 Mar 2014 14:38:26 GMT
Content-Type: text/html
Transfer-Encoding: chunked
Connection: keep-alive
X-Source: back

24d
```

```
{"message":"","cod":"200","type":"base","calctime":"","units":"imperial","
count":1,"list":[{"id":4887398,"coord":{"lat":41.850029,"lon":-87.650047},
"name":"Chicago","main":{"temp":43.74,"pressure":1002,"humidity":93,"
temp_min":41,"temp_max":46.4},"dt":1395237126,"date":"2014-03-19
13:52:06","wind":{"speed":7.78,"deg":210,"gust":7.2},"clouds":{"all":90},"
weather":[{"id":500,"main":"Rain","description":"light
rain","icon":"10d"},{"id":701,"main":"Mist","description":"mist","icon":"
50d"}],"sys":{"country":"US","population":2695598},"url":"http:\/\/
openweathermap.org\/city\/4887398"}]}
```

```
0
```

The meat of the response is the JSON data we requested, which is easy to parse, and we'll soon see how that's done in a small weather-report application that accesses *api.openweathermap.org*.

Modules and Module Loading

In the next section, I'm going to present code in the form of a *module*, so here's a brief excursion to explain how I use modules in JavaScript.

Generally, a module is a software component that implements functionality through a formally defined interface, the implementation of which is hidden inside the module. JavaScript, unlike almost all other languages, doesn't have modules built in, but you can accomplish the same thing by defining an object with an exposed interface and internal functions and variables to implement that interface.

As an example, a module defining socket functionality, in a file named *socket.js*, might look like this:

```
var Socket = (function () {
    var module_var1 = 0;
    // ... more module variables ...

    var api = {
        HttpRequest: function () {
        }
    };

    api.HttpRequest.prototype.method1 = function () {
```

```
        // ...
    };

    // ... more methods ...

    return api;

    function internal_function1() {
        // ...
    }

    // ... more internal functions ...

})();
```

The global `Socket` is the module object, and its value is set by calling an anonymous function, so anything defined inside the function is local to it and invisible to the rest of the app. Note that the function definition is enclosed in parentheses, so as not to confuse the JavaScript parser, and then it's immediately called, with the open and close parentheses on the very last line.

The anonymous function returns a module object with one method, `HttpRequest`, that's a constructor for a `HttpRequest` object. The module object is assigned to the `Socket` global variable, so you refer to the constructor as `Socket.HttpRequest`. The `Socket.HttpRequest` object has a public method, `method1`, and a module-wide variable, `module_var1`, which is internal to the `Socket` module, but visible to everything inside the module.

You use the `Socket.HttpRequest` object like this:

```
var skt = new Socket.HttpRequest();
skt.method1();
```

The *socket.js* file is only one of several utility objects we'll be defining, and it's a nuisance to keep adding `script` tags to the HTML file—made especially tricky because some will refer to others, so the order of inclusion matters. I like to include just one file, *common.html*, and have it load the other JavaScript files:

```
<script src="Socket.js"></script>
<script src="Facebook.js"></script>
<!-- ... more modules to be loaded -->
```

Now, I can list the modules I commonly use in one file. (We'll see *Facebook.js* later in this chapter.) All of the modules are in a *lib* subdirectory, so most of the *index.html* files in the examples from now on will have one `<link>` tag (for *common.html*, if needed, and one `<script>` tag for the app code):

```
<!DOCTYPE html>
<html lang="en">
<head>
```

```
        <meta charset="utf-8" />
        <title>WeatherReport</title>
        <link rel="import" href="lib/common.html">
        <script src="WeatherReport.js"></script>
    </head>
    <body>
    ...
```

I'll be following this scheme for all of the modules that I present in this book. It's probably the simplest approach that provides the essentials without getting too complicated; thus, our focus can stay on Chrome Apps. If you want something more feature-rich, you can read about the Asynchronous Module Definition (AMD) API at *github.com/amdjs/ amdjs-api*. AMD and dynamic loading are supported by RequireJS (*http://requir ejs.org/*), which works well with Chrome Apps.

Wrapping the Socket API as an Object in a Module

Our socket example works, but it's an awkward way to use sockets. The API calls aren't especially hard to code, but they're tedious to write, and doing all those string conversions is annoying. What we want are some simple wrapper functions that we can use any time we need to use sockets for HTTP requests.

It's most convenient if all of the code for these functions is placed in a single JavaScript file that defines a module. We'll implement the object `Socket.HttpRequest` as such a module, basing it on the `chrome.sockets.tcp` example code that we already have.

We don't normally think of a URL as a host plus a path; rather, we consider it one continuous string, so we'd like the `Socket.HttpRequest` object to parse it for us by using a method that we'll call open, like this:

```
var skt = new Socket.HttpRequest();
skt.open("get",
    "http://api.openweathermap.org/data/2.1/find/name" +
    "?units=imperial&cnt=2&q=Chicago");
```

I've formed the URL from two concatenated strings so that the code fits on this page. The first argument says that GET should be used, in case we want to implement POST requests, too, at some point. Here's the code for open:

```
var Socket = (function () {

var api = {
    HttpRequest: function () {
    }
};

api.HttpRequest.prototype.open = function (method, url) {
    var a = url.match(/^http:\/\/([^/]*)(.*)$/);
    this.host = a[1];
    this.path = a[2];
```

```
        this.req = "GET " + this.path + " HTTP/1.1\r\nHost: " +
            this.host + "\r\n\r\n";
    };

    return api;
})();
```

This method adds several object properties (for example, `this.host`) to the object, for use later.

Before we're ready to go further, there's a problem: the `chrome.sockets.tcp.onRe ceive` handler is global and is called for data received on *any* socket. However, we'll want to associate a receive callback with a specific `Socket.HttpRequest` instance, so the single handler will have to know what callback to call. We do that by using a global (to the module) array of `Socket.HttpRequest` instances, indexed by socket ID:

```
var activeSockets = [];
```

When a socket is created, the object reference is stored in `activeSockets`, and then the handler has a way to find out which object belongs to that socket. We can see this in the code for the `send` method, which is almost identical to the earlier example, except that some of the literals have been replaced by object properties:

```
api.HttpRequest.prototype.send = function () {
    var that = this;
    chrome.sockets.tcp.create({},
        function (createInfo) {
            activeSockets[createInfo.socketId] = that;
            chrome.sockets.tcp.connect(createInfo.socketId, that.host, 80,
                function (result) {
                    if (chrome.runtime.lastError) {
                        if (that.onerror)
                            that.onerror(chrome.runtime.lastError.message);
                    }
                    else {
                        chrome.sockets.tcp.send(createInfo.socketId,
                          str2ab(that.req),
                            function (sendInfo) {
                            }
                        );
                    }
                }
            );
        }
    );
}
```

A well-known JavaScript trap is that local functions (such as the callback in this example) have `this` set to themselves, rather than to the outer object. Consider this line:

```
chrome.sockets.tcp.connect(createInfo.socketId, that.host, 80,
```

If the code had used this.host, it would have been undefined because this would refer to the callback passed to chrome.sockets.tcp.create, not to the Socket.HttpRequest instance. The fix is to define a that variable local to the method and refer to it, as shown in the code.

If an error occurs, a onerror callback is called if it's defined, as it might be like this:

```
skt.onerror = function (msg) {
    // display the msg
};
```

To send the request, all we have to do is add a call to send to what we had before:

```
var skt = new Socket.HttpRequest();
skt.open("get",
    "http://api.openweathermap.org/data/2.1/find/name" +
    "?units=imperial&cnt=2&q=Chicago");
skt.send();
```

Now, we're ready for the chrome.sockets.tcp.onReceive handler, which can use the activeSockets array to figure out to which object the socket ID belongs:

```
chrome.sockets.tcp.onReceive.addListener(
    function (info) {
        var req = activeSockets[info.socketId];
        if (req) {
            if (info.data)
                req.receiveData(ab2str(info.data));
            else
                req.receiveData();
        }
    }
);
```

Recall from Example 4-1 that the data comes back in the form of an HTTP header followed by some JSON (if the request succeeded). The format of the response follows this pattern, assuming chunking (splitting the response into pieces), which is how openweathermap.org delivers it:

```
HTTP/1.1 <status> OK
...

<count>
<json>


0
```

Finding the status and, if it's 200 (the HTTP success code), extracting the JSON, is the job of the receiveData method. I've written it only for a single chunk; if you want, you can extend it for multiple chunks and for unchunked responses. Here's the code:

```
api.HttpRequest.prototype.receiveData = function (s) {
    var a = s.split("\r\n");
    var msg;
    if (a.length > 0) {
        if (a[0].indexOf("HTTP/1.1 ") == 0)
            this.statusText = a[0].substr(9);
        else
            this.statusText = a[0];
        this.status = parseInt(this.statusText);
    }
    else {
        this.status = 0;
        this.statusText = null;
    }
    if (this.status == 200) {
        var a = s.split("\r\n\r\n");
        var n = a[1].indexOf("{");
        var len = parseInt(a[1], 16);
        this.response = a[1].substr(n, len);
    }
    else
        this.response = null;
    if (this.onload)
        this.onload();
}
```

The app can set a callback like the following to receive the response:

```
skt.onload = function () {
    // data was received
}
```

Finally, there's an error callback, using `chrome.sockets.tcp.onReceiveError.addLis`
`tener`, which I didn't show earlier. It also uses the `activeSockets` array to find the object:

```
chrome.sockets.tcp.onReceiveError.addListener(
    function (info) {
        var req = activeSockets[info.socketId];
        if (req && req.onerror)
            req.onerror("Result Code: " + info.resultCode);
    }
);
```

Although `Socket.HttpRequest` is only for HTTP, its HTTP-ness resides in the form of data sent and how received data is interpreted. All of the socket plumbing is universal and can work for any Internet protocol.

A Weather Report App

In this section, we're going to use `Socket.HttpRequest` to implement a simple weather report app, which you can see in Figure 4-1. When you type a city and click the Get Weather button, a report displays, as shown in Figure 4-2.

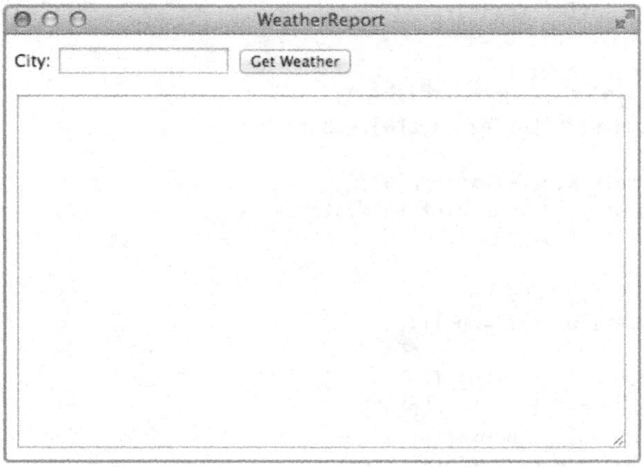

Figure 4-1. The initial Weather Report window

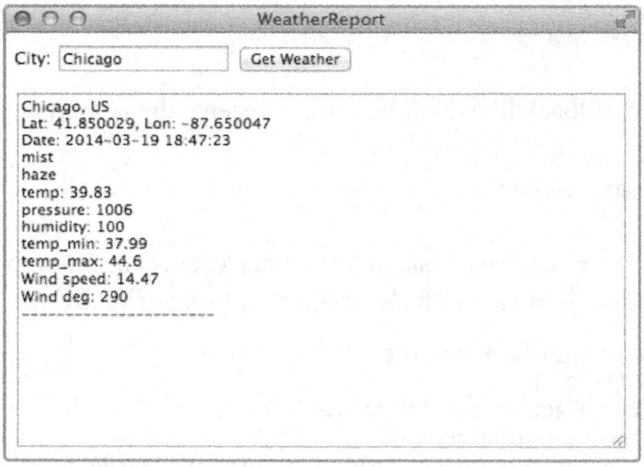

Figure 4-2. A weather report for Chicago

The *index.html* file is pretty simple (note the link and script elements):

```
<!DOCTYPE html>
<html lang="en">
<head>
    <meta charset="utf-8" />
    <title>WeatherReport</title>
    <link rel="import" href="lib/common.html">
    <script src="WeatherReport.js"></script>
</head>
```

```
<body>
    <label for="city">City:</label>
    <input type="text" id="city">
    <button id="get">Get Weather</button>
    <p>
    <textarea id="textarea" cols="60" rows="20" readonly
      style='outline: none;'></textarea>
    </p>
    <p id="message"></p>
</body>
</html>
```

The app's JavaScript file, *WeatherReport.js*, begins with the usual onload handler:

```
window.onload = function () {

var skt = new Socket.HttpRequest();

document.querySelector("#get").addEventListener("click",
    function () {
        getWeather(document.querySelector("#city").value);
    }
);

};
```

When the button is clicked, getWeather is called. It uses Socket.HttpRequest, just as we've seen in the examples earlier:

```
function getWeather(city) {
    var textarea = document.querySelector("#textarea");
    textarea.value = "Wait...";

    skt.onload = function () {
        if (skt.status === 200) {
            var obj = JSON.parse(skt.response);
            showMessage(obj.message, true);
            textarea.value = formatWeather(obj);
        }
        else
            showMessage("Error: " + skt.status);
    }

    skt.onerror = function (msg) {
        showMessage(msg);
    };
    skt.open("get", "http://api.openweathermap.org/data/2.1/find/name" +
      "?units=imperial&cnt=2&q=" + city);
    skt.send();
}
```

The showMessage function is the same one we used in Chapters 2 and 3. Because the JSON response has already been extracted if the status is 200, it's easy to convert it to a

JavaScript object by using the call to `JSON.parse`. Sometimes, the `openweather map.org` API provides a `message` property, which is displayed. Then, the report object is passed on to `formatWeather` for formatting:

```javascript
function formatWeather(value) {
    if (!value.list || value.list.count == 0)
        return "No cities found";
    var s = "";
    for (var x of value.list) {
        s += x.name;
        if (x.sys.country)
            s += ", " + x.sys.country;
        s += "\n";
        s += "Lat: " + x.coord.lat + ", Lon: " + x.coord.lon + "\n";
        s += "Date: " + x.date + "\n";
        for (var d of x.weather)
            s += d.description + "\n";
        if (x.main)
            for (var k in x.main)
                s += k + ": " + x.main[k] + "\n";
        if (x.wind)
            for (var k in x.wind)
                s += "Wind " + k + ": " + x.wind[k] + "\n";
        if (x.rain)
            s += "Rain today: " + x.rain.today + "\n";
        s += "--------------------\n";
    }
    return s;
}
```

There's no methodology that you can use to construct functions like `formatWeather`, because every API I've used formats its results differently. You just keep horsing around until you've got something you like, which is what I did. You'll find it helpful to dump out the object with `console.log` so that you can explore its properties.

The XMLHttpRequest API

There might have been something familiar to you about `Socket.HttpRequest`: it's a lot like `XMLHttpRequest`, which is built in to Chrome and most other browsers. Actually, `Socket.HttpRequest` is modeled on `XMLHttpRequest` exactly, both to provide an example of how you use sockets, and to provide an in-depth explanation of what `XMLHttpRequest` actually does under the covers.

Incidentally, although `XMLHttpRequest` is at the heart of the Ajax technique, which is widely used for dynamic websites, it has little to do with XML and, in fact, is just as often used with JSON, as we did.

The name Ajax started out life presented in all uppercase (AJAX) and until not long ago was actually an acronym that stood for Asynchronous JavaScript and XML. Today, the convention is to consider it just a name, spelled "Ajax."

I had a surprise in store all along: you can change the Weather Report example to use XMLHttpRequest by changing the following single line of code:

```
var skt = new XMLHttpRequest();
```

You also need to add any URLs you access as permissions to the *manifest.json* file, not in the socket section that was required for chrome.sockets.tcp, but as actual permissions, like this:

```
"permissions": [
    "http://api.openweathermap.org/*"
],
```

If you don't want to enumerate every URL in the permissions section, you can arrange for the app to access any and all URLs:

```
"permissions": [
    "<all_urls>"
]
```

With these minor changes, the app behaves exactly as before, but now using the built-in XMLHttpRequest API instead of one based on chrome.sockets.tcp.

For HTTP, you're definitely better off with XMLHttpRequest as opposed to doing the same thing with sockets, but XMLHttpRequest is only for HTTP and HTTPS requests. You'll go to sockets when you need to implement a nonstandard protocol, as might be used by specialized devices such as drones or programmable ball machines.

It's convenient to put a wrapper around XMLHttpRequest. This makes it even easier to use and was inspired by the popular Ajax function in jQuery, but with a very different interface. Here it is as a module in the file *Ajax.js*:

```
var Ajax = (function () {
    var api = {
        ajaxSend: function (url, responseType, successCallback, errorCallback,
          headers) {
            var req = new XMLHttpRequest();
            req.onload = function (e) {
                successCallback(req.status, req.response);
            };
            req.onerror = errorCallback;
            req.responseType = responseType ? responseType : "text";
            req.open("get", url);
            if (headers)
                for (var v in headers)
```

```
                              req.setRequestHeader(v, headers[v]);
                    req.send();
                }
        };
        return api;
    })();
```

One feature of XMLHttpRequest that we haven't used but that is implemented by the Ajax object, is a fifth argument to ajaxSend that provides headers to be added to the request. We'll need that feature later, in "Accessing Google APIs" on page 106.

To see how to use the Ajax object, here's a rewrite of getWeather from the Weather Report app we developed earlier:

```
function getWeather(city) {
    var textarea = document.querySelector("#textarea");
    textarea.value = "Wait...";

    Ajax.ajaxSend("http://api.openweathermap.org/data/2.1/find/name" +
        "?units=imperial&cnt=2&q=" + city, "json",
        function (status, obj) {
            if (status === 200) {
                showMessage(obj.message, true);
                textarea.value = formatWeather(obj);
            }
            else
                showMessage("Error: " + status);
        },
        function (e) {
            showMessage("Communication error");
            console.log('Communication error:', e);
        }
    );
}
```

We'll see more uses of the Ajax module later in this chapter when we use the chrome.identity API to access Facebook.

Identity API

Anybody can access *api.openweathermap.org*, but when you access nonpublic resources on sites such as Facebook, you must log in. In the past, apps did this by requesting a login name and password from the user and then storing that so it could be used with whatever login API the website provided. This created a few problems:

- It isn't safe to have logins and passwords stored in various places, because there's no guarantee that they're sufficiently protected.

- There's no way to revoke permission for the app to access the site, other than changing the password. (Deleting the app from your computer isn't an option if it's actually a website.)

- Permissions are all-or-nothing. There's no way to provide permission to access the site but not update it; when the app is logged in, it has all the privileges of a user.

A few years ago an API called OAuth became widely available. With OAuth, you don't provide your login and password to an app that needs to log in; rather, the app contacts the website you're trying to access (for example, Facebook) and requests the permissions it needs. You then get an authorization request from the website, not from the app. If you grant permission, the website provides a token to the app that it can use to access APIs. You can go to the website and revoke permission at any time, causing the token to become invalid. The important part is that the app never sees your login or password.

The first version of OAuth was complicated to use, but OAuth2 is much more straight-forward. It's especially easy for Chrome Apps because there's a `chrome.identi ty.launchWebAuthFlow` API that does all the work for you:

```
chrome.identity.launchWebAuthFlow(details, callback)
```

The `details` include the OAuth2 URL provided by the website and a few other options, as we'll see shortly.

You need `identity` permission in the *manifest.json* file as well as permission for any URLs you need to access. Here's the easiest way to do this:

```
"permissions": [
    "identity",
    "<all_urls>"
]
```

Accessing the Facebook API

When the `chrome.identity.launchWebAuthFlow` call is made, the user sees a login form from the website, similar to the one in Figure 4-3. Then, after successfully logging in, the user sees an authorization form (Figure 4-4) listing just the permissions requested by the app.

If the user authorizes the app, `chrome.identity.launchWebAuthFlow` calls its callback function and provides the app with an *access token*. If the user had already authorized the app in a previous launch, `chrome.identity.launchWebAuthFlow` will provide the access token without any dialogs, in effect keeping the user "logged in."

Figure 4-3. The Facebook login window

Figure 4-4. A Facebook authorization window

At any time, the user can go to the website to revoke permission for the app, as shown in Figure 4-5 for Facebook.

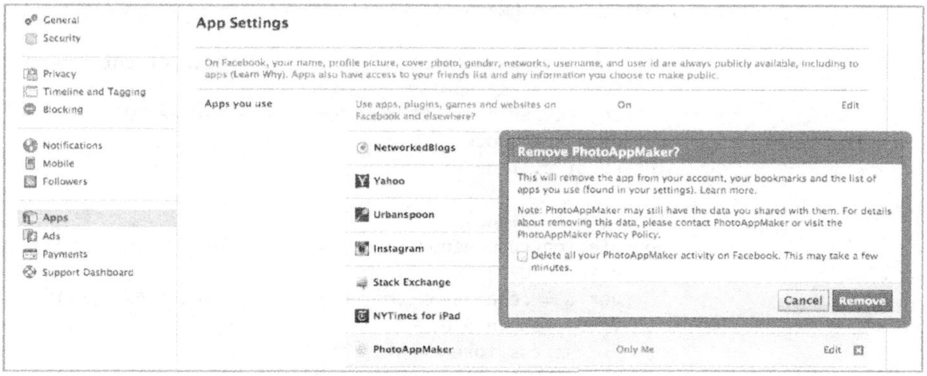

Figure 4-5. Revoking an app's Facebook authorization

What makes OAuth2 challenging to use isn't the interaction with the website—which is automated by the Chrome API—but figuring out what URL to pass to `chrome.iden tity.launchWebAuthFlow`. You'll need to study the website's developer documentation in depth; here, I'll show the details for Facebook, but, unfortunately, you'll find that every website does it differently.

Facebook uses a URL similar to the following (broken into several lines for readability):

```
https://www.facebook.com/dialog/oauth
?client_id=<clientID>
&response_type=token
&redirect_uri=<redirect_uri>
&scope=<scope>
```

The `<clientID>`, a 15-digit number, is provided by Facebook when the app is registered by the developer—yet another step that's done differently for every website, although Facebook makes it fairly easy. (Log in to Facebook and find the Create App page; doing it for apps that want to use Google APIs is described in Appendix B.)

The `<redirect_uri>` is what Facebook accesses when the OAuth2 process is completed. For Chrome Apps, there's an API for getting it: `chrome.identity.getRedirectURL`.

The `<scope>` is the list of permissions you want authorized, which is documented on the website's developer pages. For our Facebook example, we just need `user_photos`.

We'll put the call to `chrome.identity.launchWebAuthFlow` in an `authorize` method of a `Facebook` object defined in *lib/Facebook.js*:

```
var Facebook = (function () {
    var access_token = null;
    var api = {
        authorize: function (clientID, scope, callback) {
            access_token = null;
```

```
        chrome.identity.launchWebAuthFlow(
            {
                url: "https://www.facebook.com/dialog/oauth?client_id=" +
                    clientID + "&response_type=token&" +
                    "redirect_uri=" + chrome.identity.getRedirectURL() + "&" +
                    "scope=" + scope,
                interactive: true
            },
            function (responseURL) {
                console.log(responseURL);
                if (responseURL) {
                    var a = responseURL.match(/access_token=([^&]*)&/);
                    if (a.length > 0)
                        access_token = a[1];
                    callback(true);
                }
                else
                    callback(false);
            }
        );
    }
    };
    return api;
})();
```

In the first argument (`detail`) to `chrome.identity.launchWebAuthFlow`, the `interactive` property is set to `true` so we get the login/authorization interaction that we saw earlier, which is required for Facebook and most other websites that use OAuth2.

If authorization succeeds, `responseURL` is a string containing various parameters, so that we use a regular expression to extract the `access_token`, which we store in a module variable. Then, we call the app's callback by specifying `true`, indicating that the app can proceed to execute various Facebook APIs, which I'll show shortly.

I'll show the app that uses the `Facebook` object soon, but for now here's the part that calls `Facebook.authorize` (the client ID is bogus):

```
Facebook.authorize('123...345', 'user_photos',
    function () {
        getPhotos();
    }
);
```

The function `getPhotos`, which we'll see when we see the app, displays the Facebook photos.

There's one more method to look at: `Facebook.call`, which makes Facebook API calls after an app is authorized. Again, every website is different, so you need to study the developer documentation to find out how the API works. This isn't a book about accessing Facebook, so I'll just explain the one call we'll use (there are dozens of them):

```
https://graph.facebook.com/me/photos/uploaded?access_token=<access-token>
```

Facebook uses what it calls a Graph API, which works like this: we start with `me` (the logged-in user), navigate to the user's `photos`, and then to the `uploaded` photos. Each API call returns its results differently, but always as a JSON-formatted object that you must explore to find what you want, although Facebook does document the subobjects and their properties.

For photos, it's easy: the returned object is an array of `Photo` objects, each of which has properties such as `source`, the URL of the photo, `width`, and `height`. We'll use those properties in the app.

With that introduction, here's the `Facebook.call` method from *lib/Facebook.js*:

```javascript
call: function (method, successCallback, errorCallback) {
    var url = 'https://graph.facebook.com/' + method;
    if (method.indexOf('?') === -1)
        url += '?';
    else
        url += '&';
    url += 'access_token=' + access_token;
    Ajax.ajaxSend(url, "json",
        function (status, response) {
            if (response.error) {
                var err = response.error;
                if (response.error.message)
                    err = response.error.message;
                if (errorCallback)
                    errorCallback(response.error.message);
            }
            else
                successCallback(response);
```

```
            }
        );
    }
```

In building up the URL, we need to precede the `access_token` parameter with & if the method itself had a ?, which some do; otherwise, we use a ?. We send the query with `Ajax.ajaxSend` (see "The XMLHttpRequest API" on page 94).

A Facebook Photos App

With the `Facebook` object in hand, let's build a little app to show Facebook photos (mine), as presented in Figure 4-6.

Figure 4-6. The Facebook photos app

This simple app doesn't have any buttons or any options; when you launch it, it gets authorization (if isn't already authorized), gets a list of photos, and displays them in the window. The *index.html* file is pretty simple, consisting mostly of CSS to make the content `div` fill the entire window and to display "Wait…" while the photos are being fetched.

```
<!DOCTYPE html>
<html lang="en">
<head>
    <meta charset="utf-8" />
    <title>FBphotos</title>
    <link rel="import" href="lib/common.html">
```

```
    <script src="FBphotos.js"></script>
    <style>
        body, html {
            height: 100%;
            margin: 0;
        }
        #content {
            overflow-y: scroll;
            height: 100%;
            position: relative;
            background-color: black;
        }
        #wait {
            margin: 100px 100px;
            color: white;
            font-size: 30px;
        }
    </style>
</head>
<body>
    <div id="content"><p id="wait">Wait...</p></div>
</body>
</html>
```

As usual, the app file, *FBphotos.js*, puts all of the code in the onload handler to ensure that the HTML is processed and all the modules are loaded:

```
window.onload = function () {

Facebook.authorize('123...345', 'user_photos',
    function () {
        getPhotos();
    }
);
window.onresize = layoutPhotos;

// ... rest of app

};
```

Laying out the photos in the window is the job of layoutPhotos, which is also the handler for onresize events.

As I mentioned earlier, getPhotos executes the Facebook API call to retrieve the URLs of the uploaded photos, an example of which is shown here:

```
https://scontent-a.xx.fbcdn.net/hphotos-ash3/t1.0-9/s720x720/
48007_10200417185706189_1210761502_n.jpg
```

Because of a Chrome App restriction, you can't just set this URL as the src attribute of an <img> element and add it to the HTML, a technique that would work just fine in a web page. Instead, you must access the image's URL via HTTP and get the binary data coming back (compressed JPEG data) as a `Blob`, form it into a very long URL that contains the literal `Blob` data, and then use that self-contained URL in the `<img>` element. It's convenient to code a method to do that conversion in a `Photo` object, in the file *Photo.js*:

```javascript
var Photo = (function () {
    var api = {
        getBlobUri: function(url, callback) {
            Ajax.ajaxSend(url, "blob",
                function (status, response) {
                    callback(URL.createObjectURL(response));
                }
            );
        }
    };
    return api;
})();
```

The creation of the `Blob`-containing URL is done by `URL.createObjectURL`, which is built into Chrome.

With the `Photo.getBlobUri` method, we're ready to look at `getPhotos`:

```javascript
var photos;

function getPhotos() {
    Facebook.call('/me/photos/uploaded',
        function (response) {
            photos = response.data;
            var blobCount = 0;
            photos.forEach(
                function (photo) {
                    Photo.getBlobUri(photo.source,
                        function (blob_uri) {
                            photo.blob_uri = blob_uri;
                            if (++blobCount === photos.length)
                                layoutPhotos();
                        }
                    );
                }
            );
        }
    );
}
```

The `Photo.getBlobUri` callback has only three lines of code, but they're tricky:

- The returned URI is added to the `Photo` object. That's a little adventurous because the object was supplied by Facebook, but there's not much chance that Facebook will ever have a property called `blob_uri`.

- Like most things worth doing, `Photo.getBlobUri` is asynchronous, and we don't want to lay out and display the photos until we've converted all the source URLs. So, we keep a count of how many were converted and call `layoutPhotos` only when they're all done.

One way or another—because the photos were just downloaded or because the window was resized—`layoutPhotos` lays out and displays the photos:

```
function layoutPhotos() {
    var gap = 5;
    var div = document.querySelector('#content');
    while (div.firstChild)
        div.removeChild(div.firstChild);
    var totalHeight = layout(photos, div.clientWidth, div.clientHeight / 4, gap);
    var img;
    photos.forEach(
        function (photo) {
            img = new Image();
            img.src = photo.blob_uri;
            img.style['max-width'] = photo.xWidth + 'px';
            img.style['max-height'] = photo.xHeight + 'px';
            img.style['left'] = photo.xLeft + 'px';
            img.style['top'] = photo.xTop + 'px';
            img.style['position'] = 'absolute';
            div.appendChild(img);
        }
    );
    img.style['margin-bottom'] = gap + 'px'; // gap at bottom of whole div
}

function layout(photos, targetWidth, targetHeight, gap) {
    var x = gap;
    var y = gap;
    photos.forEach(
        function (photo) {
            photo.xHeight = targetHeight;
            photo.xWidth = photo.width * targetHeight / photo.height;
            var cellWidth = photo.xWidth + 5;
            if (x + cellWidth > targetWidth) {
                x = gap;
                y += targetHeight + gap;
            }
            photo.xLeft = x;
            photo.xTop = y;
            x += cellWidth;
        }
    );
}
```

The `layout` function determines where each photo goes with a very simple scheme not unlike how a word processor fills lines with ragged-right text. You can see the results in

Figure 4-6. These two functions don't do anything particularly related to Chrome Apps, so I won't go through them line by line. All they do is take the dimensions of each photo to figure out where it goes and then construct a corresponding `<img>` element, which is then appended to the HTML.

I won't show the code here, but there's a much more sophisticated layout algorithm in the Photo object (*Photos.js*) that you can find in the online example code for this book.

Accessing Google APIs

Like Facebook and many other sites, Google requires that an app be registered to get a client ID before it can use any APIs. The steps for getting a client ID through Google are enumerated in Appendix B.

Google uses OAuth2, but there's a special authorization API just for Google, used in place of `chrome.identity.launchWebAuthFlow`, called `chrome.identity.getAuthToken`:

```
chrome.identity.getAuthToken(details, callback)
```

The `details` are the same as for `chrome.identity.launchWebAuthFlow`: an object with the `interactive` property, which you'll usually set to `true`. The callback function gets the access token directly, so you don't have to extract it from a response URL, as we did earlier in the FBphotos example. If the token argument is undefined, an error occurred.

Instead of passing the client ID and scope directly to the OAuth2 call as URL parameters, `chrome.identity.getAuthToken` takes them from the manifest:

```
"permissions": [
    "identity"
],
"key": "MIIBIjANB...yyltEwIDAQAB",
"oauth2": {
    "client_id": "2546277...3kj.apps.googleusercontent.com",
    "scopes": [
        "https://www.googleapis.com/auth/drive"
    ]
}
```

The various scopes are documented along with the particular API you're using. Appendix B explains how to get the client ID and how to include a key property in the manifest so that the app ID remains fixed, because having it change during development is awkward and prone to error.

After the app is authorized by `chrome.identity.getAuthToken`, you can issue calls specified by the API you want to use. There are dozens of them at *developers.google.com/apis-explorer*.

As a simple example, the GDrive app shown in Figure 4-7 lists files on your Google Drive.

```
2013-05-29T02:16:19.295Z  articles
2013-05-24T01:37:44.177Z  Account - Dropbox.mhtml
2013-05-23T13:34:34.812Z  Backup-codes-mrochkind.txt
2013-05-06T13:13:56.408Z  EPMADD
2013-03-21T03:45:32.085Z  Untitled document
2013-03-14T14:38:40.000Z  subscriptions.txt
2013-03-08T18:50:27.153Z  GOPR0001.MP4
2013-03-05T04:00:00.962Z  Untitled document
2013-02-16T23:00:27.596Z  2013 S&T Panels
2013-02-10T15:30:16.339Z  magic_hat_and_wand.svg
2013-02-07T19:31:58.538Z  CWA 7-Feb-2013
2013-02-03T19:43:24.760Z  ImageMagick Machine
2012-12-06T19:00:37.767Z  Untitled document
2012-12-06T15:07:05.242Z  AppDev book proposal
2012-12-06T01:54:23.618Z  Scratchpad tips and tricks
2012-12-06T01:54:01.506Z  Gunbarrel website
2012-12-06T01:53:57.834Z  Serial Numbers
2012-12-06T01:53:49.237Z  new one
2012-11-30T19:29:43.631Z  CWA
2012-11-28T19:35:10.986Z  Scratchpad
2012-11-26T17:46:26.613Z  Important Numbers
```

Figure 4-7. Files on my Google Drive

The *index.html* file is similar to ones we've been using in other examples:

```html
<!DOCTYPE html>
<html lang="en">
<head>
    <meta charset="utf-8" />
    <title>GDrive</title>
    <link rel="import" href="lib/common.html">
    <script src="GDrive.js"></script>
</head>
<body>
    <textarea id="textarea" cols="55" rows="20" readonly
        style='outline: none;'></textarea>
</body>
</html>
```

An object in *Google.js* wraps the calls needed to access Google APIs, very similar to *Facebook.js* that we saw in "Accessing the Facebook API" on page 97:

```javascript
var Google = (function () {
    var access_token;

    var api = {
        authorize: function (callback) {
            chrome.identity.getAuthToken(
                {
```

```
                    'interactive': true
                },
                function(token) {
                    access_token = token;
                    callback(token !== undefined);
                }
            );
        },

        call: function (method, successCallback, errorCallback) {
            var url = 'https://www.googleapis.com/' + method;
            Ajax.ajaxSend(url, "json",
                function (status, response) {
                    if (response && response.error && response.error.message)
                        errorCallback(response.error.message);
                    else if (status == 200)
                        successCallback(response);
                    else
                        errorCallback('Result code: ' + status);
                },
                function (e) {
                    if (errorCallback)
                        errorCallback('Communication error');
                },
                {
                    Authorization: 'Bearer ' + access_token
                }
            );
        }
    };
    return api;
})();
```

Google API calls generally have the form `https://www.googleapis.com/<method>`,
where *<method>* is the method (e.g., *drive/v2/files*). Note in the `call` method that
we send the access token along as an `Authorization` header, which is a bit more convenient than supplying it as a URL query parameter. That uses the fifth argument to
`Ajax.ajaxSend` that I mentioned earlier.

The entire `GDrive` app code is surprisingly compact:

```
window.onload = function () {

Google.authorize(
    function () {
        var ta = document.querySelector('#textarea');
        ta.value = 'Wait ...';
        Google.call('drive/v2/files?q=trashed%3dfalse',
            function (response) {
                var s = '';
                response.items.forEach(
                    function (file) {
```

```
                        s += file.modifiedDate + '  ' + file.title + '\n';
                }
            );
            ta.value = s;
        },
        function (msg) {
            ta.value = 'Error: ' + msg;
        }
    );
    }
);

};
```

Notice the method string:

```
drive/v2/files?q=trashed%3dfalse
```

The `trashed=false` parameter value is written with the equals sign escaped as %3d. This is because it's the value of the q parameter, not a top-level query parameter in its own right.

As GDrive illustrates, using Google APIs from Chrome Apps is much like using any other API, except for the special, Google-only, OAuth2 authorization.

WebSockets

HTTP was originally designed as a way for web browsers to fetch web pages. It has since been coopted for use by web APIs, as we've seen. Parameters describing the request are specified by paths and query parameters (or by POST data), and the requested data must be extracted from the response. This approach, though very widely used, is inefficient for two reasons:

- Supplying all those headers with every request and response slows down communication and requires extra processing.
- All interaction must be initiated from the client.

The second issue is occasionally worked around by having the client issue a long-term request, which the server responds to when it has something to say, possibly minutes or even hours after the request was issued. This can become complicated if the client wants to do some other communication in the interim or if the long-term request times out; in both cases, the request must be reissued.

Much better would be to use a symmetrical protocol by which either client or server can send a message and the overhead of all those headers is eliminated. That's what WebSockets (part of the HTML5 effort) are all about. They're not specific to Chrome Apps, but they do work well with them.

WebSockets API

Using WebSockets is considerably easier than using XMLHttpRequest. First, the client creates a connection to the server with the constructor, like this:

```
var ws = new WebSocket('ws://23.21.124.185:5002');
```

The special ws protocol indicates that the connection is to a WebSocket. After the object is instantiated, a message can be sent by using send:

```
ws.send(data);
```

The data can be a string, an ArrayBuffer, or a Blob. A message is received with an onmessage handler:

```
ws.onmessage = function (event) {
    if (event.data) {
        // do something with data
    }
    else
        // no data was received
};
```

Those are the basics. There is one additional API call, close, and a few additional events such as onopen, but not many—WebSockets really is very simple.

WebSockets is only a client API; there is no corresponding server API. To build a server, you need to follow Internet Engineering Task Force (IETF) document RFC6455, which defines the WebSocket Protocol in terms of the raw data being transmitted on the sockets. (Recall from "Socket API" on page 81 that I characterized sockets as the underlying API of the Internet.)

Example WebSocket Server

There is a Chrome API for server-side sockets (chrome.sockets.tcpServer), so it's possible to implement a WebSocket server as a Chrome App. But, WebSocket servers are normally built by using server technologies. Because implementing a WebSocket server is a distraction from our focus on Chrome Apps, I won't describe the example one I've built in detail, but I've included it in the example code for this book. It accesses the New York City MTA (Metropolitan Transportation Authority) Bus Time service to provide a WebSocket interface that supplies bus status.

The example server is implemented with Node.js, for which there's a good WebSocket library. I ran the server on an Amazon Elastic Computer Cloud (EC2) instance that is accessible (when I'm running it) at IP address 23.21.124.185, port 5002. (Sorry, it's not available to you, although its source code and the MTA Bus Time server are.)

Example WebSocket Client

After you connect to the example server, it begins sending status-update messages every minute. The messages contain information about buses on the M4 line (what stop they're approaching, whether they're making progress, and so on), which runs between Penn Station and The Cloisters, about as far north as Manhattan goes. Figure 4-8 shows a typical status display in the app, called NYCBusWS, where, for example, bus 3840 is approaching 101 Street making normal progress. Figure 4-9 shows that it's reached that stop a short time later.

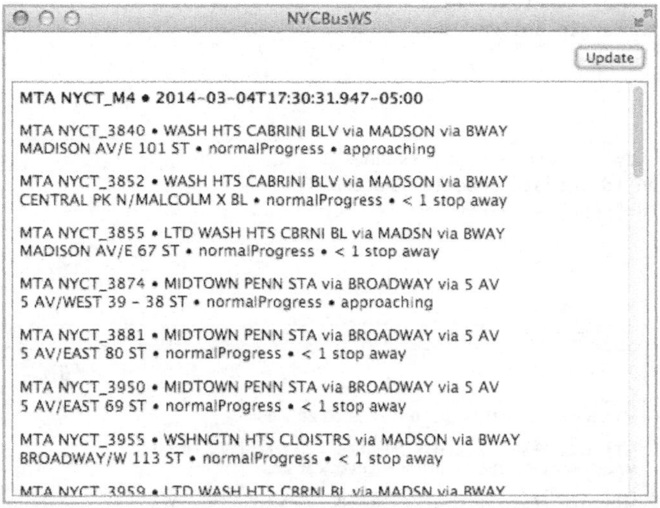

Figure 4-8. Updated status of buses on the M4 route

Here's the *index.html* file:

```
<!DOCTYPE html>
<html lang="en">
<head>
    <meta charset="utf-8" />
    <title>NYCBusWS</title>
    <link rel="import" href="lib/common.html">
    <script src="NYCBusWS.js"></script>
    <style>
        body, html {
            height: 100%;
            width: 100%;
            margin: 0;
            margin-top: 5px;
        }
        #results {
```

```
                height: 85%;
                width: 95%;
                margin: 0 auto;
                padding: 5px;
                overflow: auto;
                border: 1px solid gray;
            }
            #message {
                margin-left: 10px;
            }
            #update {
                float: right;
                margin-right: 10px;
                margin-bottom: 10px;
            }
        </style>
    </head>
    <body>
        <span id="message"> </span>
        <button id="update">Update</button>
        <div id="results"></div>
    </body>
</html>
```

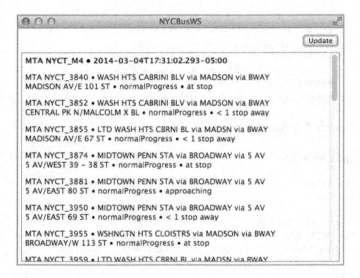

Figure 4-9. Status of buses on the M4 route

If you don't want to wait for the next status report to come from the server, you can click the Update button to get the status right away. It sends an update request to the server like this:

```
ws.send('update');
```

Using WebSockets requires no special permissions or anything else in the *manifest.json* file.

As usual, the app's JavaScript code is entirely in the `window.onload` handler:

```
window.onload = function () {

var ws = new WebSocket('ws://23.21.124.185:5002'); // Bus status server
ws.onclose = function () {
    showMessage('Not connected');
};
ws.onopen = function () {
    showMessage('Connected', true);
    ws.onmessage = function (event) {
        if (event.data) {
            showStatus(JSON.parse(event.data));
        }
        else
            showMessage('No data received');
    };
};
ws.onerror = function (e) {
    console.log(e);
}

document.querySelector("#update").addEventListener("click",
    function () {
        ws.send('update');
    }
);

// ... rest of app

};
```

Messages are shown by using `showMessage`, which is what we've seen in earlier examples. (See "Local Files" on page 22.) Observe that setting the `ws.onmessage` handler is deferred until a callback to the `ws.onopen` handler confirms that the WebSocket is connected; this is just to make sure that we don't execute setup code too soon.

When data arrives from the server, it's converted to a JavaScript object with `JSON.parse` and then displayed by using `showStatus`:

```
function showStatus(obj) {
    var buses = [];
    var lineRef;
    obj.Siri.ServiceDelivery.VehicleMonitoringDelivery.forEach(
        function (vmd) {
            vmd.VehicleActivity.forEach(
                function (va) {
```

```
                    var mvj = va.MonitoredVehicleJourney;
                    buses.push(mvj);
                    lineRef = mvj.LineRef;
                }
            );
        }
    );
    buses.sort(
        function(a, b) {
            return (a.VehicleRef < b.VehicleRef) ? -1 :
                (a.VehicleRef > b.VehicleRef) ? 1 : 0;
        }
    );
    var s = "<b>" + lineRef + " &bull; " +
      obj.Siri.ServiceDelivery.ResponseTimestamp + "</b>";
    buses.forEach(
        function (bus) {
            s += "<p>" + bus.VehicleRef + " &bull; " +
            bus.DestinationName + "<br>";
            s += bus.MonitoredCall.StopPointName + " &bull; " +
            bus.ProgressRate + " &bull; " +
            bus.MonitoredCall.Extensions.Distances.PresentableDistance;
        }
    );
    document.querySelector('#results').innerHTML = s;
}
```

As I mentioned in "A Weather Report App" on page 91, you need to work on this sort of display code a bit as you come to terms with the JSON that the server returns.

This app is pretty simple, but that's because most of the work is being done on the server. To build the server, I had to register it with the MTA, figure out its APIs, and incorporate it into a WebSocket server.

Just to be clear, the WebSocket protocol is different from the HTTP protocol, and you can't use WebSockets to execute APIs that expect HTTP interaction (so-called REST APIs). As yet, no mainstream websites that I know of have a WebSocket API (it's pretty new), but they are increasingly being used internally, within client/server applications. (The bus status WebSocket server was written by me for this book, not by the MTA.)

Google Cloud Messaging

So far in this chapter, we've confined our communication to executing APIs provided by servers. Now, it's time to look at Google Cloud Messaging (GCM), which can send messages from a Google server to applications to provide information about software updates, weather alerts, news flashes, calendar events, or anything else that needs to be efficiently broadcast.

This kind of messaging is also called *push messaging*, because these messages are pushed from server to client, not pulled by the client from the server. The corresponding Chrome API was actually called `chrome.pushMessaging`, but that API was very difficult to use from the server side and has since been replaced by `chrome.gcm`, which is compatible with GCM for Android and is much easier to use.

Figure 4-10 shows the overall GCM architecture. You begin by creating a project on the Google Developers Console, identified by its *project number* (shown at the bottom of Figure 4-10). (More about project numbers shortly.) A Chrome App that wants to use GCM executes the `chrome.gcm.register` call to get a *registration ID*, which is unique for each Chrome App (identified by its app ID), user, and project number. The Chrome App uploads that registration ID to the app server, the same server that handles the server-side of the application through whatever API has been designed for it by the developer. The app server stores the registration IDs (in a database or a file) for all clients to which it might want to send messages.

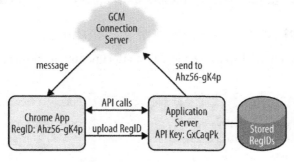

Figure 4-10. Google Cloud Messaging architecture

To send a GCM message, the app server sends to the GCM Connection Server (operated by Google) the message, the API key (obtained from the Google Developers Console), and a list of registration IDs that the message is to go to. The GCM Connection Server then sends the messages to the Chrome Apps associated with those registration IDs. The messages are received by `chrome.gcm.onMessage` handlers that the apps have set up.

For the Chrome App this is extremely efficient, because once the `chrome.gcm.onMessage` handler is set up, there's nothing further to do until a message arrives. In fact, the Chrome App doesn't even have to be running—Chrome will activate it automatically when a message arrives.

Example Application Server

Here we'll see the code for a simple GCM-receiving Chrome App that receives GCM messages about buses at a stop on Fifth Avenue in New York. The example app server is a variation on the one used in "WebSockets" on page 109. It also queries the New York MTA Bus Time server, but it's written in PHP instead of JavaScript running on Node.js. The implementation of this app server isn't directly related to Chrome Apps (it would also serve Android apps), so it's discussed, and the example PHP program is shown, in Appendix C. There I also describe how to send GCM messages from Amazon Simple Notification Service, which, unlike GCM itself, can also handle Apple Push Notification Service and Amazon Device Messaging.

A typical GCM message sent to the Chrome App is:

```
12:45:50 -- M4 at stop; M4 1 stop away@5 AV/WEST 47 - 46 ST
```

For simplicity the app server only monitors one stop, so the stop name after the @ is always the same. As we'll see, all the Chrome App has to do when it receives the message is set the window title to the stop name and show the rest of the message in its window.

Example Client

The Chrome App client displays the last 10 status updates, as shown in Figure 4-11.

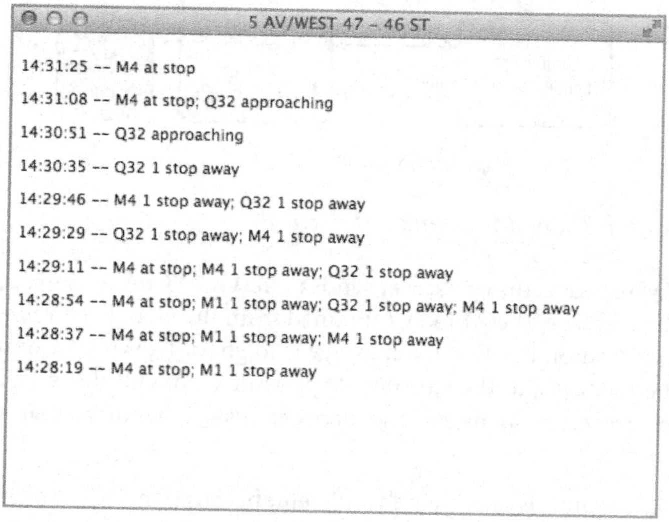

Figure 4-11. Last 10 bus-status updates

The first thing a GCM client has to do is get a registration ID so it can tell the app server where to send messages. This is done with `chrome.gcm.register`:

```
chrome.gcm.register(senderIDs, callback)
```

senderIDs is an array of sender IDs, which are project numbers assigned by Google when a project is created (see Figure 4-10). In our examples, there is only one project, but a single client could be interested in messages from several projects. The callback is called with the registration ID as its argument.

One difference between this example client, called NYCBusGCM, and those we've seen previously, is that all of the GCM-related code goes into the *background.js* file, not the app's JavaScript file that's referenced from its HTML file. This is to allow GCM messages to be received and handled even if the app isn't running. Chrome remembers which events had handlers and reloads the background script automatically when such an event occurs and the script is inactive.

It's necessary to register a sender ID (project number) only once, provided the registration ID is retained by the app for further use. It makes sense, then, to do the registration when the app is first installed or updated, and then to save the registration ID in local storage (see "Setting and Getting Local Storage" on page 56). That's what's done for chrome.runtime.onInstalled in *background.js*:

```
chrome.runtime.onInstalled.addListener(
    function() {
        chrome.storage.local.get("registered",
            function(result) {
                if (!result["registered"]) {
                    var senderIDs = ["806...503"];
                    chrome.gcm.register(senderIDs,
                        function (registrationID) {
                            console.log(registrationID);
                            if (chrome.runtime.lastError)
                                console.log(chrome.runtime.lastError);
                            else
                                sendRegistrationID(registrationID);
                        }
                    );
                }
            }
        );
    }
);
```

If there is a new registration ID, it's sent to the server by sendRegistrationID:

```
function sendRegistrationID(registrationID) {
    // Should use https
    Ajax.ajaxSend("http://basepath.com/servers/gcmv2-bus.php?regid=" +
        registrationID, 'json',
        function (status, response) {
            if (status == 200)
                chrome.storage.local.set(
                    {
```

```
                registered: true
            }
        );
    else
        console.log('Error sending registrationID');
    }
);
}
```

The server is *basepath.com/servers/gcmv2-bus.php* (details are in Appendix C); the `re
gid` parameter tells it to store a registration ID and then to send messages to that reg-
istration ID when there's something to send. As the comment indicates, a registration
ID needs to be kept secure, so `https` should have been used, but the website I use for
examples isn't set up for SSL.

Note that `Ajax.ajaxSend` is being executed from the background script, so the technique we've been using of having it loaded by a *common.html* file referenced from *in-
dex.html* won't work. Rather, it has to be loaded along with *background.js* from the
manifest, which lists two scripts instead of one. While we're looking at *manifest.json*,
note that it requests three permissions, `gcm`, `storage` (so the registration ID can saved),
and `"http://basepath.com/*"` (so the registration ID can be uploaded to the server):

```
{
    "app": {
        "background": {
            "scripts": [
                "background.js",
                "lib/Ajax.js"
            ]
        }
    },
    "manifest_version": 2,
    "name": "NYCBusGCM",
    "version": "1.0.0",
    "permissions": [
        "gcm",
        "storage",
        "http://basepath.com/*"
    ]
}
```

The app also has a window, which is created the normal way, except that it's saved in a
global so we can post messages to it from elsewhere in the background script, as we'll
see shortly:

```
var win;

chrome.app.runtime.onLaunched.addListener(
    function (launchData) {
        chrome.app.window.create('index.html', null,
            function (createdWindow) {
```

```
                win = createdWindow.contentWindow;
            }
        );
    }
);
```

Note that the Chrome window object is what's passed to the chrome.app.window.cre
ate callback, and that the Document Object Model (DOM) window (what you normally
manipulate with JavaScript) is in createdWindow.contentWindow.

That's all the setup we need to enable the app to receive GCM messages, but we still need
to add a handler for the messages. It writes the message to the log (essential during
development to understand what's going on) and then posts it to the application window:

```
chrome.gcm.onMessage.addListener(
    function(message) {
        console.log('chrome.gcm.onMessage', message);
        win.postMessage(message, '*');
    }
);
```

(Posting and receiving window messages is standard DOM stuff; it's not unique to
Chrome Apps.)

This example's *index.html* is about as simple as one can be:

```
<!DOCTYPE html>
<html lang="en">
<head>
    <meta charset="utf-8" />
    <title>NYCBusGCM</title>
    <script src="NYCBusGCM.js"></script>
</head>
<body>
</body>
</html>
```

The window's JavaScript is simple, too:

```
var msgs = Array();

window.addEventListener("message",
    function (messageEvent) {
        showStatus(messageEvent.data.data.message);
    }
);

function showStatus(message) {
    var body = document.querySelector('body');
    body.innerHTML = '';
    var a = message.split('@');
    if (a.length > 1)
```

```
        document.title = a[1];
    msgs.push(a[0]);
    if (msgs.length > 10)
        msgs.shift();
    for (var i = msgs.length - 1; i >= 0; i--)
        body.insertAdjacentHTML('beforeend',
            "<p>" + msgs[i]);
}
```

Observe that the message received by the `message` handler is in `messageEvent.data`, which is the message received from GCM. It in turn has a `data` property with a `message` property, which is why the string sent from the app server is referred to as `messageEvent.data.data.message`.

The `showStatus` function just breaks out the stop name (following the @), sets it as the window title, and displays the status that preceded it. All the `push` and `shift` stuff is for limiting the display to the last 10 status updates.

Summary of IDs, Numbers, and Keys

It took me a while to get all the GCM credentials straight, so I thought I'd do you a favor and summarize it all in one place:

- Each GCM project you create with the Google Developers Console has a unique *project number*.
- That project number is also known as a *sender ID*; this is what you send to get a *registration ID*.
- The registration ID uniquely identifies the combination of the app (by app ID), the user, and the project.
- An app server needs an *API key*, which you get from the Google Developers Console (see Appendix C for details).
- To cause a GCM message to be sent, the app server passes the API key, the list of registration IDs, and the message to the *GCM Connection Server*.
- One added twist: If you use something other than Google's GCM Connection Server to send messages, you might find that a registration ID is referred to as a *device token*.

 If you're using `chrome.pushMessaging` (the predecessor API to `chrome.gcm`) things are much worse. If you're struggling with client IDs, client secrets, redirect URIs, refresh tokens, and access tokens, you have the wrong API. Thankfully, `chrome.gcm` dispenses with those horrors. The 50 hours I spent chasing them down is lost and gone forever, but now at least Google has set things right.

App-to-App Messaging

So far, we've see how GCM can send messages from the cloud to an app that's asked for them, and we've also seen how to send a message to a window within an app, by using the standard `window.postMessage` DOM API.

It's also possible for a Chrome App to send a message to another app running on the same computer. You can do this by using the `chrome.runtime.sendMessage` API:

```
chrome.runtime.sendMessage(appId, message, options, responseCallback)
```

You need the app ID of the the app you want to send the message to, which is available from the Extensions page. To keep it from changing, you can fix it, as explained in Appendix B.

The `message` can be a string, array, or object. The only available `option` is rarely used, so I won't go into it, but you can check the API documentation (*http://bit.ly/sendmes sage_api*) for the details. The callback is called when the exchange is complete. An error occurred if `chrome.runtime.lastError` is defined in the callback; otherwise, the callback argument is the receiver's response.

The receiving app should set an `onMessageExternal` listener:

```
chrome.runtime.onMessageExternal.addListener(callback)
```

When a message arrives, the callback is called with three arguments: the message, a `MessageSender` object that provides information about the sender (see the documentation for details), and a function that the callback can call to send a response, which is its single argument. If you want the response function to work after the callback returns, save it in a variable and return `true` from the event callback.

You can also send a message by using `chrome.runtime.connect`, which keeps the port open and thus is more efficient for lots of messages than is `chrome.runtime.sendMes sage`. I won't go into the details of `chrome.runtime.connect` here.

To show how app-to-app messaging works, we'll modify the bus-status Chrome App to get rid of its window and instead send a message to a different app. The new app, `NYCBusGCM-s`, now has only three files: *background.js*, *Ajax.js* (needed to send the registration ID to the app server), and, as always, *manifest.json*. There are no permissions required to use `chrome.runtime.sendMessage`.

The only change to *background.js* from the example in Figure 4-11 is to the `onMes sage` handler that receives GCM messages:

```
chrome.gcm.onMessage.addListener(
    function(message) {
        console.log('chrome.gcm.onMessage', message);
        chrome.runtime.sendMessage('lgibpahbcalokboffnkpdcelgobbmkfd',
          message.data.message, {},
```

```
            function (response) {
                if (chrome.runtime.lastError)
                    console.log('chrome.runtime.sendMessage error',
                        chrome.runtime.lastError);
                else
                    console.log(response);
            }
        );
    }
);
```

When a GCM message arrives, it's sent to the app with app ID lgibpahbcalokboffnkpd
celgobbmkfd. That app, called ReceiveMessage, doesn't use GCM, so its *back-
ground.js* file is as simple as can be:

```
chrome.app.runtime.onLaunched.addListener(
    function (launchData) {
        chrome.app.window.create('index.html');
    }
);
```

Its *manifest.json* is also simple, devoid of permissions, except that it has a key property
so its app ID is fixed (see Appendix B):

```
{
    "app": {
        "background": {
            "scripts": [ "background.js" ]
        }
    },
    "manifest_version": 2,
    "name": "ReceiveMessage",
    "version": "1.0.0",
    "key": "MIIBIjANBgkqhki...cv1dsGtG5UbWrj5aQIDAQAB"
}
```

The *index.html* file is similar to what the earlier bus-status app had:

```
<!DOCTYPE html>
<html lang="en">
<head>
    <meta charset="utf-8" />
    <title>ReceiveMessage</title>
    <script src="ReceiveMessage.js"></script>
</head>
<body>
</body>
</html>
```

The app's JavaScript sets up an onMessageExternal handler in window.onload:

```
window.onload = function () {
    chrome.runtime.onMessageExternal.addListener(
        function(message, sender) {
```

```
            console.log('chrome.runtime.onMessageExternal', message);
            showStatus(message);
        }
    );
};
```

The function `showStatus` is identical to the one in Figure 4-11, and, indeed, when `ReceiveMessage` is running and receiving messages, its window shows the same information as that shown in Figure 4-11.

Notifications

There's yet another kind of messaging: the transient display of a notification that appears in the upper-right corner of the screen, as shown in Figure 4-12.

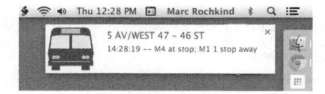

Figure 4-12. A notification about bus status

Sending a screen notification uses the `chrome.notifications` API, primarily the call to create a notification:

```
chrome.notifications.create(notificationId, options, creationCallback)
```

The optional `notificationId` is a unique identifier that you make up that's associated with the notification. This way, if a notification with the same ID is sent, any earlier ones are first cleared. There are a bunch of options, which you can read about in the `chrome.notifications` API documentation (*http://bit.ly/notifications_api*); we'll use the four that are required when you create a notification:

type
:   `basic`, `image`, `list`, or `progress` (we'll use `basic`)

iconUrl
:   An icon to appear in the notification

title
:   The notification title

message
:   The notification message

Recall from Figure 4-11 that the bus-status messages have this form:

```
12:45:50 -- M4 at stop; M4 1 stop away@5 AV/WEST 47 - 46 ST
```

We want the stop name (after the @) to be the notification title, and whatever precedes it to be the message. Here's the onMessage handler in *background.js* that does the splitting and the creation of the notification (shown in Figure 4-12):

```javascript
chrome.gcm.onMessage.addListener(
    function(message) {
        console.log('chrome.gcm.onMessage', message);
        var a = message.data.message.split('@');
        var title = 'Bus Status';
        if (a.length > 1)
            title = a[1];
        chrome.notifications.create(
            '',
            {
                type: 'basic',
                iconUrl: 'icon128-bus.png',
                title: title,
                message: a[0]
            },
            function (notificationID) {
            }
        );
    }
);
```

Because we have an icon (examples up to now have omitted them), we might as well use it in the manifest, too. We also need notifications permission:

```json
{
    "app": {
        "background": {
            "scripts": [
                "background.js",
                "lib/Ajax.js"
            ]
        }
    },
    "manifest_version": 2,
    "name": "NYCBusGCM",
    "version": "1.0.0",
    "icons": {
        "128": "icon128-bus.png"
    },
    "permissions": [
        "gcm",
        "storage",
        "notifications",
        "<all_urls>"
```

```
        ]
    }
```

Unlike the example in "App-to-App Messaging" on page 121, here the app is complete; no app such as `ReceiveMessage` is needed to show the bus status, because notifications do it; nor is there any `onLaunched` event handler, because the app is never launched, only loaded. There are only four files: *background.js*, *Ajax.js*, *icon128-bus.png*, and *manifest.json*.

Moreover, the app continues to work and show notifications even if it's inactive (as long as it's installed, of course). Figure 4-13 demonstrates that it goes inactive if no status arrives for about 15 seconds.

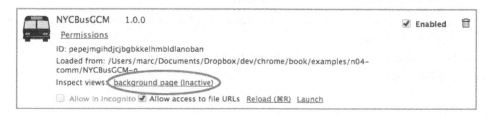

Figure 4-13. An app going inactive

For a background page (not other JavaScript files), Chrome remembers which handlers were set. The page is unloaded when it's no longer needed (no windows and no consoles open), destroying all the handlers (but not the fact that they once existed) along with all the other code. When an event that it wanted to handle occurs, the page is reloaded. It executes from the top, as it did when it was first installed, reestablishing the handlers, and then the handler for the event that just occurred is called. In this way, apps that only occasionally need to execute take up very few resources, and certainly none for their code and associated data.

Chapter Summary

We've seen a lot of different approaches to messaging in this chapter, some unique to Chrome Apps, some part of HTML5, and some as old as the Internet:

- The Socket API provides basic Internet communication. You can use it to implement any Internet protocol.

- For the HTTP protocol, whether to fetch web pages or execute REST APIs, you can use the standard JavaScript `XMLHttpRequest` API, wrapped by a convenient `Ajax` object.

- There's a `chrome.identity` API for handling OAuth2, with a special call just for accessing Google APIs. After the app is authorized, you invoke API operations via HTTP.

- HTML5 includes WebSockets, which are easier to use and more efficient than HTTP protocols, but they do require somewhat exotic server-side programming. The Chrome App end is easy.

- Google Cloud Messaging (GCM) can send messages from the cloud to any running apps that have registered to receive them. You can even send GCM messages from Amazon Simple Notification Service and from other commercial servers.

- If you just want to go from window to window within an app, you can use the old and standardized `window.postMessage`.

- The `chrome.runtime` API can send messages between Chrome Apps on the same computer.

- The `chrome.notifications` API can display a transient notification at the top of the user's screen.

CHAPTER 5

Graphics and Imaging

Many Chrome Apps don't just display text and forms; they display graphics of all sorts, both those drawn by the app and those brought into the app, such as photographs. Many of the related APIs are part of HTML5 and aren't unique to Chrome Apps, but their use in Chrome Apps does have its peculiarities, as I'll describe in this chapter. I'll also show you how to use the `mediaGalleries` API that is (as of this writing) unique to Chrome Apps.

Outputting Graphics

Until now, all of our examples showed fairly mundane user interfaces, built up from simple HTML objects, mostly text areas and buttons. However, desktop apps need to be much snazzier, with more-advanced GUIs.

The next few sections describe six different ways to create a user interface: simple text, HTML tables, positioned HTML, drawing on a canvas, Scalable Vector Graphics (SVG), and creating a PDF. Next, we'll look at how to display images, chiefly JPEGs. Finally, we'll investigate the Chrome `mediaGalleries` API, which makes it straightforward for your app to access media files stored on the local computer.

Calendar Example

To show all the different ways of displaying graphics from a Chrome App, we'll implement the same calendar example each way. The calendar-related part of the app, which calculates the months and days, will stay the same; only the output code will change as we go through all six variations. Figure 5-1 shows the first variation, a plain-vanilla calendar that displays as just text.

```
February 2014

Su Mo Tu We Th Fr Sa
                    1
2  3  4  5  6  7  8
9  10 11 12 13 14 15
16 17 18 19 20 21 22
23 24 25 26 27 28


March 2014

Su Mo Tu We Th Fr Sa
                    1
2  3  4  5  6  7  8
9  10 11 12 13 14 15
16 17 18 19 20 21 22
23 24 25 26 27 28 29
30 31
```

Figure 5-1. A plain calendar rendered as text

The *manifest.json* file is straightforward, as shown here:

```
{
    "app": {
        "background": {
            "scripts": [ "background.js" ]
        }
    },
    "manifest_version": 2,
    "name": "Calendar",
    "version": "1.0.0",
    "permissions": [
        {
            "fileSystem": [
                "write"
            ]
        },
        "webview"
    ]
}
```

The *background.js* file is as minimal as they get:

```
chrome.app.runtime.onLaunched.addListener(
    function (launchData) {
        chrome.app.window.create('index.html');
    }
);
```

The *index.html* file is simple, too. The CSS is designed to make the div that contains the calendar scroll:

```
<!DOCTYPE html>
<html lang="en">
<head>
    <meta charset="utf-8" />
    <title>Calendar</title>
    <link rel="import" href="lib/common.html">
    <script src="Calendar.js"></script>
    <style>
        body, html {
            height: 100%;
            width: 100%;
            margin: 0;
        }
        #holder {
            height: 100%;
            width: 100%;
            margin: 0 auto;
            overflow: auto;
            position: absolute;
        }
    </style>
</head>
<body>
    <div id="holder"><div id="calendar"></div></div>
</body>
</html>
```

Now comes the *Calendar.js* file that contains the calendar-producing code. This code depends on an `OutputText` object to do the actual rendering (plain text, in this first case):

```
var output = OutputText;

buildCalendar((new Date()).getFullYear());

function buildCalendar(year) {
    output.start();
    window.resizeTo(output.pageWidth(), 800);

    for (var month = 0; month < 12; month++) {
        if (month > 0)
            output.addPage();
        changeMonth(month);
        var row = 1;
        for (var day = 1; day <= 31; day++) {
            var date = new Date(year, month, day);
            if (date.getFullYear() != year || date.getMonth() != month)
                break; // day does not exist in this month
            var dayOfWeek = date.getDay();
            if (dayOfWeek === 0 && day > 1)
                row++;
            output.text(row, dayOfWeek, 'date', day.toString(), 5, 20);
```

```
            }
        drawGrid(row);
    }
    output.write();

    function changeMonth(monthToShow, wantLines) {
        var m = ['January', 'February', 'March', 'April', 'May',
            'June', 'July', 'August', 'September', 'October',
            'November', 'December'][monthToShow];
        output.text(0, 0, 'month', m + ' ' + year, 0, 24);
        ['Sunday', 'Monday', 'Tuesday', 'Wednesday',
            'Thursday', 'Friday', 'Saturday'].forEach(
            function (weekday, index) {
                output.text(0, index, 'weekday', weekday, 0, 0);
            }
        );
    }

}
```

We build the calendar by going through the months, from 1 to 12, and then the days of each month, from 1 to 31, stopping when we get to a day that doesn't exist (for example, 31-April or 29-Feb in a non–leap year). The call to drawGrid at the end of the for loop for the months is empty for text output, because no grid is drawn:

```
function drawGrid(numRows) {
}
```

We'll see the grid in subsequent examples.

OutputText, and the other output objects we'll introduce later, has these methods:

OutputText.start()
    Start the output, doing whatever setup work is needed.

OutputText.pageWidth()
    Return the page width in pixels.

OutputText.addPage()
    Begin a new page. This is needed before every month but the first.

OutputText.text(row, col, type, s, xOffset, yOffset)
    Output text in row row of the month's page, and in week column col (for example, column 1 for Monday). type is month for a month title (for example, January 2014), weekday for a weekday name (for example, Monday), and date for a day number (for example, 27). The text to output is x, and it's offset by xOffset and yOffset, in pixels, from the start of row and col. You will see more clearly how to use OutputText as we progress through the examples.

```
OutputText.write()
```
Write the output if it's been accumulated in a buffer.

```
OutputText.line(x1, y1, x2, y2)
```
Draw a line from the point (x1, y1) to (x2, y2), measured in pixels, with the origin at the upper-left corner of the page. (This is not used in the first, text-only, example.)

In the code for our text-only calendar, note that the month title and weekday names are written on row 0 of each page, and the dates are written in rows 1 through 4, 5, or 6, depending on the number of weeks in which the month's days occur. For example, 1-March-2014 was on a Saturday; thus the 31 days in March for this particular year span six weeks, requiring that many rows of dates, as you can see in Figure 5-1.

Rendering the Calendar as Text

Following is the code for OutputText, which outputs the text calendar in Figure 5-1. Notice that the xOffset and yOffset arguments of OutputText.text are ignored, and that OutputText.line doesn't do anything:

```
var calDiv = document.querySelector("#calendar");

var OutputText = (function () {
    var prevRow = -1;
    var para;

    var api = {
        cellWidth: 0,
        cellHeight: 0,

        start: function () {
            calDiv.style['font-family'] = 'monospace';
        },

        text: function (row, col, type, s, xOffset, yOffset) {
            if (type === 'weekday')
                s = s.substr(0, 2);
            else if (type === 'date' && s.length === 1)
                s = ' ' + s;
            if (row !== prevRow || col === 0) {
                para = document.createElement('p');
                para.style['margin-left'] = '10px';
                for (var i = 0; i < col; i++)
                    para.insertAdjacentHTML('beforeend', '   ');
                calDiv.appendChild(para);
            }
            para.insertAdjacentHTML('beforeend', s + ' ');
            prevRow = row;
        },
```

```
        addPage: function () {
            calDiv.insertAdjacentHTML('beforeend', '<hr>');
        },

        pageWidth: function () {
            return 150;
        },

        line: function (x1, y1, x2, y2) {
        },

        getTextWidth: function (s, fontSize) {
            return 0;
        },

        write: function () {
        }
    };
    return api;
})();
```

There are a few of things to note about OutputText.text:

- We've set a monospaced font in OutputText.start, to make it very easy to line up the columns. In later examples, we'll use Times, which is a proportional font that makes the positioning less straightforward.

- We show just the first two letters of each weekday name, so that the names line up with the dates. For the same reason, we pad one-digit dates to two characters.

- The row !== prevRow || col === 0 condition means that we've gone to a new row or we're at column 0, in either case of which we need to start a new paragraph. The column 0 case is for handling the weekday names, because they, along with the month title, are in row 0.

- If the first week of the month (a new paragraph) doesn't begin on a Sunday, we must add padding to move the date to the correct horizontal position, which is what the for loop does.

 If you can follow this text example, you're all set to keep up as we look at the next five versions of Output objects, because, as I mentioned earlier, the buildCalendar function never changes.

Rendering the Calendar as a Table

A text-only calendar is fine for a reference, but if you want to hang it on the wall, you'll want something more like the one shown in Figure 5-2. Because it's mostly a grid of rows and columns, the obvious way to render it is as an HTML table.

Figure 5-2. Our calendar rendered as table

Rather than setting up a separate app example for each rendering illustration, I've instead combined them into one example that shows six windows. We haven't yet encountered a *background.js* file that creates more than one window on an onLaunched event, but here's one that creates six:

```
chrome.app.runtime.onLaunched.addListener(
    function (launchData) {
        chrome.app.window.create('index.html');
        chrome.app.window.create('index.html',
            {
            },
            function (createdWindow) {
                createdWindow.contentWindow.outputType = 'Table';
            }
        );
        chrome.app.window.create('index.html',
```

```
                {
                },
                function (createdWindow) {
                    createdWindow.contentWindow.outputType = 'HTML';
                }
            );
            chrome.app.window.create('index.html',
                {
                },
                function (createdWindow) {
                    createdWindow.contentWindow.outputType = 'Canvas';
                }
            );
            chrome.app.window.create('index.html',
                {
                },
                function (createdWindow) {
                    createdWindow.contentWindow.outputType = 'SVG';
                }
            );
            chrome.app.window.create('index.html',
                {
                },
                function (createdWindow) {
                    createdWindow.contentWindow.outputType = 'PDF';
                }
            );
        }
    );
```

Each window has a different value for the outputType property of the DOM window,
which is accessed as createdWindow.contentWindow, where createdWindow is the argument to the chrome.app.window.create callback function—again, something else
we haven't had to use until now.

Because each of the windows loads the same index.html file (which we've already seen)
it's up to the *Calendar.js* file to decide how to render the calendar, based on the value of
the outputType property. That's done by setting the global output to the corresponding
object via this switch statement:

```
if (!window.outputType)
    window.outputType = 'Text';

var output;

switch (window.outputType) {
case 'Text':
    output = OutputText;
    break;
case 'Table':
    output = OutputTable;
```

```
        break;
    case 'HTML':
        output = OutputHTML;
        break;
    case 'Canvas':
        output = OutputCanvas;
        break;
    case 'SVG':
        output = OutputSVG;
        break;
    case 'PDF':
        output = OutputPDF;
    }
    document.title = 'Calendar - ' + window.outputType;
```

Observe that in *Calendar.js* the property is referenced as `window.outputType`, because `window` is the DOM window; in *background.js* it was referenced as `createdWindow.con tentWindow.outputType`.

Because the `buildCalendar` function was written to reference the rendering object as `output`, the appropriate rendering takes place according to how the `switch` statement sets `output`.

As a preview of coming attractions, Figure 5-3 shows five of the windows: the text and table versions (which we already saw) along with the HTML, Canvas, and SVG versions. The PDF rendering at the right of Figure 5-3 was captured in a PDF reader app (Preview, on Mac OS X.)

Whereas `OutputText` started a new paragraph, `OutputTable` starts a new `<tr>` element, and the padding for months that don't start on a Sunday is done by appending `<td>` elements:

```
var OutputTable = (function () {
    var sizeBig = 20;
    var sizeSmall = 14;
    var marginHorz = 36;
    var marginVert = 36;
    var prevRow = -1;
    var table, tr;

    var api = {
        cellWidth: 100,
        cellHeight: 80,
        margins: {
            top: marginVert,
            bottom: marginVert,
            left: marginHorz,
            right: marginHorz
        },

        start: function () {
```

```
        table = document.createElement('table');
        table.border = 0;
        table.cellPadding = 0;
        table.style['border-collapse'] = 'collapse';
        table.style['margin-left'] = this.margins.left + 'px';
        table.style['margin-bottom'] = this.margins.bottom + 'px';
        calDiv.appendChild(table);
    },

    text: function (row, col, type, s, xOffset, yOffset) {
        var that = this;

        if (type === 'weekday') {
            xOffset = (this.cellWidth - this.getTextWidth(s, 'small')) / 2;
            yOffset = output.cellHeight * .8;
        }
        if (row !== prevRow || col === 0) {
            if (prevRow > 0)
                while (tr.childNodes.length < 7)
                    appendTd(tr, null, true);
            tr = document.createElement('tr');
            table.appendChild(tr);
            prevRow = row;
        }
        while (tr.childNodes.length < col)
            appendTd(tr, null, true);
        if (type === 'month')
            appendTd(tr, s, false, 7);
        else
            appendTd(tr, s, row > 0);

        function appendTd(tr, s, border, colSpan) {
            var td = document.createElement('td');
            td.width = that.cellWidth + 'px';
            td.height = that.cellHeight + 'px';
            if (colSpan) {
                td.colSpan = 7;
                td.style['text-align'] = type === 'month' ? 'center' : 'left';
                td.style['vertical-align'] = 'bottom';
            }
            else
                td.style['vertical-align'] = 'top';
            if (border)
                td.style.border = '1px solid black';
            if (s) {
                var p = document.createElement('p');
                p.style.fontFamily = 'Times';
                var fSize = type === 'weekday' ? sizeSmall : sizeBig;
                p.style.fontSize = fSize + 'px';
                p.style['margin-top'] = ((yOffset || 0) -
                    fSize * .6) + 'px'; // Move up to position at baseline.
                p.style['margin-left'] = (xOffset || 0) + 'px';
```

```
                    p.style['margin-bottom'] = 0;
                    p.style['margin-right'] = 0;
                    p.innerText = s;
                    td.appendChild(p);
                }
                tr.appendChild(td);
            }
        },

        addPage: function () {
        },

        pageWidth: function () {
            return this.margins.left + 7 * this.cellWidth + this.margins.right;
        },

        line: function (x1, y1, x2, y2) {
            // table has the lines
        },

        getTextWidth: function (s, fontSize) {
            return measureText(s,
              fontSize === 'small' ? sizeSmall : sizeBig);
        },

        write: function () {
            for (var c = tr.childNodes.length; c < 7; c++)
                api.text(prevRow, c, 'date');
        }
    };
    return api;
})();
```

The month titles are written into <td> elements that span all seven columns. Most of the code has to do with setting up CSS for the HTML elements to handle the offset arguments to OutputTable.text and to handle horizontal and vertical alignment. This code isn't hard to follow, but it's hard to explain the principles behind it, except to say that I kept revising it until the table looked the way I wanted it to. That's generally how CSS gets written, in any app. We'll see later that the graphical rendering techniques—Canvas, SVG, and PDF—are much easier to work with when it comes to positioning.

HTML elements such as <p> use the top for positioning (CSS top attribute), whereas the graphical techniques (Canvas, SVG, and PDF) use the baseline, as shown in Figure 5-4.

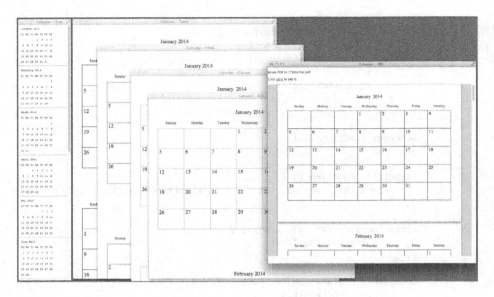

Figure 5-3. calendar rendered six different ways

The `buildCalendar` function assumes baseline positioning, which is why `OutputTa ble.text` adjusts the text up in the internal `appendTd` function. (We'll see the same thing in `OutputHTML`.) An adjustment of .6 of the font size seems to do the trick:

```
p.style['margin-top'] = ((yOffset || 0) - fSize * .6) + 'px';
```

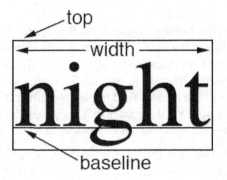

Figure 5-4. Text location and width

Weekday names need to be centered in their cells, which is done by computing their x offset, for which we need to know their width in pixels (see Figure 5-4). You do this by using the `OutputTable.getTextWidth` method, which calls `measureText` (see

Example 5-1), a function based on one contributed to Stack Overflow (*http://bit.ly/ calculate_text_width*).

Example 5-1. Function to measure the width of text

```
function measureText(text, fontSize) {
    var div = document.createElement('div');
    document.body.appendChild(div);
    div.style.fontFamily = 'Times';
    div.style.fontSize = fontSize + 'px';
    div.style.position = 'absolute';
    div.style.left = -1000;
    div.style.top = -1000;
    div.innerHTML = text;
    var width = div.clientWidth;
    document.body.removeChild(div);
    return width;
}
```

All this function does is add a <div> element to the document, measure it, and then get rid of it.

The OutputTable.write method fixes a quirk of tables when the border-collapse attribute is set to collapse: empty cells on the last row don't have rules, as shown in the left window in Figure 5-5. The problem is fixed by writing a suitable number of empty cells, as shown in the right window. This is another reason why outputting tables requires a lot of tuning before things look the way you want them to.

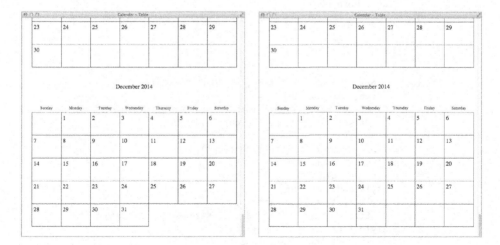

Figure 5-5. Calendar with and without missing cells

Rendering the Calendar as Positioned HTML

All right, one more HTML-based rendering before we get into the juicy graphical stuff, this time with what I call "positioned HTML." What we're going to do is output HTML <p> and <hr> elements, using CSS pixel positioning to place them exactly where we want them. This is actually easier than using tables because we don't need to wrestle with the automatic layout that tables want to control. It's a technique that probably ought to be used more often than it is.

One HTML oddity that we'll exploit is that, at least in Chrome, you can draw a vertical line with an <hr> element. All you need to do is define the height greater than the width.

Here's the code for OutputHTML:

```
var OutputHTML = (function () {
    var sizeBig = 20;
    var sizeSmall = 14;
    var marginHorz = 36;
    var marginTop = 36;

    var api = {
        cellWidth: 100,
        cellHeight: 80,
        pageOffset: marginTop,
        margins: {
            top: marginTop,
            bottom: 0,
            left: marginHorz,
            right: marginHorz
        },

        start: function () {
        },

        text: function (row, col, type, s, xOffset, yOffset) {
            if (type === 'weekday') {
                xOffset = (this.cellWidth - this.getTextWidth(s, 'small')) / 2;
                yOffset = output.cellHeight * .8;
            }
            var p = document.createElement('p');
            p.innerText = s;
            p.style.margin = 0;
            p.style.padding = 0;
            p.style.fontFamily = 'Times';
            var fSize = type === 'weekday' ? sizeSmall : sizeBig;
            p.style.fontSize = fSize + 'px';
            p.style.position = 'absolute';
            p.style.top = (this.pageOffset + row * this.cellHeight + yOffset -
                fSize * .6) + 'px'; // Move up to position at baseline.
            p.style.left = (this.margins.left + col * this.cellWidth +
                xOffset) + 'px';
```

```
        if (type === 'month')
            p.style.width = 7 * (this.cellWidth) + 'px';
        else
            p.style.width = this.cellWidth + 'px';
        p.style['text-align'] = type === 'month' ? 'center' : 'left';
        calDiv.appendChild(p);
    },

    addPage: function () {
        this.pageOffset += 8 * this.cellHeight;
    },

    pageWidth: function () {
        return this.margins.left + 7 * this.cellWidth + this.margins.right;
    },

    line: function (x1, y1, x2, y2) {
        var hr = document.createElement('hr');
        hr.setAttribute('noshade', true);
        hr.style.position = 'absolute';
        hr.style.top = (this.pageOffset + Math.min(y1, y2)) + 'px';
        hr.style.left = (this.margins.left + Math.min(x1, x2)) + 'px';
        if (x1 === x2) {
            hr.style.width = '.1px';
            hr.style.height = (Math.abs(y2 - y1) - 1) + 'px';
        }
        else {
            hr.style.width = (Math.abs(x2 - x1) - 1) + 'px';
            hr.style.height = '.1px';
        }
        calDiv.appendChild(hr);
    },

    getTextWidth: function (s, fontSize) {
        return measureText(s,
            fontSize === 'small' ? sizeSmall : sizeBig);
    },

    write: function () {
    }
};
    return api;
})();
```

This object is much simpler than `OutputTable`. Now, the lines are actually drawn by using the `OutputHTML.line` method; `OutputText` didn't draw lines at all, and `Output Table` used table borders.

Here, as in `OutputTable`, `buildCalendar` expects text to be vertically positioned on the baseline, which is how Canvas, SVG, and PDF output behave, whereas a `<p>` element's top attribute refers to its top (refer back to Figure 5-4). This difference is handled, as before, in `OutputTable.text` by fudging the paragraph up a bit, the results of which you can see in Figure 5-6.

Figure 5-6. Calendar rendered as positioned HTML

HTML5 Canvas

New in HTML5, a canvas allows you to draw pixels on a raster-based, fixed-sized area that you define by using a `<canvas>` element. Unlike all other HTML elements, there's no way to specify what's on the canvas with HTML—for that, you need to use the Java-Script Canvas API.

The canvas holds only the pixels you've placed there, and nothing else. It has no memory of the drawing operations themselves (rectangles, lines, text, and so on). After you draw it, you cannot modify or delete a shape, although you can certainly draw over it. Also, you can't attach event handlers to shapes, because they don't exist on the canvas, although you can certainly attach event handlers to the `<canvas>` element as a whole, because it does exist.

That much said, drawing on a canvas is pretty convenient, and it affords the sort of operations you'd expect in a modern graphics package. After a canvas is drawn, it's also possible to get its pixels as an image and even write them out as a file, such as a PNG or a JPEG.

A good source of detailed information is the book *HTML5 Canvas, Second Edition* by Steve Fulton and Jeff Fulton (O'Reilly). Here I'll just introduce a few basic Canvas API calls; there are many more that I won't cover.

A Simple Canvas Example

We'll first look at a simple canvas example and then show the `OutputCanvas` object, which can draw a calendar onto a canvas. The simple example utilizes this *index.html* file, which does nothing more than create a `<canvas>` element:

```
<!DOCTYPE html>
<html lang="en">
<head>
    <meta charset="utf-8" />
    <title>Canvas Example</title>
    <script src="Canvas.js"></script>
  </head>
<body style='margin: 0;'>
<canvas width="510" height="510"></canvas>
</body>
</html>
```

Because we'll be writing the canvas to a JPEG file, we need `write` permission on the `filesystem`:

```
"permissions": [
    {
        "fileSystem": [
            "write"
        ]
    }
]
```

The *background.js* is the usual boring one that just opens a window (one window!).

This example draws the shapes shown in Figure 5-7.

First comes the `canvas` object itself and the two-dimensional context within which we actually draw:

```
var canvas = document.querySelector('canvas');
var context = canvas.getContext('2d');
```

 For now, only 2d is officially supported; there's also `webgl` for 3D, but as of this writing it's experimental.

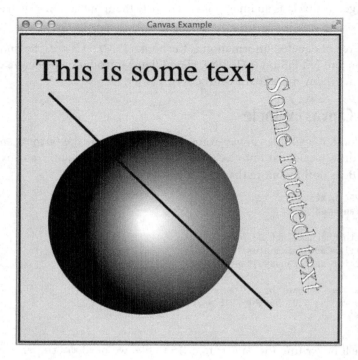

Figure 5-7. Output from our canvas example

Next, we draw the outer black border and the gray interior:

```
context.fillStyle = '#ddd';
context.strokeStyle = 'black';
context.lineWidth = 3;
context.fillRect(5, 5, 500, 500);
context.strokeRect(5, 5, 500, 500);
```

The arguments of the `fillRect` method are the starting x and y coordinates (upper left of the rectangle) and the width and height. The `strokeRect` method is similar.

There's no actual circle method; instead, you create an arc path and fill it, as shown by this code, which draws a circle with a gradient fill:

```
var gradient = context.createRadialGradient(200, 310, 0, 260, 310, 150);
gradient.addColorStop(.1, "white");
gradient.addColorStop(1, "black");

context.beginPath();
context.arc(200, 310, 150, 0, 2 * Math.PI);
context.fillStyle = gradient;
context.fill();
```

The first three arguments to `createRadialGradient` are the x and y coordinates of the center of the starting circle, followed by its radius. The last three arguments are for the ending circle. The `addColorStop` method sets a color transition for the gradient; its arguments are a position in the range 0 to 1 between the start and end, and a color. Here, white is located 10 percent from the start (the inner circle), and black is at the end.

The arguments to `arc` are the x and y coordinates of the center, the radius, and the starting and ending angles in radians. For a circle, the start angle is 0° and the end is 360°, which is 2π radians. The `fill` method closes the path and fills the circle with the gradient.

Next, let's add some text at the top of the drawing:

```
context.font = "50px Times";
context.fillText('This is some text', 30, 80);
```

The last two arguments to `fillText` are the x and y coordinates. The y coordinate is that of the baseline (again, refer back to Figure 5-4).

Here's some rotated text:

```
context.save();
context.translate(420, 250);
context.rotate(Math.PI / 180 * 80);
context.textAlign = "center";
context.fillStyle = "white";
context.lineWidth = 1;
context.fillText("Some rotated text", 0, 0);
context.strokeText("Some rotated text", 0, 0);
context.restore();
```

The `translate` and `rotate` methods rotate the entire context, not specifically the text. The `fillText` method then draws in this modified coordinate system. The text is also stroked, to create the outlined effect that you can see in Figure 5-7. The context is saved before the translation and rotation, and then restored, so subsequent canvas operations won't be affected.

Finally, here's code to stroke a line from (50, 100) to (400, 450) in the original coordinates system and to call `saveFile` to save the drawing in a file (which we're going to see next):

```
context.lineWidth = 4;
context.beginPath();
context.moveTo(50, 100);
context.lineTo(400, 450);
context.stroke();

saveFile(canvas);
```

The `saveFile` function creates a `Blob` from the canvas and then writes it to a file chosen by the user.

All the file API calls are explained in Chapter 2.

```
function saveFile(cvs) {
    var blob = dataURItoBlob(cvs.toDataURL('image/jpeg'));
    chrome.fileSystem.chooseEntry(
        {
            type: 'saveFile',
            suggestedName: 'canvas.jpg'
        },
        function(entry) {
            writeFileEntry(entry, blob,
                function(e) {
                    if (e.target.error)
                        errorHandler(e);
                    else
                        console.log('Saved.');
                }
            );
        }
    );
}

function writeFileEntry(entry, blob, callback) {
    if (entry)
        entry.createWriter(
            function(writer) {
                writer.onerror = errorHandler;
                writer.truncate(0);
                writer.onwriteend = function () {
                    writer.write(blob);
                    writer.onwriteend = callback;
                };
            },
            errorHandler
        );
}

function errorHandler(e) {
    if (e.target.error)
        console.log(e.target.error.message);
    else
        console.log(e);
}
```

Here's the code that converts a canvas to a blob, based on code posted on Stack Overflow (*http://bit.ly/blob_from_dataurl*):

```
function dataURItoBlob(dataURI, dataTYPE) {
    if (!dataTYPE)
        dataTYPE = 'image/jpeg';
    var binary = atob(dataURI.split(',')[1]);
    var array = [];
    for(var i = 0; i < binary.length; i++)
        array.push(binary.charCodeAt(i));
    return new Blob([new Uint8Array(array)], {type: dataTYPE});
}
```

The technique here is that we first get a data URI by using the Canvas API toDataURL call, and then we convert its data to a Uint8Array, from which we can directly create a Blob. The resulting JPEG looks exactly like the drawing in Figure 5-7.

Drawing the Calendar by Using a Canvas

Because a canvas is fundamentally graphical, it's easier to draw the calendar into a canvas than it is to mess around with tables and HTML, for which positioning was a design afterthought. We've already seen all of the canvas operations in OutputCanvas, except for measureText, which is built in to the Canvas API, so we don't need the function that appeared in Example 5-1. Here's the code, which is much more straightforward than the earlier output objects:

```
var OutputCanvas = (function () {
    var sizeBig = 20;
    var sizeSmall = 14;
    var marginHorz = 36;
    var marginTop = 36;
    var canvas;
    var ctx;

    var api = {
        cellWidth: 100,
        cellHeight: 80,
        pageOffset: marginTop,
        margins: {
            top: marginTop,
            bottom: 0,
            left: marginHorz,
            right: marginHorz
        },

        start: function () {
            canvas = document.createElement('canvas');
            canvas.width = this.pageWidth();
            canvas.height = 12 * 8 * this.cellHeight;
            calDiv.appendChild(canvas);
            ctx = canvas.getContext('2d');
        },
```

```
text: function (row, col, type, s, xOffset, yOffset) {
    var x, y;
    var fontSize = type === 'weekday' ? sizeSmall : sizeBig;

    if (type === 'weekday') {
        xOffset = (this.cellWidth - this.getTextWidth(s, 'small')) / 2;
        yOffset = output.cellHeight * .8;
    }
    ctx.font = fontSize + "px serif";
    if (type === 'month') {
        var titleWidth = this.getTextWidth(s, fontSize);
        x = (this.pageWidth() - titleWidth) / 2;
        y = this.pageOffset + yOffset;
    }
    else {
        x = this.margins.left + col * this.cellWidth + xOffset;
        y = this.pageOffset + row * this.cellHeight + yOffset;
    }
    ctx.fillText(s, x, y);
},

addPage: function () {
    this.pageOffset += 8 * this.cellHeight;
},

pageWidth: function () {
    return this.margins.left + 7 * this.cellWidth + this.margins.right;
},

line: function (x1, y1, x2, y2) {
    ctx.lineWidth = .5;
    ctx.beginPath();
    ctx.moveTo(this.margins.left + x1, this.pageOffset + y1);
    ctx.lineTo(this.margins.left + x2, this.pageOffset + y2);
    ctx.stroke();
},

getTextWidth: function (s, fontSize) {
    ctx.font = (fontSize === 'small' ? sizeSmall : sizeBig) + "px serif";
    return ctx.measureText(s).width;
},

write: function () {
}
};
return api;

})();
```

Figure 5-8 shows the calendar rendered onto a canvas (the "Calendar - Canvas" window in Figure 5-3).

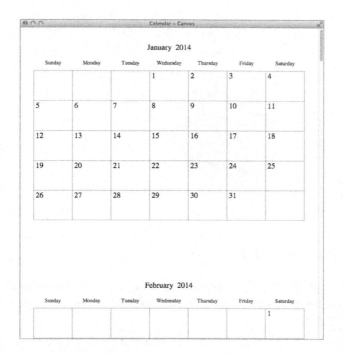

Figure 5-8. Calendar rendered onto a canvas

Scalable Vector Graphics (SVG)

Unlike a canvas, which retains only the pixels, an SVG image is composed of discrete objects, which are represented in the DOM. This means that you can construct an SVG image directly in an HTML file, like this:

```
<!DOCTYPE html>
<html lang="en">
<head>
    <meta charset="utf-8" />
    <title>Simple SVG Example</title>
  </head>
<body>
<svg>
    <circle cx="100" cy="100" r="90" fill="gray"/>
</svg>
</body>
</html>
```

Figure 5-9 shows the output in Chrome (as an HTML page, not as an app).

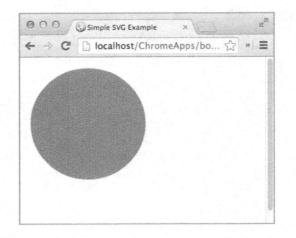

Figure 5-9. SVG circle shown in browser

The *only* way to draw an SVG image is by adding elements to an <SVG> tag; there's no drawing API as there is with canvases, for which the API is the only way to draw. They're opposites in this respect.

Canvases came with HTML5, but SVG is much older, having been standardized by the W3C since 1999. You can study the API at www.w3.org/TR/SVG (*http:// www.w3.org/TR/SVG*), or you can get the book *SVG Essentials, Second Edition* by J. David Eisenberg and Amelia Bellamy-Royds (O'Reilly).

Another SVG Example

In this section, we'll look at a more elaborate example—this time as a Chrome App— which draws some shapes similar to those we drew with a canvas (Figure 5-7). Figure 5-10 presents the SVG version.

This app's *background.js* just opens a window loaded from *index.html*, and its *manifest.json* requests no permissions. Here's the *index.html* file:

```
<!DOCTYPE html>
<html lang="en">
<head>
    <meta charset="utf-8" />
    <title>SVG Example</title>
    <script src="SVG.js"></script>
  </head>
<body style='margin: 0;'>
<svg width="510" height="510">
    <defs>
        <radialGradient id="circleGrad">
            <stop offset="10%" stop-color="white" />
```

```
                  <stop offset="100%" stop-color="black" />
             </radialGradient>
         </defs>
         <rect x="5" y="5" width="500" height="500" stroke-width="3"
           stroke="black" fill="#ddd" />
         <circle cx="200" cy="310" r="150" fill="url(#circleGrad)"/>
         <text font-size="50" font-family="Times" x="430" y="50"
           fill="white" stroke="black"
           transform="rotate(80 400,40)">
             Some rotated text
         </text>
         <line x1="50" y1="100" x2="400" y2="450"  stroke-width="4"
           stroke="black" />
     </svg>
     </body>
     </html>
```

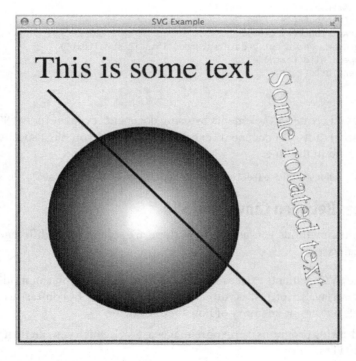

Figure 5-10. Output from SVG example

In the <defs> element, there's a definition for a gradient, somewhat like the one we saw in "A Simple Canvas Example" on page 143, except here we didn't need to define a center or starting and ending circles.

Next comes the background gray rectangle with a black border, represented by a single <rect> element. Then, the circle filled by the gradient that we defined. After that, some rotated text, both filled and stroked, and finally the line.

But where's the horizontal text, "This is some text"? That element is created by the JavaScript in *SVG.js* (referenced from the *index.html* file):

```
window.onload = function () {

var svg = document.querySelector('svg');
var text = document.createElementNS("http://www.w3.org/2000/svg", "text");
text.setAttribute('font-family', 'Times');
text.setAttribute('font-size', 50);
text.setAttribute('x', 30);
text.setAttribute('y', 80);
var textNode = document.createTextNode('This is some text');
text.appendChild(textNode);
svg.appendChild(text);

};
```

Notice that you create SVG elements by using document.createElementNS (NS stands for namespace), not with document.createElement, and you must specify the namespace, as we did in this line:

```
var text = document.createElementNS("http://www.w3.org/2000/svg", "text");
```

Differences Between Canvas and SVG

Apart from the methods you use to draw, there are several other differences between SVG and Canvas:

- Because SVG elements exist as long as the drawing does, you can modify or delete them from JavaScript, just as you can any DOM element. By contrast, a canvas keeps its pixels but has no memory of how they got there.

- Many drawing programs can export images as SVG, which you can then incorporate into an HTML file.

- You can attach event handlers to SVG elements (as we'll see later).

- SVG images scale as the resolution of the window changes, whereas a canvas never changes from the resolution at which it was drawn.

This last point is demonstrated in Figure 5-11, which shows the canvas and SVG examples zoomed in a browser to 500 percent. The SVG scales right up, whereas the pixels for the canvas version just get bigger. Although this is an important difference in many web applications, it doesn't matter much in Chrome apps, because an app window can't zoom. (To prepare the figure, I had to create the drawings in a browser window.)

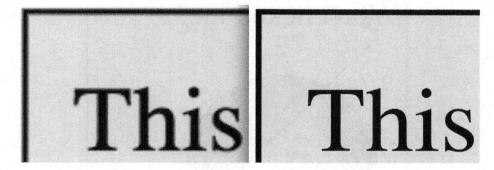

Figure 5-11. Zooming in shows the scalability of SVG

To show how to attach an event handler to an SVG element, here's some additional code added to *SVG.js*:

```
text.addEventListener('click',
    function (e) {
        textNode.data = "You clicked me.";
    }
);
```

Now, when you click on the text at the top of Figure 5-10, you see the results depicted in Figure 5-12.

How do you decide whether to use a canvas or an SVG? Here are some considerations:

- If you're going to draw in JavaScript, calling the Canvas API is much easier than creating SVG elements, modifying their attributes, and inserting them into parent elements.

- If you have hundreds or thousands of shapes, a canvas will be much more efficient because all those shapes don't have to persist as DOM elements. Thus, a canvas is probably a better choice for games and other highly interactive applications.

- If you need scalability or need to add event handlers, SVG is a better choice.

- If a designer rather than a programmer is to draw the image, SVG is more approachable.

- There are several canvas JavaScript libraries (KineticJS, EaselJS, Fabric, Paper, and so on) that make drawing easier; there are far fewer SVG libraries.

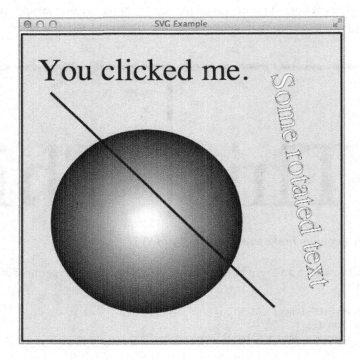

Figure 5-12. The output from SVG example after clicking the text at the top

Drawing the Calendar by Using SVG

Figure 5-13 shows the calendar rendered via SVG; it's almost indistinguishable from the canvas version in Figure 5-8.

Figure 5-13. Our calendar rendered as SVG

The code for OutputSVG is similar to OutputCanvas, too, when you account for the fact that, instead of drawing shapes, SVG elements are created:

```
var OutputSVG = (function () {
    var sizeBig = 20;
    var sizeSmall = 14;
    var marginHorz = 36;
    var marginTop = 36;
    var svg;

    var api = {
        cellWidth: 100,
        cellHeight: 80,
        pageOffset: marginTop,
        margins: {
            top: marginTop,
            bottom: 0,
            left: marginHorz,
            right: marginHorz
        },

        start: function () {
            svg = document.createElementNS("http://www.w3.org/2000/svg", "svg");
            svg.setAttribute('width', this.pageWidth());
```

```
            svg.setAttribute('height', 12 * 8 * this.cellHeight);
            calDiv.appendChild(svg);
        },

        text: function (row, col, type, s, xOffset, yOffset) {
            var x, y;
            var fontSize = type === 'weekday' ? sizeSmall : sizeBig;

            if (type === 'weekday') {
                xOffset = (this.cellWidth - this.getTextWidth(s, 'small')) / 2;
                yOffset = output.cellHeight * .8;
            }
            if (type === 'month') {
                var titleWidth = this.getTextWidth(s, fontSize);
                x = (this.pageWidth() - titleWidth) / 2;
                y = this.pageOffset + yOffset;
            }
            else {
                x = this.margins.left + col * this.cellWidth + xOffset;
                y = this.pageOffset + row * this.cellHeight + yOffset;
            }
            var text = createSVGText(s, fontSize);
            text.setAttribute('x', x);
            text.setAttribute('y', y);
            svg.appendChild(text);
        },

        addPage: function () {
            this.pageOffset += 8 * this.cellHeight;
        },

        pageWidth: function () {
            return this.margins.left + 7 * this.cellWidth + this.margins.right;
        },

        line: function (x1, y1, x2, y2) {
            var line = document.createElementNS("http://www.w3.org/2000/svg",
                "line");
            line.setAttribute('x1', this.margins.left + x1);
            line.setAttribute('y1', this.pageOffset + y1);
            line.setAttribute('x2', this.margins.left + x2);
            line.setAttribute('y2', this.pageOffset + y2);
            line.setAttribute('stroke', 'black');
            line.setAttribute('stroke-width', .5);
            svg.appendChild(line);
        },

        getTextWidth: function (s, fontSize) {
            var text = createSVGText(s, fontSize);
            svg.appendChild(text);
            var w = text.getComputedTextLength();
            svg.removeChild(text);
```

```
                return w;
        },

        write: function () {
        }
    };
    return api;

    function createSVGText(s, fontSize) {
        var text = document.createElementNS("http://www.w3.org/2000/svg", "text");
        text.setAttribute('font-family', 'Times');
        text.setAttribute('font-size', fontSize);
        var textNode = document.createTextNode(s);
        text.appendChild(textNode);
        return text;
    }

})();
```

Creating PDFs

If you've been reading this book all the way to this point, you've learned about files, databases, networking, and graphics, but you might be wondering why I never mentioned printing. After all, typical productivity apps for Mac OS X, Windows, and Linux provide a way to print, and Google clearly wants Chrome Apps to be on a par with them someday. Here's why I haven't mentioned printing: you can't do it. There's no Chrome or HTML API for printing, other than for printing a whole window. Instead, you create a PDF file and let the user print it outside of the app.

There's no standard API for PDFs either, but there are a few third-party JavaScript libraries you can use. I've tried only jsPDF, which has some rough edges, but it works, so that's the one I'll describe here. You can read about it and download it from *github.com/MrRio/jsPDF* and *parall.ax/products/jspdf*. (*.ax* is the top-level domain for the Åland Islands. Cute!)

One thing about all the PDF libraries I've looked at, including those for PHP, is that you build up the PDF file, but nothing is output until you explicitly write it. That's the chief motivation for having the `write` method in all of the `Output` objects we've been studying. In a conventional web app that creates a PDF from JavaScript, there's no good place to write it to, because all files are sandboxed. But, we know from Chapter 2 and what we've already seen in this chapter that you can easily write a PDF to an external file. We'll see the code for that shortly.

Because the *file://* protocol isn't allowed, there's no way to open the PDF as an external file in an app window or even in a browser window. However, as we'll see when we get to the `OutputPDF` calendar object, you can read the `FileEntry` for the PDF as a data URL and refer to it that way, either as a link to a browser (outside of the Chrome App) or as a `<webview>` element placed directly in the Chrome App window. Of course, the user can certainly locate the file manually (the user previously chose the location and name for it) and open it manually, by double-clicking it, for example.

A Simple PDF Example

Let's begin our look at jsPDF with a simple example that creates a two-page PDF, as illustrated in Figure 5-14.

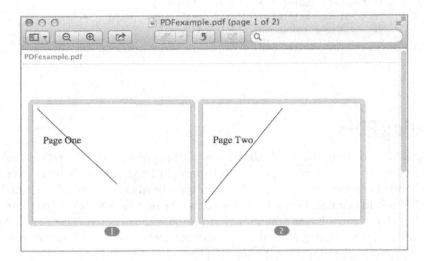

Figure 5-14. Output from PDF example shown in the Mac OS X Preview app

The *index.html* file is about as simple as it can be:

```
<!DOCTYPE html>
<html lang="en">
<head>
    <meta charset="utf-8" />
    <title>PDF Example</title>
    <link rel="import" href="lib/common.html">
    <script src="PDF.js"></script>
</head>
<body>
</body>
</html>
```

The *background.js* file is also minimal:

```
chrome.app.runtime.onLaunched.addListener(
    function (launchData) {
        chrome.app.window.create('index.html');
```

```
    }
);
```

Because the example will write a PDF to a file, you need to request `fileSystem` permission in the manifest.json file, which we've seen a bunch of times already:

```
"permissions": [
    {
        "fileSystem": [
            "write"
        ]
    }
]
```

To use *PDF.js*, it's necessary to include several files that come with it, loaded by *common.html*, but I'll postpone showing exactly what's loaded and how until later, when I explain how the calendar is rendered as a PDF.

Here's the code using *PDF.js* for this simple example:

```
var pdf = new jsPDF('l', 'pt', 'letter');
pdf.setFont('Times', 'Roman');
pdf.setFontSize(50);
pdf.text('Page One', 50, 200);
pdf.setLineWidth(3);
pdf.lines([[400, 400]], 20, 20);
pdf.addPage();
pdf.text('Page Two', 50, 200);
pdf.setLineWidth(3);
pdf.lines([[-390, 500]], 400, 20);
pdf.output('save');
```

Here are some hints to reading the nonobvious parts of the code:

- The constructor specifies landscape orientation (as opposed to portrait), dimensions in points, and letter-size paper.

- The origin is at the upper left of the page.

- The arguments to the `lines` method mean that the line starts at the point given by the last two arguments and extends to the point given by the first argument, which is relative to the starting point. The complex first argument allows for Bezier curves, but here I'm just drawing a line. See the documentation at *mrrio.github.io/jsPDF/doc* for all the gory details.

- The `output` method as it comes is set up to show the PDF in a browser window, but that won't work with Chrome Apps, because the app's window is not a browser window. Instead, there's an undocumented `save` argument that invokes a global `saveAs` method that you must supply:

```
saveAs(blob, options)
```

The `blob` argument is a `Blob` representing the PDF, and the `options` argument is whatever was passed as a second argument to `output` (which in the preceding example is nothing). My implementation of `saveAs` lets the user choose a file and then saves the PDF to that file:

```
function saveAs(blob, options) { // Must be global.
    chrome.fileSystem.chooseEntry(
        {
            type: 'saveFile'
        },
        function (entry) {
            if (entry)
                saveToEntry(blob, options, entry);
        }
    );
}

function saveToEntry(blob, options, entry) {
    entry.createWriter(
        function(writer) {
            writer.onerror = errorHandler;
            writer.truncate(0);
            writer.onwriteend = function () {
                writer.write(blob);
                writer.onwriteend = function () {
                    if (options.callback)
                        options.callback(blob, entry);
                };
            };
        },
        errorHandler
    );
}

function errorHandler(e) {
    console.log(e);
}
```

The various file API calls were described in Chapter 2.

I've implemented things so that a callback function can be supplied to `output`, which allows the calling app to arrange to do more with the PDF than just write it to a file. For instance, here's a version that displays the saved path to the user, using `chrome.file System.getDisplayPath`, which is described in Chapter 2:

```
pdf.output('save',
    {
        callback: function (blob, entry) {
            chrome.fileSystem.getDisplayPath(entry,
                function callback(displayPath) {
                    document.querySelector("body").
                        insertAdjacentHTML('beforeend',
                        '<p>Wrote PDF to ' + displayPath);
                }
            );
        }
    }
);
```

You can see the output in Figure 5-15.

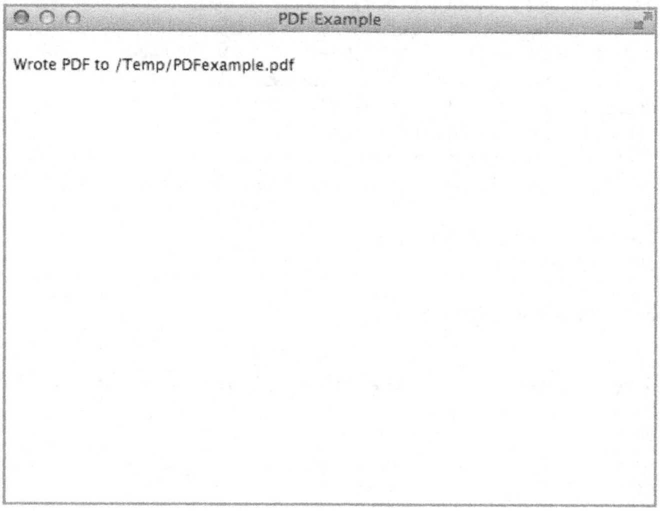

```
┌──────────────────────────────────────────────┐
│ ● ○ ○                PDF Example               │
│ Wrote PDF to /Temp/PDFexample.pdf              │
│                                                │
│                                                │
│                                                │
│                                                │
│                                                │
│                                                │
│                                                │
│                                                │
│                                                │
│                                                │
│                                                │
└──────────────────────────────────────────────┘
```

Figure 5-15. PDF example window showing the saved path

Although jsPDF's built-in output option to show a PDF won't work with Chrome Apps, you can do the same thing by generating a data URL from the Blob, somewhat similar to what we did to show images in "Accessing the Facebook API" on page 97. It's also useful to provide a link so that the PDF will show in a browser—as long as the link specifies target="_blank" so that it's shown in the default browser. (Recall that Chrome Apps are forbidden to do any navigation within themselves.)

Here's another version of a call to output that displays a link and also shows the PDF in a <webview> element:

```
pdf.output('save',
    {
```

```
            callback: function (blob, entry) {
                chrome.fileSystem.getDisplayPath(entry,
                    function callback(displayPath) {
                        document.querySelector("body").
                          insertAdjacentHTML('beforeend',
                           '<p>Wrote PDF to ' + displayPath);
                        showPDF(blob);
                    }
                );
            }
        }
    );

    function showPDF(blob) {
        var reader = new FileReader();
        reader.onload = function(event) {
            document.querySelector("body").
              insertAdjacentHTML('beforeend',
              'Click <a target="_blank" href="' + event.target.result +
               '">here</a> to see it in a browser.');
            document.querySelector("body").
              insertAdjacentHTML('beforeend',
              '<p><webview src="' + event.target.result +
               '" style="width:100%; height:700px;"></webview>');
        };
        reader.onerror = function(e) {
            console.log(e);
        };
        reader.readAsDataURL(blob);
    }
```

To use a webview, you need webview permission in the *manifest.json* file:

```
"permissions": [
    {
        "fileSystem": [
            "write"
        ]
    },
    "webview"
]
```

Figure 5-16 shows the output in the Chrome App window. If you click on the link, you see the same PDF in a browser. If you hover the mouse pointer over the embedded PDF in the Chrome App window, you see some controls, but only the zooming controls work. Unfortunately, clicking the save and print icons does nothing. That's not true of the PDF display in a browser, of course—there, the controls actually work. (There's no need for the user to save the PDF in a file, because it has already been saved in a location of the user's choosing.)

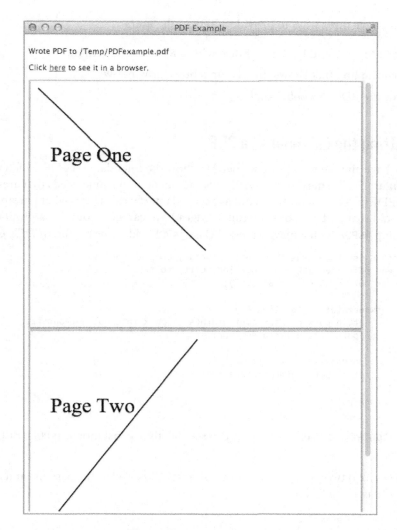

Figure 5-16. PDF example window showing embedded PDF

Thus, you have three ways to provide a PDF to the user:

- Save it to a file and let the user deal with it as he or she sees fit.
- Provide a link that shows the PDF in a browser window.
- Show the PDF in a `webview`.

Outputting the Calendar as a PDF

We now have almost everything we need to show the calendar as a PDF, which you can
see in Figure 5-17. There are two API calls the calendar example needs that are present
in the jsPDF implementation, but not as exposed interfaces. (This is what I meant earlier
when I said that jsPDF had some rough edges.) We can get around that limitation by
subclassing `jsPDF` with a new, extended class `jsPDFX`, like this (in the *jsPDFX.js* file):

```
function jsPDFX(orientation, unit, format, compressPdf) {
    var pdf = new jsPDF(orientation, unit, format, compressPdf);
    var pdfx = Object.create(pdf);

    pdfx.getWidth = function (s) {
        return pdfx.getStringUnitWidth(s) * pdfx.internal.getFontSize() /
            pdfx.internal.scaleFactor;
    };
    pdfx.getPageSize = function () {
        return pdfx.internal.pageSize;
    };
    return pdfx;
}
```

In the `OutputPDF` code that we're going to see shortly, we instantiate `jsPDFX` rather than
`jsPDF`.

We need to load two plug-ins that come with jsPDF as well as the base file and our two
files *saveAs.js* and *jsPDFX.js*:

```
<script src="saveAs.js"></script>
<script src="jsPDFX.js"></script>
<script src="jspdf.js"></script>
<script src="jspdf.plugin.standard_fonts_metrics.js"></script>
<script src="jspdf.plugin.split_text_to_size.js"></script>
```

Now, with all of that set up, we can code `OutputPDF`:

```
var OutputPDF = (function () {
    var sizeBig = 20;
    var sizeSmall = 14;
    var pdf;

    var api = {
        cellWidth: 100,
```

```
cellHeight: 80,
margins: {
    top: 36,
    bottom: 0,
    left: 0,
    right: 0
},

start: function () {
    pdf = new jsPDFX('l', 'pt', 'letter');
    this.margins.left = this.margins.right =
      (pdf.getPageSize().width - 7 * this.cellWidth) / 2;
    pdf.setFont('Times', 'Roman');
},

text: function (row, col, type, s, xOffset, yOffset) {
    var x, y;

    if (type === 'weekday') {
        xOffset = (this.cellWidth - this.getTextWidth(s, 'small')) / 2;
        yOffset = output.cellHeight * .8;
    }
    pdf.setFontSize(type === 'weekday' ? sizeSmall : sizeBig);
    if (type === 'month') {
        var titleWidth = pdf.getWidth(s);
        var pageSize = pdf.getPageSize();
        x = (pageSize.width - titleWidth) / 2;
        y = this.margins.top + yOffset;
    }
    else {
        x = this.margins.left + col * this.cellWidth + xOffset;
        y = this.margins.top + row * this.cellHeight + yOffset;
    }
    pdf.text(s, x, y);
},

addPage: function () {
    pdf.addPage();
},

pageWidth: function () {
    return pdf.getPageSize().width;
},

line: function (x1, y1, x2, y2) {
    pdf.setLineWidth(1);
    pdf.lines([[x2 - x1, y2 - y1]], x1 + this.margins.left,
      y1 + this.margins.top);
},

getTextWidth: function (s, fontSize) {
    pdf.setFontSize(fontSize === 'small' ? sizeSmall : sizeBig);
```

```
                return pdf.getWidth(s);
            },

            write: function () {
                pdf.output('save',
                    {
                        callback: function (blob, entry) {
                            chrome.fileSystem.getDisplayPath(entry,
                                function callback(displayPath) {
                                    document.querySelector("#calendar").
                                        insertAdjacentHTML('beforeend',
                                            '<p>Wrote PDF to ' + displayPath);
                                    showPDF(blob);
                                }
                            );
                        }
                    }
                );
            }
        };
        return api;

        function showPDF(blob) {
            var reader = new FileReader();
            reader.onload = function(event) {
                document.querySelector("#calendar").
                    insertAdjacentHTML('beforeend',
                        'Click <a target="_blank" href="' + event.target.result +
                            '">here</a> to see it in a browser.');
                document.querySelector("#calendar").
                    insertAdjacentHTML('beforeend',
                        '<p><webview src="' + event.target.result +
                            '" style="width:100%; height:680px;"></webview>');
            };
            reader.onerror = function(e) {
                console.log(e);
            };
            reader.readAsDataURL(blob);
        }
    })();
```

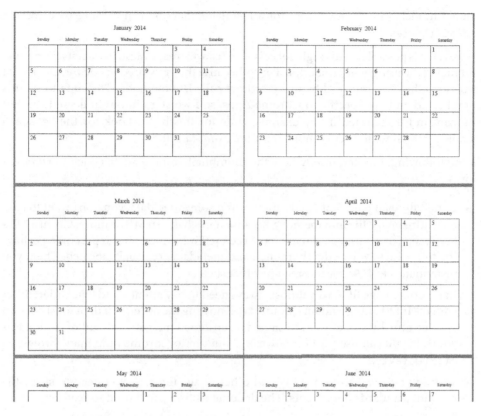

Figure 5-17. The calendar rendered as PDF

Working with Images

As I explained in "Accessing the Facebook API" on page 97, you can easily show an image by using a standard HTML <img> element, as long as you're showing a data URL containing Blob data representing the image. You can't refer to the image's URL directly with an http or file protocol as you would in a web page. The code to do that was incorporated into a getBlobUri method of a Photo object.

Accessing Image Thumbnails and Metadata

There are APIs for getting FileEntry objects referring to images, as we'll see in "The mediaGalleries API" on page 173, but there are no other Chrome APIs for dealing with images themselves. Unlike other platforms you might have used (for example, Mac OS X), Chrome provides no way to get thumbnails or metadata (date/time, F-number, camera model, and so on), except for a few fields that you can retrieve by using the mediaGalleries API.

However, it is possible—although not easy—to read an image file to extract its thumbnail and metadata entirely in JavaScript. This is because they're stored inside the file in data structures that you can read by using ordinary file I/O methods. The code to do it is complicated and not specific to Chrome Apps, so I won't go into it in detail here, but you can find it included in the example code for this book. Look for the Metadata example (which we'll discuss shortly) for the *exifdata.js* file.

In the following, I sketch briefly how the thumbnail and metadata code in *exifdata.js* works:

- Generally, if all you want is a thumbnail and some metadata, you don't want to read the entire image file into memory, because it might be 10 MB or more. Given a File (a subclass of Blob), you can use its slice method to pick off just part of it, perhaps the first 64 KB, where the thumbnail and metadata are usually located. Then, you instantiate a FileReader to read just that slice.

- In reading image files, you almost always need to pay attention to byte order: little-endian (Intel) or big-endian (Motorola). Knowing the order, you then must convert two- or four-byte quantities to signed or unsigned integers. Instead of coding this yourself, you can use a little-known API built in to Chrome (and many browsers) called DataView.

- To find your way around JPEG and other image formats, you need to study the relevant standards documents. The documents that you'll want to read are:

  "Parsing Exif client-side using JavaScript" (*http://bit.ly/parsing_exif_using_js*)

  "Description of Exif file format" (*http://bit.ly/exif_description*)

  JPEG File Interchange Format (*http://bit.ly/jpeg_file_interchange*)

  JPEG File Interchange Format File Format Summary (*http://bit.ly/jpeg_file_inter change_summary*)

  TIFF Revision 6.0 (*http://bit.ly/tiff_6*)

In *exifdata.js*, all of the above is incorporated into an ExifData object that you instantiate with a FileEntry as an argument, like this:

```
var exifdata = new ExifData.Exif(fileEntry);
```

Then, you can extract the metadata and thumbnail URL by using the getMetadata method, like this:

```
exifdata.getMetadata(
    function (metadata, thumbURL) {
        // do something with metadata and thumbURL
```

```
    }
);
```

The `metadata` argument is a string that you can display directly as, for example, the `innerText` of a `<p>` element, and `thumbURL` is a data URL suitable for direct use as the `src` attribute of an `<img>` element. To see how you use those two arguments, we'll look at an example app that displays an image, its thumbnail, and its metadata, as demonstrated in Figure 5-18.

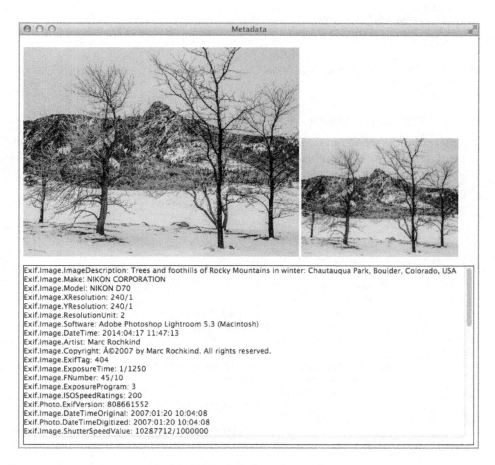

Figure 5-18. An image, embedded thumbnail, and metadata

The *background.js* and *manifest.json* files for this example are nothing special, except that `fileSystem` permission is needed because the example will use `chrome.fileSys tem.chooseEntry` to open the image file (see "External Files" on page 42).

The *index.html* file shows the image, its thumbnail, and its metadata:

```
<!DOCTYPE html>
<html lang="en">
<head>
    <meta charset="utf-8" />
    <title>Metadata</title>
    <link rel="import" href="lib/common.html">
    <script src="Metadata.js"></script>
</head>
<body>
    <p>
        <img id="img" width="450"></img>
        <img id="thumb"></img>
    </p>
    <p id="metadata"
      style="height: 300px; overflow: scroll; border: 1px solid black;"></p>
</body>
</html>
```

For this example, *common.html* just loads the *exifdata.js* file.

The interesting file is *Metadata.js*, which implements the app. Note that there's really no user interface; the app just brings up the open-file dialog when it loads:

```
window.onload = function () {

chrome.fileSystem.chooseEntry(
    {
        type: 'openFile'
    },
    function (fileEntry) {
        if (fileEntry) {
            fileEntry.file(
                function (file) {
                    document.querySelector('#img').src =
                      URL.createObjectURL(file);
                }
            );
            (new ExifData.Exif(fileEntry)).getMetadata(
                function (metadata, thumbURL) {
                    if (thumbURL)
                        document.querySelector('#thumb').src= thumbURL;
                    if (metadata)
                        document.querySelector('#metadata').innerText= metadata;
                }
            );
        }
    }
);

};
```

As you know by now, Chrome Apps aren't allowed to display the path to a file directly in the src attribute of an `<img>` element, so we call URL.createObjectURL to convert a

File to a self-contained data URL for the image, which can be displayed. The `getMetadata` method also provides a data URL for the thumbnail, so you can use it directly, as well, in the following line:

```
document.querySelector('#thumb').src= thumbURL;
```

We'll see another use of the `ExifData` object in "The mediaGalleries API" on page 173.

Image Rendering Quality

There are three ways to show an image in a Chrome App window:

- By using the `<img>` element, as we've already seen several times.
- By using the `drawImage` method of a canvas context.
- By using an SVG `<image>` element.

Usually, you'll use whatever works with the graphical approach you're using, but, if you're free to choose your API, there's a difference you should know about: if you're not showing the image at its actual size, the HTML `<img>` and SVG `<image>` elements do a much better job of rendering than the canvas `drawImage` method does.

To see this, consider the example app shown in Figure 5-19. In the figure the same 2411 x 2411 image has been reduced to 200 x 200, first by using an HTML `<img>` element, then by using Adobe Lightroom (a profesional-grade image-processing application), next by using the SVG `<image>`, and finally, by a canvas `drawImage` call. Looking at the lines (the ropes holding the sails), you can clearly see that the reduction done by the Canvas API is inferior to the others.

Let's look briefly at the code for this example. The *background.js* and *manifest.json* files are nothing special (no permissions), so we'll skip those. Here's the *index.html* file:

```
<!DOCTYPE html>
<html lang="en">
<head>
    <meta charset="utf-8" />
    <title>ImageResize</title>
    <script src="ImageResize.js"></script>
</head>
<body>
Original 2411x2411; reduced to 200x200
<table cellspacing="0" cellpadding="5">
<tr>
<td>
    <img src="boat.jpg" width="200" height="200" id="boat">
    <br>
    Reduced in HTML
<td>
    <img src="boat-200.jpg" width="200" height="200">
```

```
    <br>
    Reduced in Lightroom
<tr>
<td>
    <svg height="200" width="200">
        <image xlink:href="boat.jpg" x="0" y="0" height="200" width="200" />
    </svg>
    <br>
    Reduced by SVG
<td>
    <canvas id="cvs" width="200" height="200" style='display:inline;'></canvas>
    <br>
    Reduced by Canvas
</table>
</body>
</html>
```

Figure 5-19. A large image reduced by using four algorithms

The HTML and SVG renderings use the original 2411 x 2411 *boat.jpg* image file, and
the Lightroom example uses a 200 x 200 image exported from Lightroom,
boat-200.jpg. The canvas code is in *ImageResize.js*:

```
window.onload = function () {
    var canvas = document.querySelector('#cvs');
    var canvasContext = canvas.getContext('2d');
```

```
    var img = document.querySelector('#boat');
    canvasContext.drawImage(img, 0, 0, 200, 200);
};
```

I don't know why Chrome's canvas does so poorly, but I can guess: SVG is very old, even
older than Chrome, so when the first version of Chrome was built, its developers quite
naturally shared code between the core HTML, which certainly included the <img>
element's implementation, and their implementation of SVG. Canvas came along much
later and was probably done by a different group who then stuck it into Chrome. Maybe
someday the discrepancy I've shown will go away; all I can report is what I see now.

The mediaGalleries API

An app can call chrome.fileSystem.chooseEntry to access an individual media file
(image, video, or music), or even a directory of files, but it's convenient if the media
directories on the user's computer can be accessed automatically, without the user having
to choose them. That's what the mediaGalleries API is for. It's only for accessing media
galleries, the files in them (as FileEntry objects), and some very limited metadata. You
can't use it to do anything with the media itself, such as cropping a photo or editing an
audio track.

The Principal mediaGalleries API Methods

I'll discuss the principal mediaGalleries methods here; you can read about the others
in the Chrome API documentation (*http://bit.ly/mediaGalleries*).

You usually begin by requesting an array of the media galleries present on the computer
with chrome.mediaGalleries.getMediaFileSystems. Each gallery acts like a FileSys
tem; after you have a FileSystem object, you can operate on it with the API that we saw
in "Local Files" on page 22. Here's the call:

```
chrome.mediaGalleries.getMediaFileSystems(details, callback)
```

If the manifest requests the allAutoDetected permission, the galleries that the Chrome
API knows about are automatically accessed:

```
"permissions": [
    {
        "mediaGalleries": [
            "allAutoDetected"
        ]
    }
]
```

Here's an example call:

```
chrome.mediaGalleries.getMediaFileSystems(
    {interactive: 'yes'},
```

```
    function (mediaFileSystems) {
        console.log(mediaFileSystems);
    }
);
```

The `callback` argument to `chrome.mediaGalleries.getMediaFileSystems` is called with an array of `DOMFileSystem` objects, one per gallery, as you can see from the first few lines of the log, which has been formatted for readability:

```
[DOMFileSystem, DOMFileSystem, DOMFileSystem, DOMFileSystem,
  DOMFileSystem, DOMFileSystem]
    0: DOMFileSystem
        name: "chrome-extension_fnn...-1"
        root: DirectoryEntry
        __proto__: DOMFileSystem
    1: DOMFileSystem
        name: "chrome-extension_fnn...-2"
        root: DirectoryEntry
        __proto__: DOMFileSystem
    ...
```

There's not much useful in the log, not even the names of the galleries. We'll see how to get something more informative in a moment.

If the first argument to `chrome.mediaGalleries.getMediaFileSystems` has an `interactive` value of `yes`, as it does in the preceding code example, a dialog box opens in which the user can manually select a gallery as well as view the list of galleries added to, as shown in Figure 5-20. (I don't know how the empty item got there.)

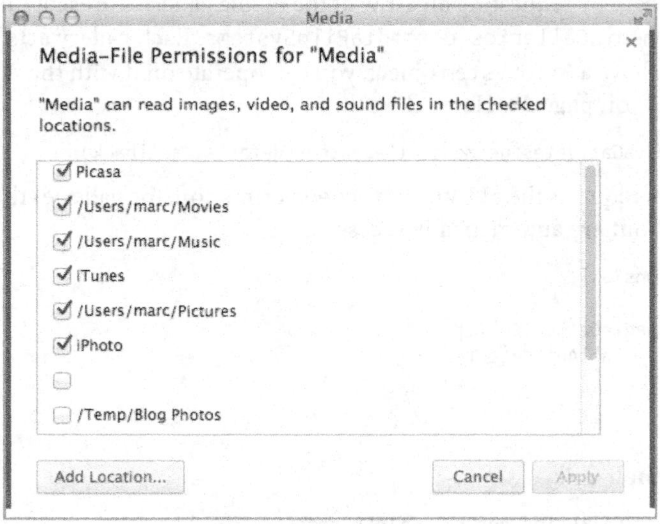

Figure 5-20. The dialog for choosing media galleries

The other choices for `interactive` are `no`, which suppresses the dialog, and `if_need ed`, which shows the dialog only if no galleries were automatically discovered.

The `chrome.mediaGalleries.getMediaFileSystemMetadata` method provides more information about a media gallery:

```
var mData = chrome.mediaGalleries.getMediaFileSystemMetadata(item)
```

The argument is a mediaGallery (`DOMFileSystem` object) as retrieved by `chrome.media Galleries.getMediaFileSystems`. Note that this method is synchronous; the metadata is its return value.

Here's some code that displays metadata from each gallery:

```
chrome.mediaGalleries.getMediaFileSystems(
    {interactive: 'yes'},
    function (mediaFileSystems) {
        mediaFileSystems.forEach(
            function(item, indx, arr) {
                var mData =
                    chrome.mediaGalleries.getMediaFileSystemMetadata(item);
                console.log(mData);
            }
        );
    }
);
```

The log shows the following:

```
Object {galleryId: "1", isAvailable: true, isMediaDevice: false,
isRemovable: false, name: "iTunes"} Media.js:175
Object {galleryId: "2", isAvailable: true, isMediaDevice: false,
isRemovable: false, name: "/Users/marc/Music"} Media.js:175
Object {galleryId: "3", isAvailable: true, isMediaDevice: false,
isRemovable: false, name: "/Users/marc/Pictures"} Media.js:175
Object {galleryId: "4", isAvailable: true, isMediaDevice: false,
isRemovable: false, name: "/Users/marc/Movies"} Media.js:175
Object {galleryId: "6", isAvailable: true, isMediaDevice: false,
isRemovable: false, name: "Picasa"} Media.js:175
Object {galleryId: "8", isAvailable: true, isMediaDevice: false,
isRemovable: false, name: "iPhoto"}
```

Now we can see things that make sense. The galleries have names such as "iTunes," "/Users/marc/Music," and so on.

For each gallery, represented by a `DOMFileSystem` object, the `root` member gives its `DirectoryEntry`, so you can use the filesystem API calls in Chapter 2 to get at the actual directory and media files in the gallery, as we'll see in the media browser example that's coming up next.

A Media Browser

At this juncture, we can combine what we know about the mediaGalleries API, file and directory I/O, displaying images, and accessing metadata with the ExifData object to build an example app that provides navigation in a pane at the left of the window and the media itself in a pane on the right, as shown in Figure 5-21. Figures 5-22, 5-23, and 5-24 show an audio track, a video, and an image, respectively. For images only, the ExifData object from "Accessing Image Thumbnails and Metadata" on page 167 is used to display thumbnails in the navigation (left) pane and metadata under the photo in the right pane.

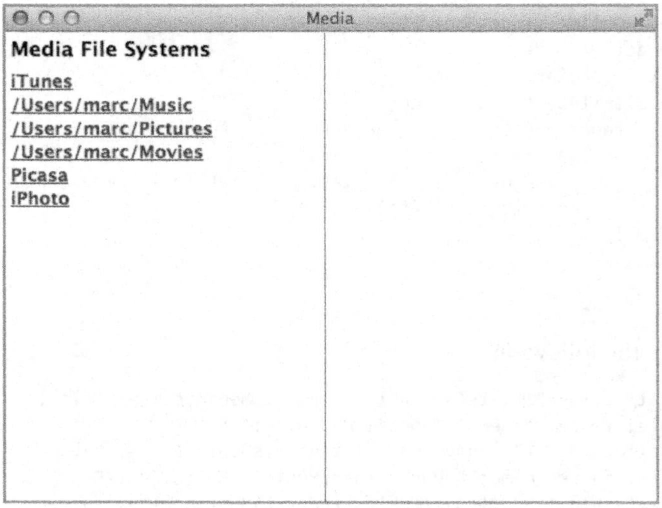

Figure 5-21. Media browser showing the media filesystems

As usual for most of our examples, the *background.js* file is nothing special. The *manifest.json* file requests permission to access all of the media galleries and to read what's there. It also requests fileSystem permission, which is needed by ExifData:

```
{
    "app": {
        "background": {
            "scripts": [ "background.js" ]
        }
    },
    "manifest_version": 2,
    "name": "Media",
    "version": "1.0.0",
    "permissions": [
        {
```

```
            "mediaGalleries": [
                "read",
                "allAutoDetected"
            ]
        },
        "fileSystem"
    ]
}
```

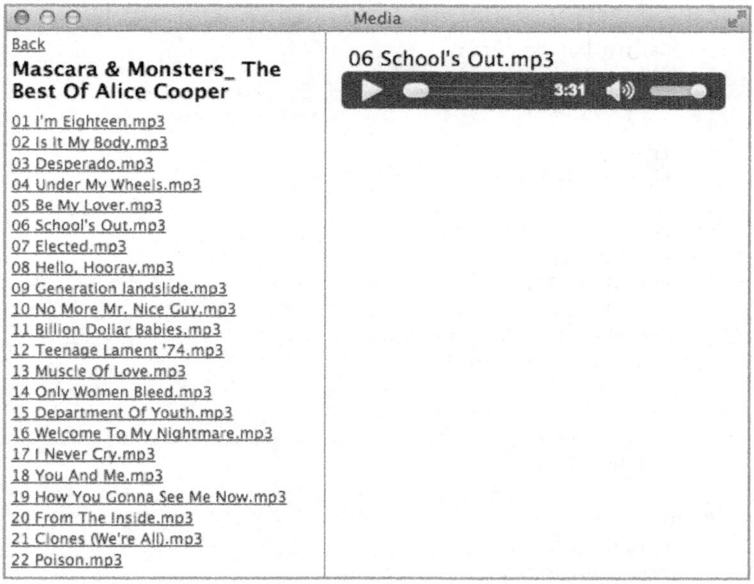

Figure 5-22. Media browser showing an audio track

The *index.html* file is somewhat lengthy, but all it really does is set up the two panes as cells in a table. The navigation pane on the left has an `id` of `tdtoc`, and the content pane on the right is assigned an `id` of `content`. That pane has two divisions: `view` for the media, and, for images, `metadata` for the metadata:

```html
<!DOCTYPE html>
<html lang="en">
<head>
    <meta charset="utf-8" />
    <title>Media</title>
    <link rel="import" href="lib/common.html">
    <script src="Media.js"></script>
    <style>
        body, html {
            width: 100%;
            height: 100%;
```

```css
        margin: 0;
        font-size: 12px;
    }
    table {
        border-collapse: collapse;
        height: 100%;
        width: 100%;
        margin: 0 auto;
        position: absolute;
    }
    p {
        margin-bottom: 2px;
        margin-top: 2px;
        margin-left: 5px;
    }
    td, tr {
        height: 100%;
    }
    #toc {
        width: 250px;
        height: 100%;
        overflow: auto;
        border-right: 1px solid gray;
        /*margin-left: 5px;*/
    }
    #tdtoc {
        width: 250px;
        height: 100%;
    }
    #content {
        height: 100%;
        overflow: auto;
    }
    #view {
        padding: 10px;
        font-size: 16px;
    }
    #heading {
        margin-bottom: 8px;
        margin-top: 4px;
        font-size: 16px;
        font-weight: bold;
    }
    .thumbnail {
        vertical-align: middle;
        margin-right: 5px;
        display: block;
    }
    .de {
        font-weight: bold;
        font-size: 14px;
    }
```

```
        </style>
    </head>
    <body>
        <link rel="import" href="stuff.html">
        <table><tr>
            <td id="tdtoc"><div id="toc"></div></td>
            <td><div id="content"><div id="view"></div><p id="metadata"></p></div></td>
        </tr></table>
    </body>
</html>
```

Figure 5-23. Media browser showing a video

Note that some of the CSS, such as that for #heading, is for elements that aren't present in the HTML but will be added dynamically from the JavaScript.

Now onto *Media.js*. The only tricky part is the implementation of the Back link at the top of the navigation pane (see Figure 5-22). To implement it, there is a global (global to the onload handler, that is) variable to hold a stack:

```
var stack = [];
```

Figure 5-24. Media browser showing an image

Each time a directory is visited, the code calls the doDirectoryEntry function (which we'll see in its entirety soon), and an object containing that DirectoryEntry and its name is pushed onto the stack:

```
function doDirectoryEntry(de, name) {
    stack.push({ item: de, name: name });
    // rest of function
}
```

Then, when the Back link is clicked, the DirectoryEntry for the directory being shown in the navigation pane is discarded from the top of the stack, and the one just under it, which represents the last one visited, is popped and then shown in the navigation pane:

```
stack.pop();
var x = stack.pop();
doDirectoryEntry(x.item, x.name);
```

We'll see the stack-manipulation code in context as we review the entire implementation.

Here's how the app begins, by showing the media galleries in the navigation page (refer to Figure 5-21):

```
window.onload = function () {

var entriesHolder;
var stack;

getMediaFileSystems();

function getMediaFileSystems() {
    stack = [];
    document.querySelector('#toc').innerHTML =
      '<p id="heading">Media File Systems</p>';
    chrome.mediaGalleries.getMediaFileSystems(
        {interactive: 'yes'},
        function (mediaFileSystems) {
            var id = 0;
            entriesHolder = [];
            mediaFileSystems.forEach(
                function(item, indx, arr) {
                    var mData =
                      chrome.mediaGalleries.getMediaFileSystemMetadata(item);
                    document.querySelector('#toc').insertAdjacentHTML(
                      'beforeend',
                      '<p><a href="" class="de" id=' + id++ + '>' +
                        mData.name + '</a>');
                    entriesHolder.push(item.root);
                }
            );
        }
    );
}

// ... rest of app ...
};
```

Here's a bit of narration to help you follow this code:

- As we've done before, the entire application is in the onload handler.

- The DirectoryEntry for each gallery (item.root, in the loop) is saved in the en
  triesHolder array, so we can find it later when the user clicks the corresponding
  link.

- The index into entriesHolder, represented by the id variable, is set as the id of
  the <a> element for that item in the navigation pane.

- The <a> elements have a class of de, which will be important in detecting clicks,
  as we're about to see.

When the user clicks anything in the navigation pane, the app must determine what was
clicked and then take the appropriate action. The click might have been on the Back

link, a directory, or a media file. That's all done by the onclick event handler for the navigation pane:

```
document.querySelector('#toc').onclick = function (e) {
    if (e.target && e.target.nodeName == 'A') {
        if (e.target.id === 'back') {
            if (stack.length > 1) {
                stack.pop();
                var x = stack.pop();
                doDirectoryEntry(x.item, x.name);
            }
            else
                getMediaFileSystems();
        }
        else if (e.target.className === "de") {
            doDirectoryEntry(entriesHolder[parseInt(e.target.id)],
                e.target.innerText);
        }
        else if (e.target.className === "media") {
            showMedia(entriesHolder[parseInt(e.target.id)]);
        }
    }
    return false;
}
```

Because the click could be anywhere at all in the toc division, we need to access e.tar get to see if we're on an <a> element and, if we are, what kind of element it is:

- If its id is back, it's the Back link.
- If its class is de, it's a directory.
- If its class is media, it's a media file.
- Otherwise, the click is ignored.

For directories, the id gives the index into entriesHolder, so the saved DirectoryEn try can be accessed, and the doDirectoryEntry function is called with that and the name that appeared as arguments. For media files, showMedia is called, although here the object in entriesHolder is a FileEntry.

Here's doDirectoryEntry:

```
function doDirectoryEntry(de, name) {
    stack.push({ item: de, name: name });
    if (!name)
        name = de.name;
    document.querySelector('#toc').innerHTML = '';
    document.querySelector('#toc').insertAdjacentHTML(
        'beforeend',
        '<p><a href="" id="back">Back</a>');
    document.querySelector('#toc').insertAdjacentHTML(
```

```
                'beforeend',
              '<p id="heading">' + name + '</p>');
        var id = 0;
        entriesHolder = [];
        var dr = de.createReader();
        dr.readEntries(
            function (entries) {
                entries.forEach(
                    function(item, indx, arr) {
                        if (item.isDirectory) {
                            document.querySelector('#toc').insertAdjacentHTML(
                              'beforeend',
                              '<p><a href="" class="de" id=' + id++ + '>' +
                                item.name + '</a>');
                            entriesHolder.push(item);
                        }
                        else {
                            var toc = document.querySelector('#toc');
                            var p = document.createElement('p');
                            toc.appendChild(p);
                            // img as object so closure below will grab it
                            var img = document.createElement('img');
                            img.className = 'thumbnail';
                            p.appendChild(img);
                            var a = document.createElement('a');
                            a.className = 'media';
                            a.id = id++;
                            a.href = '';
                            a.innerText = item.name;
                            p.appendChild(a);
                            entriesHolder.push(item);
                            (new ExifData.Exif(item)).getMetadata(
                                function (metadata, thumbURL) {
                                    if (thumbURL) {
                                        img.width = '125';
                                        img.src= thumbURL;
                                        p.style['margin-top'] = '10px';
                                        p.style['margin-bottom'] = '10px';
                                    }
                                    item.metadata = metadata;
                                }
                            );
                        }
                    }
                );
            },
            function (e) {
                console.log(e);
            }
        );
}
```

This function basically adds appropriate HTML to the navigation pane. Each item in the directory is either another directory, for which an <a> element with a class of de is added, or a media file. The only strange part is that an img object is created and appended for every media file, even if it's not an image. Then, an ExifData object is used to read its metadata, which produces a thumbURL only for images. The way the code is organized, if it's not an image, the img won't get a src attribute. (If you're bothered by sourceless img tags, you can rework the code to avoid them. I'm not bothered by them.)

It was this example that motivated me to write code in ExifData to extract thumbnails. The first version used the actual, full-size image to display the thumbnails, but that was ridiculously slow, because some of my JPEGs are several megabytes in size, and some of my image directories have hundreds of images. Taking 10 minutes to display the contents of a directory in the navigation pane is obviously unacceptable. By extracting the thumbnails, the process takes only a few seconds, even for large directories. And, as you can see from the code, this is an asynchronous operation, so the user is free to click a link without having to wait for all the thumbnails to display.

All we have left is showMedia:

```
function showMedia(item) {
    var viewDiv = document.querySelector('#view');
    var metadataDiv = document.querySelector('#metadata');
    viewDiv.innerHTML = '';
    metadataDiv.innerHTML = '';
    viewDiv.insertAdjacentHTML('beforeend', '<p>' + item.name + '</p>');
    item.file(
        function (file) {
            chrome.mediaGalleries.getMetadata(file, {},
                function (metadata) {
                    if (metadata && metadata.mimeType) {
                        var element;
                        var mediaType = metadata.mimeType.split('/')[0];
                        var elementName = mediaType === 'image' ? 'img' :
                            mediaType;
                        element = document.createElement(elementName);
                        element.setAttribute("controls", "controls");
                        viewDiv.appendChild(element);
                        element.style['max-width'] = '700px';
                        element.style['max-height'] = '700px';
                        element.src = URL.createObjectURL(file);
                    }
                }
            );
        },
        error
    );
    if (item.metadata)
        metadataDiv.innerText = item.metadata;
}
```

This function shows the media and its metadata, if any (only images have any). To show the media, an element is added to the right pane. The type of element is determined by these two magical lines of code:

```
var mediaType = metadata.mimeType.split('/')[0];
var elementName = mediaType === 'image' ? 'img' : mediaType;
```

The mediaType is given as the first part of the mimeType (audio/mpeg, video/mp4, image/jpeg, and so on). For images, we want an <img> element. Otherwise, we want a <video> or <audio> element, for which we use the mediaType directly.

For <video> and <audio> elements, we want controls, which we get with this line:

```
element.setAttribute("controls", "controls");
```

Images don't have controls, but setting that attribute does no harm, so we keep the code simple by setting it anyway.

What? That's all? Indeed it is. From the functionality of this useful little app, you might have expected a lot more code, but there isn't any more. Lots of little tricks—like using the id to hold the index into entriesHolder, going for metadata thumbnails even when there aren't any, and using the mimeType to generate the correct media-showing element—have all kept things very simple.

Chapter Summary

In this chapter, we went into various graphics and imaging APIs, including drawing with absolutely positioned HTML elements, HTML5 Canvas, SVG, and PDF. We've also examined some quirky issues with images and explained how to use the mediaGalleries API.

CHAPTER 6

Miscellaneous APIs

This chapter discusses a grab-bag of Chrome APIs, none of which warrants a full chapter of its own. Some of them are pretty useful, and others you'll want to read about but will probably never use.

Alarms

JavaScript has always had a way to set one-time or periodic alarms by using the `setIn terval` and `setTimeout` functions, but their lifetime was limited to the lifetime of the program. When it stops, they're gone.

With the Chrome alarm APIs, you can set an alarm that lasts as long as the app is installed, even if its background page goes inactive. You create such an alarm with `chrome.alarms.create`:

```
chrome.alarms.create(name, alarmInfo)
```

The second argument is an object that has the following three properties:

`when`
> When the alarm should first fire, in milliseconds past the current time (`Date.now()`)

`delayInMinutes`
> How long to delay until the alarm first fires

`periodInMinutes`
> How long to wait between firings

One of the `when` and `delayInMinutes` properties is required, and `periodInMinutes` should be present only if you want the alarm to fire more than once.

When an alarm fires, it triggers a `chrome.alarms.onAlarm` event, the callback function of which receives an `Alarm` object as its argument, indicating which alarm fired. Its most important property is `name`.

You clear an alarm by using `chrome.alarms.clear`:

```
chrome.alarms.clear(name, callback)
```

The callback function has a Boolean argument that indicates whether the alarm was cleared.

There are also APIs to get information about existing alarms and to clear all alarms, which you can read about in the documentation (*http://bit.ly/alarms_apis*).

To see how alarms work, here's an example that displays a notification reminding you to stretch every 20 minutes, as shown in Figure 6-1. When the alarm fires, the notification is generated with the `chrome.notifications` API that we saw back in "Notifications" on page 123.

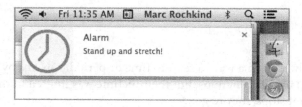

Figure 6-1. An alarm notification

This example has no HTML or JavaScript files other than *background.js*. Its *manifest.json* requests `alarms` and `notifications` permissions:

```json
{
    "app": {
        "background": {
            "scripts": [
                "background.js"
            ]
        }
    },
    "manifest_version": 2,
    "name": "Alarm",
    "version": "1.0.0",
    "icons": {
        "128": "icon128-alarm.png"
    },
    "permissions": [
        "alarms",
        "notifications"
```

```
            ]
        }
```

The icon is the one shown in Figure 6-1. We use this both for the app and for its notifications, as we're about to see.

Here's *background.js*, which is the entire app:

```
chrome.runtime.onInstalled.addListener(
    function() {
        chrome.alarms.create("alarm-stretch",
            {
                when: Date.now() + 10 * 1000, // in 10 seconds
                periodInMinutes: 20
            }
        );
    }
);

chrome.alarms.onAlarm.addListener(
    function(alarm) {
        chrome.notifications.create(
            '',
            {
                type: 'basic',
                iconUrl: 'icon128-alarm.png',
                title: "Alarm",
                message: 'Stand up and stretch!'
            },
            function (notificationID) {
            }
        );
    }
);
```

Recall from "Notifications" on page 123 that after *background.js* executes, the background page goes inactive because there's no window active (see Figure 6-2), although Chrome remembers that it had set a listener for the chrome.alarms.onAlarm event. When that event occurs (every 20 minutes, in this case), *background.js* is executed, thereby reestablishing that event's handler, and then the event is handled by invoking the handler function, which generates the notification that pops up on the screen.

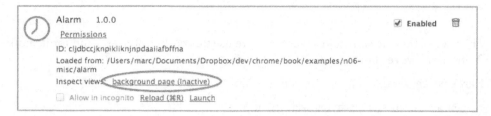

Figure 6-2. The alarm app going inactive

Context Menus

If you right-click (or control-click on a Mac) with the mouse pointer inside a Chrome App window, nothing happens unless the app was loaded unpacked, in which case you get some debugging options, such as Reload App or Inspect Element. But you can create your own context menu by using `chrome.contextMenus.create`:

```
chrome.contextMenus.create(createProperties, callback)
```

Each call creates just one menu item; if you want several items, you must make a call for each one. The `createProperties` argument has a bunch of properties having to do with the style of the menu item (normal, checkbox, and so on), its title, the context in which it's effective, and so forth. I'll just get into the basic properties; you can read about the others in the `chrome.contextMenus` documentation (*http://bit.ly/contextMenus*).

The second argument is a callback that indicates that the item was created, with `chrome.runtime.lastError` being set if an error occurred.

The *background.js* page for the simple example we'll look at just creates a window loaded with *index.html*, which has just a paragraph of introductory text:

```html
<!DOCTYPE html>
<html lang="en">
<head>
    <meta charset="utf-8" />
    <title>Context Menus</title>
    <script src="contextMenus.js"></script>
</head>
<body>
    <p id="para">Right-click to choose something.</p>
</body>
</html>
```

The manifest requests `contextMenus` permission:

```
{
    ...
    "permissions": [
        "contextMenus"
```

```
        ]
}
```

Here's the app's JavaScript file, *contextMenus.js*, which creates two menu items and a handler that's called when the user clicks an item:

```
window.onload = function () {

function done() {
    if (chrome.runtime.lastError)
        console.log(chrome.runtime.lastError);
}

chrome.contextMenus.create(
    {
        id: "menu-item-1",
        title: "Menu Item 1"
    },
    done
);
chrome.contextMenus.create(
    {
        id: "menu-item-2",
        title: "Menu Item 2"
    },
    done
);

chrome.contextMenus.onClicked.addListener(
    function (info) {
        document.querySelector('#para').innerText =
          "You clicked " + info.menuItemId;
    }
);

};
```

As of this writing, the documentation for context menus (*http://bit.ly/contextMenus*) is in pretty bad shape. For example, it refers to extensions instead of apps, and it indicates that certain properties are required or prohibited for "event pages," by which is meant the app's background script, which I always name *background.js*. In fact, these rules seem to apply to all uses of context menus, which is either a bug or a documentation error. I suspect that it's the latter.

Anyway, when you run the app, right-clicking brings up the context menu shown in Figure 6-3. In the figure, the first menu item was chosen earlier, resulting in the text that's shown in the window (put there by the event handler), and the second menu item is about to be chosen.

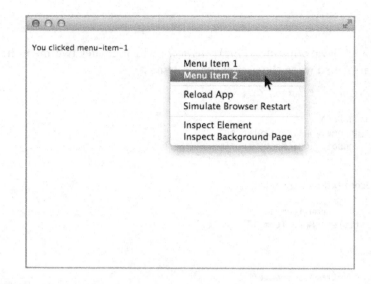

You clicked menu-item-1

Menu Item 1
Menu Item 2

Reload App
Simulate Browser Restart

Inspect Element
Inspect Background Page

Figure 6-3. Choosing an item from a context menu

Location

The location API provides a way to determine the app's geographical location or, to be more precise, the location of the device on which it's running. You start by calling `chrome.location.watchLocation` to cause a `chrome.location.onLocationUpdate` event to be fired initially and whenever the location changes:

```
chrome.location.watchLocation(name, requestInfo)
```

The first argument names the request, but it's optional and you can supply an empty string if you want. The second argument, also optional, is an object that provides parameters such as the minimum distance and minimum time between location updates. Both default to zero, which means that all changes are reported. You can read about the details at *developer.chrome.com/apps/location*.

To see the API in action, here's a simple example with the usual boring *background.js* and *manifest.json* files, except that you need `location` permission:

```
{
    ...
    "permissions": [
        "location"
    ]
}
```

The *index.html* file has a <p> element to report the location. There's also an initial "Wait…" notice, because getting the location takes a few seconds:

```
<!DOCTYPE html>
<html lang="en">
<head>
    <meta charset="utf-8" />
    <title>Location</title>
    <script src="location.js"></script>
</head>
<body>
    <p id="para">Wait...</p>
</body>
</html>
```

Here's the important part, the *location.js* file. This just shows the location when it changes:

```
window.onload = function () {

chrome.location.watchLocation('', {});

chrome.location.onLocationUpdate.addListener(
    function(position) {
        document.querySelector('#para').innerText = "You are at " +
            position.coords.latitude + ' ' + position.coords.longitude;
    }
);

};
```

Figure 6-4 shows the result, and it's pretty accurate. Because my desktop computer rarely moves, the chrome.location.onLocationUpdate event occurred only once, but had it been a more portable device that did move while the app was running, one or more subsequent updates would have occurred.

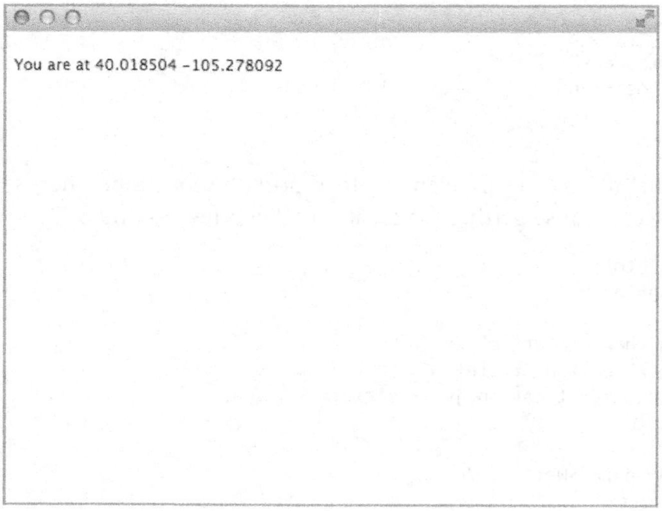

Figure 6-4. An app showing current location

Text-to-Speech

With the `tts` (text-to-speech) API, you can make your app talk. The primary call is `chrome.tts.speak`, which utters the text supplied as its first argument:

```
chrome.tts.speak(utterance, options, callback)
```

The optional second argument is an object with properties that control the voice to be used, the speech rate, the pitch, and so on, although not every implementation supports every possibility. You can find more details at *developer.chrome.com/apps/tts*. The optional callback is called right away, perhaps before the speech even started, so you can check `chrome.runtime.lastError` to see if an error occurred.

You can call `chrome.tts.getVoices` to get a list of the available voices:

```
chrome.tts.getVoices(
    function(voices) {
        console.log(voices);
    }
);
```

Part of the output from this call is shown in Figure 6-5.

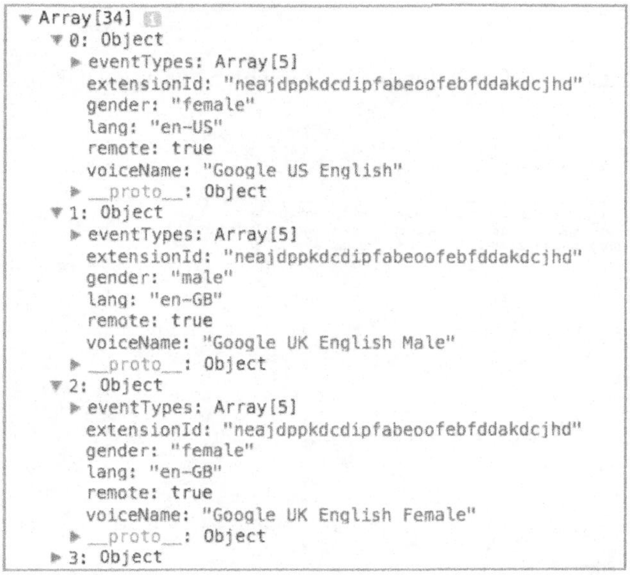

```
▼ Array[34] 🔳
  ▼ 0: Object
    ▶ eventTypes: Array[5]
      extensionId: "neajdppkdcdipfabeoofebfddakdcjhd"
      gender: "female"
      lang: "en-US"
      remote: true
      voiceName: "Google US English"
    ▶ __proto__: Object
  ▼ 1: Object
    ▶ eventTypes: Array[5]
      extensionId: "neajdppkdcdipfabeoofebfddakdcjhd"
      gender: "male"
      lang: "en-GB"
      remote: true
      voiceName: "Google UK English Male"
    ▶ __proto__: Object
  ▼ 2: Object
    ▶ eventTypes: Array[5]
      extensionId: "neajdppkdcdipfabeoofebfddakdcjhd"
      gender: "female"
      lang: "en-GB"
      remote: true
      voiceName: "Google UK English Female"
    ▶ __proto__: Object
  ▶ 3: Object
```

Figure 6-5. Available voices for the tts API

A speaking example we'll look at has the usual *background.js* and *manifest.json* files, the latter with tts permission:

```
{
    ...
    "permissions": [
        "tts"
    ]
}
```

The *index.html* file has a text area in which you can type whatever you want spoken, and a button that starts the speech:

```
<!DOCTYPE html>
<html lang="en">
<head>
    <meta charset="utf-8" />
    <title>Text-to-Speech</title>
    <script src="tts.js"></script>
</head>
<body>
    <p>
        <textarea id="textarea" cols="55"
          rows="20">Text-to-speech example.</textarea>
    </p>
    <button id="speak">Speak</button>
```

```
</body>
</html>
```

You can see this user interface in Figure 6-6, for which I've typed part of a famous speech.

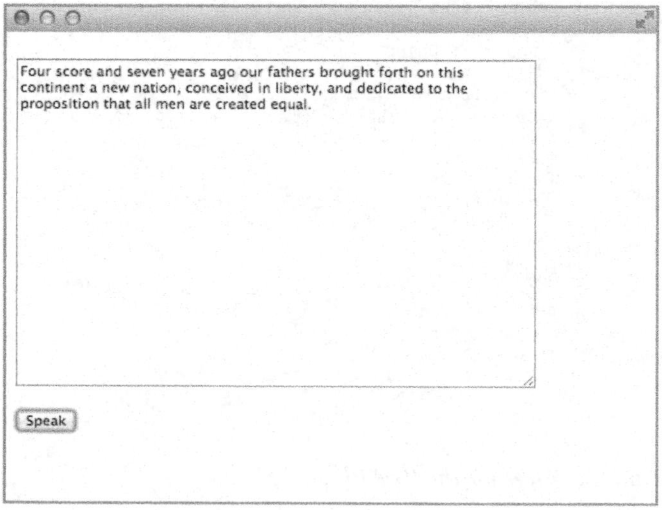

Figure 6-6. Text-to-speech example

Here's the *tts.js* file:

```
window.onload = function () {

document.querySelector("#speak").onclick = function () {
    chrome.tts.speak(
        document.querySelector("#textarea").value,
        {
            voiceName: "Google UK English Female",
            onEvent: function(event) {
                console.log('Event ' + event.type + ' at ' + event.charIndex);
                if (event.type === 'error')
                    console.log('Error: ' + event.errorMessage);
            }
        },
        function() {
            if (chrome.runtime.lastError)
                console.log('Error: ' + chrome.runtime.lastError.message);
        }
    );
};

};
```

`chrome.tts.speak` is called with two options: `voiceName`, taken from Figure 6-5, and a callback function that indicates various events during the speaking. The Gettysburg Address sounds strange in a female English voice, but that's computers for you.

System Queries

There are a few simple APIs for getting information about the system—specifically, CPU usage, displays, memory, network, and storage:

```
chrome.system.cpu.getInfo(callback)
chrome.system.display.getInfo(callback)
chrome.system.memory.getInfo(callback)
chrome.system.network.getNetworkInterfaces(callback)
chrome.system.storage.getInfo(callback)
```

Each callback function has a single argument that provides the requested information. There are some additional APIs, for such things as ejecting a storage device; you can read about these on the relevant pages, such as *developer.chrome.com/apps/system_storage*.

Each info query has its own permission in the *manifest.json* file:

```
{
    ...
    "permissions": [
        "system.cpu",
        "system.display",
        "system.memory",
        "system.network",
        "system.storage"
    ]
}
```

In the example program we'll look at, *background.js* is as usual and the *index.html* file has no user interface at all because the output will be displayed on the console log:

```
<!DOCTYPE html>
<html lang="en">
<head>
    <meta charset="utf-8" />
    <title>System</title>
    <script src="system.js"></script>
</head>
<body>
</body>
</html>
```

Here's *system.js*:

```
window.onload = function () {

chrome.system.cpu.getInfo(
```

```
    function (info) {
        console.log(info);
    }
);

chrome.system.display.getInfo(
    function (info) {
        console.log(info);
    }
);

chrome.system.memory.getInfo(
    function (info) {
        console.log(info);
    }
);

chrome.system.network.getNetworkInterfaces(
    function (networkInterfaces) {
        console.log(networkInterfaces);
    }
);

chrome.system.storage.getInfo(
    function (info) {
        console.log(info);
    }
);

};
```

The output is shown in Figures 6-7, 6-8, 6-9, 6-10, and 6-11.

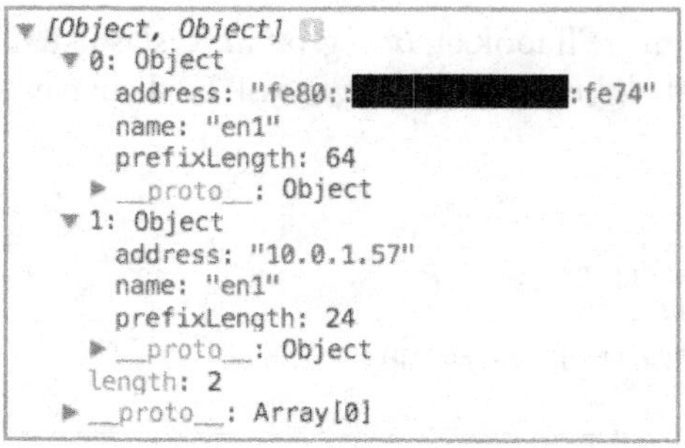

Figure 6-7. Network information

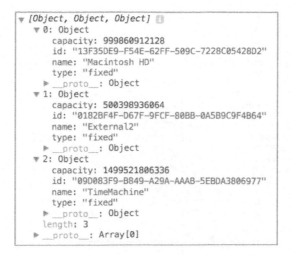

Figure 6-8. Storage information

Figure 6-9. Display information

```
▼ Object 🔲
    archName: "x86_64"
  ▼ features: Array[6]
        0: "mmx"
        1: "sse"
        2: "sse2"
        3: "sse3"
        4: "ssse3"
        5: "sse4_1"
        length: 6
      ▶ __proto__: Array[0]
    modelName: "Intel(R) Core(TM)2 Duo CPU      E7600  @ 3.06GHz"
    numOfProcessors: 2
  ▼ processors: Array[2]
    ▼ 0: Object
      ▼ usage: Object
          idle: 260146510
          kernel: 7267948
          total: 284714271
          user: 17299813
        ▶ __proto__: Object
      ▶ __proto__: Object
    ▼ 1: Object
      ▼ usage: Object
          idle: 263885903
          kernel: 5686043
          total: 284713796
          user: 15141850
        ▶ __proto__: Object
      ▶ __proto__: Object
      length: 2
    ▶ __proto__: Array[0]
  ▶ __proto__: Object
```

Figure 6-10. CPU information

```
Object {availableCapacity: 221597696, capacity: 8589934592}
```

Figure 6-11. Memory information

Camera

There are no Chrome APIs for operating the computer's camera; for that, you use the standard HTML5 media stream APIs. However, you do need to request `videoCapture` permission in the manifest.json file:

```
{
    ...
    "permissions": [
        "videoCapture"
    ]
}
```

Figure 6-12 shows an example app. The larger image is a live video of me fiddling with my computer. I smiled up at the camera and clicked the Take Photo button, resulting in the still capture in the smaller image.

Figure 6-12. Live video (on left) and a captured image

As you've come to expect, *background.js* is nothing special. Here's the *index.html* file it references:

```
<!DOCTYPE html>
<html lang="en">
<head>
    <meta charset="utf-8" />
    <title>Camera</title>
    <script src="camera.js"></script>
</head>
<body>
    <video id="video" autoplay></video>
    <button id="shutter">Take Photo</button>
    <img id="img"></img>
</body>
</html>
```

The first thing the app must do is connect the `<video>` element in the HTML to the camera with the HTML5 `navigator.webkitGetUserMedia` API (details in the "Media-Stream API" article (*http://bit.ly/mediastream_api*) on the Mozilla Developer Network):

```
window.onload = function () {

var img = document.querySelector('#img');
var video = document.querySelector('#video');
```

```
navigator.webkitGetUserMedia({video: true, audio: true},
    function(localMediaStream) {
        video.src = window.URL.createObjectURL(localMediaStream);
        video.onloadedmetadata = function(e) {
            // ... video is loaded ...
        };
    },
    function(e) {
        console.log('Error:', e);
    }
);

};
```

The first callback function receives a MediaStream object, which is converted to an object URL and then set as the <video> element's src property. A handler for the onloaded metadata event is also set, but it doesn't do anything in the example.

The second callback (third argument) to navigator.webkitGetUserMedia is an error callback.

After navigator.webkitGetUserMedia completes, video appears in the larger image, as shown in Figure 6-12.

Following is the code for the button and its handler, also in the window.onload function:

```
var maxWidth = 300;

function capture() {
    var canvas = document.createElement('canvas');
    canvas.width = maxWidth;
    canvas.height = video.videoHeight * maxWidth / video.videoWidth;
    canvas.getContext('2d').drawImage(video, 0, 0, canvas.width, canvas.height);
    var data = canvas.toDataURL('image/png');
    img.setAttribute('src', data);
}

document.querySelector('#shutter').onclick = capture;
```

Because the captured image can't be directly set into an <img> element, it's first drawn into a canvas (see "HTML5 Canvas" on page 142) and then a data URL extracted from that canvas is set as the src property of the <img> element. That makes the still appear in the window (see Figure 6-12).

Bluetooth, USB, and Serial APIs

Chrome provides APIs for connecting to three kinds of external devices: Bluetooth, USB, and serial. The APIs supply functionality to discover which devices are available and to open them in some sense, but the actual data sent back and forth is device-specific. This is similar to the situation with data files: the APIs handle discovering what's there, opening a connection, and transmitting data, but the actual data depends on the file: JPEG, Excel spreadsheet, some sort of calendar, or whatever. Chrome APIs don't help with the data itself, only with the plumbing.

There are too many APIs, too many devices, and too many complications to discuss in depth here, so I'll just explain some basic Bluetooth operations, and if you want to deal with these hardware devices, you can consult the relevant documentation pages for `chrome.bluetooth` (*http://bit.ly/bluetooth_api*), `chrome.bluetoothLowEnergy` (*http://bit.ly/bluetoothLowEnergy*), `chrome.bluetoothSocket` (*http://bit.ly/bluetooth Socket*), `chrome.usb` (*http://bit.ly/usb_api*), and `chrome.serial` (*http://bit.ly/seri al_api*).

To use Bluetooth, you include a `bluetooth` section in your *manifest.json* file; there are no permissions:

```
{
    ...
    "bluetooth": {
        "uuids": [ "1105", "1106" ],
        "socket": true
    }
}
```

The `uuids` are numbers that identify Bluetooth profiles that the app will be using. Profiles are specific data formats that are defined as part of various Bluetooth standards. This example specifies two, although it doesn't do any actual data communication, as we'll see.

The *background.js* is the usual one that just opens a window. The *index.html* has a Discover button and a text area for results, and it also has some CSS for buttons that the JavaScript will add dynamically:

```
<!DOCTYPE html>
<html lang="en">
<head>
    <meta charset="utf-8" />
    <title>Bluetooth</title>
    <script src="bluetooth.js"></script>
    <style>
        .device {
            display: block;
            margin-top: 5px;
        }
    </style>
</head>
<body>
    <button id="discover">Discover</button>
    <p>
        <textarea id="textarea" cols="55" rows="20" readonly
          style='outline: none;'></textarea>
```

```
    </p>
  </body>
</html>
```

The app in *bluetooth.js* first queries for all existing device connections with the
`chrome.bluetooth.getDevices` API:

```
chrome.bluetooth.getDevices(callback)
```

The example makes this call and then shows the devices in the window as a series of
buttons:

```
window.onload = function () {

chrome.bluetooth.getDevices(
    function(devices) {
        devices.forEach(updateDeviceName);
    }
);

function updateDeviceName(device) {
    log('\nadded: ' + device.name);
    console.log(device);
    var b = document.createElement('button');
    b.className = 'device';
    b.innerText = 'Connect to ' + device.name;
    b.device = device;
    b.onclick = function (e) {
        connectTo(e.srcElement.device);
    };
    document.body.appendChild(b);
};

function log(msg) {
    var m = (typeof(msg) == 'object') ? JSON.stringify(msg) : msg;
    console.log(m);
    document.querySelector("#textarea").value += m + '\n';
}

};
```

You can see these buttons in Figure 6-13. I'll show the `connectTo` function a bit later.

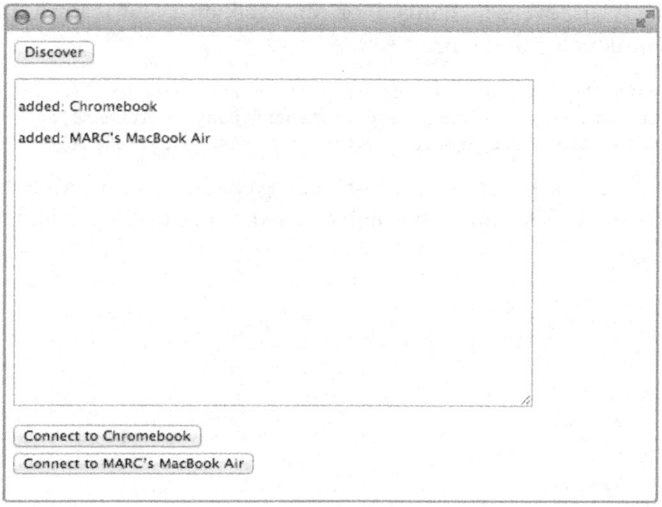

Figure 6-13. Initial list of devices with connection buttons

If a device is subsequently activated somehow for Bluetooth (the details are up to the device and the OS), the app can discover them by using chrome.bluetooth.startDiscovery:

```
chrome.bluetooth.startDiscovery(callback)
```

Because discovery uses a lot of resources, it's important to stop it at some point with chrome.bluetooth.stopDiscovery:

```
chrome.bluetooth.stopDiscovery(callback)
```

The example calls chrome.bluetooth.startDiscovery when you click the Discover button, and then it calls chrome.bluetooth.stopDiscovery 30 seconds later:

```
document.querySelector("#discover").onclick = function () {
    chrome.bluetooth.startDiscovery(
        function() {
            log('\ndiscovery started');
            // Stop discovery after 30 seconds.
            setTimeout(
                function() {
                    chrome.bluetooth.stopDiscovery(function() {});
                    log('\ndiscovery stopped');
                },
                30000
            );
        }
    );
};
```

When a device is discovered, changed, or removed, an event is fired. Here's the code that sets up handlers for these three events.

```
chrome.bluetooth.onDeviceAdded.addListener(updateDeviceName);
chrome.bluetooth.onDeviceChanged.addListener(updateDeviceName);
chrome.bluetooth.onDeviceRemoved.addListener(removeDeviceName);
```

The `updateDeviceName` function in the preceding example is what added the button for a device. Figure 6-14 shows an additional device that was discovered after the Discover button was clicked.

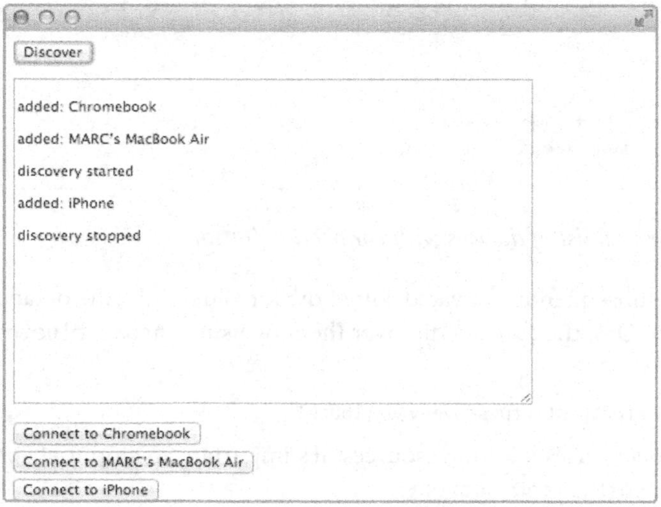

Figure 6-14. The list of devices after clicking the Discover button

The `removeDeviceName` function removes the corresponding button (the device connection itself has already been removed):

```
function removeDeviceName(device) {
    log('\ndeleted: ' + device.name);
    for (var d of document.body.children) {
        if (d.className === 'device' && d.device.address === device.address)
            document.body.removeChild(d);
    }
}
```

That's really all this example can do. Here's the `connectTo` function that acts as the button `onclick` handler, which creates a Bluetooth socket:

```
function connectTo(device) {
    var uuid = '1106';
    var onConnectedCallback = function() {
```

```
        if (chrome.runtime.lastError) {
            console.log("Connection failed: " +
                chrome.runtime.lastError.message, device.name);
        }
        else {
            console.log('Connected OK');
            // ... use connection as defined by profile ...
        }
    };

    chrome.bluetoothSocket.create(
        function(createInfo) {
            console.log(createInfo);
            // ... should save createInfo.socketId ...
            chrome.bluetoothSocket.connect(createInfo.socketId,
                device.address, uuid, onConnectedCallback);
        }
    );
}
```

Attempting to connect results in an error, because I made no serious attempt to determine the correct profile for any of the devices, much less implement that profile. That's work for a Bluetooth expert, but at least you have some idea of how things operate from the Chrome API perspective.

Internationalization and Localization

Internationalization is designing your application so that it's reasonably easy to configure it for a specific language and/or culture. The configuration job is called *localization*. Because both words are hard to type and pronounce, they're often abbreviated by the count of their interior letters: i18n and l10n.

Internationalization mostly involves three kinds of information that varies depending on language and culture:

- Strings
- Dates and times
- Numbers, including currency and percentages

Localization is mostly translating the strings from the language of the developer to some other language. After you have internationalized dates and numbers, localization is automatic and doesn't require any human creativity and decision making.

To the extent possible, it's generally a good idea to globalize your user interface so as to reduce the amount of localization. For example, if you represent a date as 2014-06-12, users around the world will know what you mean. If you instead represent it as "June 12, 2014", you will need to internationalize and then localize the month name. The same goes for the horrible choice 6/12/2014. (Even if you show it as 12/6/2014 for European users, you still have problems, for how are they to know that you've localized it?)

Another example of globalization is using icons instead of words to represent actions, although even then you have to make sure that the icons are globally meaningful.

(As you already know, outside of this section, I haven't internationalized any of my examples, because that would make the source code harder to follow.)

Internationalizing and Localizing Strings

Most systems for internationalizing and localizing strings, including the Chrome App system, work like this:

- In the code, each literal string is replaced by a key into a dictionary of strings.
- There's one dictionary per supported language, identified by a language identifier such as en, de, or es.
- At runtime, the effective language is chosen by the user or from a system-wide setting.
- Localizing for a specific language involves taking an existing dictionary, usually the one that the developer created, and translating the strings to create a new dictionary.

For Chrome Apps, you get a localized string with the call:

```
chrome.i18n.getMessage("messagename")
```

In this example, *messagename* is the key. In the manifest and CSS files, you refer to an internationalized string with the notation MSG_*messagename*. You can't use that notation in HTML files—you have to modify strings with JavaScript, as I'm about to show.

A language dictionary, which must be named *messages.json*, is coded in JSON as in this example, for English (locale en):

```
{
  "hello": {
    "message": "Hello",
    "description": "The word 'Hello', to appear in the main window."
  },
  "goodbye": {
    "message": "Goodbye",
    "description": "The word 'Goodbye', to appear in the main window."
  }
}
```

For each key, there's a message property that supplies the localized string, and an optional description that's an aid to the translator.

Here's the corresponding Spanish dictionary:

```
{
  "hello": {
    "message": "Hola",
    "description": "The word 'Hello', to appear in the main window."
  },
  "goodbye": {
    "message": "Adiós",
    "description": "The word 'Goodbye', to appear in the main window."
  }
}
```

The text needs to be in UTF-8, so make sure you're using a text editor that supports that encoding.

You put each *messages.json* in a folder named for its locale (*en*, *es*, and so on), and you put the local folders in a folder named *_locales*, as shown in Figure 6-15.

Figure 6-15. Source files set up for I18N

You have to add a `default_locale` property to the manifest, like this:

```
{
    "app": {
        "background": {
            "scripts": ["background.js"]
        }
    },
    "manifest_version": 2,
    "name": "I18N",
    "version": "1.0.0",
    "default_locale": "en"
}
```

The *background.js* file in the example is the usual one that just opens a window. Here's the *index.html* file:

```
<!DOCTYPE html>
<html lang="en">
<head>
    <meta charset="utf-8" />
    <title>I18N</title>
```

```
        <script src="i18n.js"></script>
    </head>
    <body>
        <h1 id=hello_phrase>[hello goes here]</h1>
        <h1 id=goodbye_phrase>[goodbye goes here]</h1>
    </body>
</html>
```

What actually appears at runtime is determined by the JavaScript in *i18n.js*:

```
window.onload = function () {
    document.querySelector("#hello_phrase").innerHTML =
        chrome.i18n.getMessage("hello");
    document.querySelector("#goodbye_phrase").innerHTML =
        chrome.i18n.getMessage("goodbye");
}
```

So, assuming that the computer's locale is set to English, when the app is first launched you see what's shown in Figure 6-16.

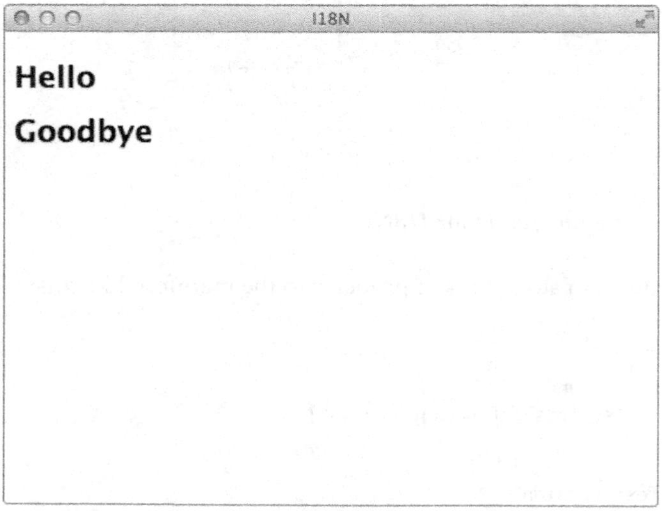

Figure 6-16. An app localized for English

If you then set your computer's locale to Spanish (how you do that varies with your operating system), relaunch Chrome, and then launch the app, you get what's shown in Figure 6-17.

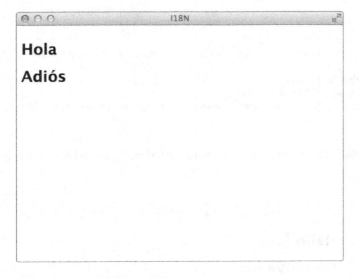

Figure 6-17. An app localized for Spanish

In practice, here's how you should internationalize strings:

- Create *messages.json* files for two locales as you develop the app, so that you can test that the internationalization mechanism works.

- Choose your native locale (English, for me) for one of them and code the strings as they should appear in that locale.

- Pick any other locale for the other *messages.json* file. If you know that language, go ahead and enter the strings. If not, put in bogus strings for testing (as I'll show in a bit).

- As you develop the user interface, switch locales occasionally to ensure that strings are being handled properly.

- To localize the app, give the dictionary you developed in your native language to the translator, and then place the *messages.json* file that he or she produces into the proper folder. Then, provide a test version of the app to the translator so that he or she can verify that the translation went as expected.

- Unfortunately, most people will be unable to translate a JSON file without making a few errors that mess up the JSON notation, so you'll likely need to fix the files that you get back.

Because I know only one language, here's an ersatz German dictionary I might use during development:

```
{
  "hello": {
    "message": "Hello [de]",
    "description": "The word 'Hello', to appear in the main window."
  },
  "goodbye": {
    "message": "Goodbye [de]",
    "description": "The word 'Goodbye', to appear in the main window."
  }
}
```

Changing the locale to de results in what's shown in Figure 6-18, which is good enough for testing.

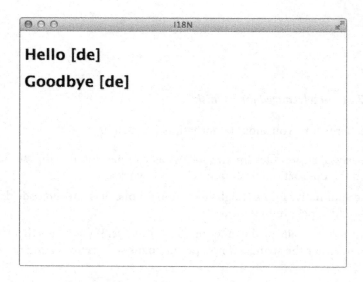

Figure 6-18. An app localized for ersatz German

There are a few more features of the i18n API that I didn't cover here; if you'd like more information, see the chrome.i18n documentation (*http://bit.ly/i18n_api*) for the full treatment.

Internationalizing Numbers

Numbers can be handled with ECMAScript (what standard JavaScript is called) facilities, not unique to Chrome Apps. I'll give the highlights here, and you can read all the details at the ECMAScript Internationalization API (*http://bit.ly/internationaliza tion_api*).

Countries vary in whether they use commas to group digits and a period to mark the decimal point, or vice versa. The simplest way to format a decimal number for the current locale is to construct a `Number` object and call its `toLocaleString` method, like this:

```
var num = new Number(1234.56);
var s = num.toLocaleString();
```

You can also explicitly choose the locale with an argument to `toLocaleString`:

```
function decimalNumbers() {
    var num = new Number(1234.56);
    console.log("Decimal format, user's language:", num.toLocaleString());
    console.log("Decimal format, German:", num.toLocaleString("de"));
}
```

Figure 6-19 illustrates what appears on the console.

```
Decimal format, user's language: 1,234.56
Decimal format, German: 1.234,56
```

Figure 6-19. A number localized for English and German

For currency, `toLocaleString` takes a second argument that indicates the currency. For the current locale, you need to supply an explicit argument. You can get the current locale by using `navigator.language` (see also Figure 6-20):

```
function currencyNumbers() {
    var lang = navigator.language;
    var num = new Number(1234.56);
    console.log("Currency format, pound sterling, user's language:",
      num.toLocaleString(lang, {style: "currency", currency: "GBP"}));
    console.log("Currency format, pound sterling, German:",
      num.toLocaleString("de", {style: "currency", currency: "GBP"}));
}
```

```
Currency format, pound sterling, user's language: £1,234.56
Currency format, pound sterling, German: 1.234,56 £
```

Figure 6-20. A number in pounds sterling localized for English and German

You can also handle percent (see also Figure 6-21):

```
function percentNumbers() {
    var lang = navigator.language;
    var num = new Number(1234.56);
    console.log("Percent format, user's language:",
      num.toLocaleString(lang, {style: "percent"}));
    console.log("Percent format, German:",
      num.toLocaleString("de", {style: "percent"}));
}
```

```
Percent format, user's language: 123,456%
Percent format, German: 123.456 %
```

Figure 6-21. Percentage localized for English and German

Internationalizing Dates

There are only a couple of ways to represent numbers in any locale ($1234.56 or $1,234.56, for US English), but there are numerous ways to represent dates: 6/12/14, 6/12/2014, June 12 2014, 12-June-2014, 2014-06-12, 2014 June 12, 12 June 2014, and 2014-June-12 are all the same date. Add time, and it gets worse: you can have 12-hour or 24-hour time, with various forms of A.M./P.M. notations, a time zone expressed as letters (for example, MST) or a time offset, and so on.

So, even without any attempt at localization, dates and times are messy. With localization, they're messier.

You can handle dates, like numbers, by using ECMAScript standard facilities. You can go to the ECMAScript Internationalization API documentation (*http://bit.ly/interna tionalization_api*) for more detail than I'll present here.

At first, things seem easy—all you do is the following:

```
var d = new Date("2014-06-12");
console.log("Local time, user's language:", d.toLocaleString(lang));
console.log("Local time, German:", d.toLocaleString("de"));
```

Figure 6-22 reveals what you get.

```
Local time, user's language: 6/11/2014 6:00:00 PM
Local time, German: 11.6.2014 18:00:00
```

Figure 6-22. A date localized in default format for English and German

There are three problems here:

- A time is shown even though none was specified.
- The ambiguous format MM/DD/YYYY or DD.MM.YYYY is used, even though I have my computer set to use the format YYYY-MM-DD. It seems that Chrome ignores the computer's date-format setting.
- The date seems to be wrong!

The seemingly wrong date was caused by `2014-06-12` being interpreted as `2014-06-12T00:00:00-00:00` (midnight, UTC) and then being translated to Mountain Daylight Time, which moves it six hours backward to 6 P.M. on 11-June-2013.

You can solve the shifting-date problem easily by passing a time-zone option to toLo
caleString, one of several options it takes as its second argument. The principal ones
are listed in Table 6-1.

Table 6-1. toLocaleString options

Option	Values
timeZone	UTC or an IANA time-zone name (see iana.org/time-zones), such as America/Denver or Europe/Bucharest
hour12	Whether to use 12-hour time; true or false
weekday	narrow, short, long
era	narrow, short, long
year	numeric, 2-digit
month	numeric, 2-digit, narrow, short, long
day	numeric, 2-digit
hour	numeric, 2-digit
minute	numeric, 2-digit
second	numeric, 2-digit
timeZone Name	short, long

Because the options are properties of an object, you can't specify the order. For instance:

```
{year: "numeric", month: "numeric", day: "numeric"}
```

and:

```
{year: "numeric", day: "numeric", month: "numeric"}
```

are the same.

Here are some examples:

```
var d = new Date("2014-06-12T12:00:00-00:00");
var options1 = {
    year: "numeric",
    month: "long",
    day: "numeric"
};
console.log("Local date, user's language:", d.toLocaleString(lang, options1));
console.log("Local date, German:", d.toLocaleString("de", options1));
var options2 = {
    year: "numeric",
    month: "short",
```

```
    day: "numeric",
    hour: "2-digit",
    minute: "2-digit",
    second: "2-digit",
    timeZone: "America/Denver",
    timeZoneName: "short"
};
console.log("Local date, user's language:", d.toLocaleString(lang, options2));
console.log("Local date, German:", d.toLocaleString("de", options2));
```

The console output is shown in Figure 6-23.

```
Local date, user's language: June 12, 2014
Local date, German: 12. Juni 2014
Local date, user's language: Jun 12, 2014 6:00:00 AM MDT
Local date, German: 12. Jun 2014 06:00:00 GMT-06:00
```

Figure 6-23. Example dates localized for English and German

Here's a function to provide a date in the global YYYY-MM-DD format without using
toLocaleString at all. Note that the Date methods it does call all return results in the
local time zone:

```
function getDateLocal(d) {
    return d.getFullYear() + "-" + (101 + d.getMonth()).toString().slice(-2) +
        "-" + (100 + d.getDate()).toString().slice(-2);
}

var d = new Date("2014-06-12T12:00:00-00:00");
console.log("Local date, YYYY-MM-DD:", getDateLocal(d));
```

Figure 6-24 displays the output.

```
Local date, YYYY-MM-DD: 2014-06-12
```

Figure 6-24. A date in global format

I like to write dates in the form DD-MMM-YYYY, where MMM is the month in English,
because it's a little more readable to most people than the YYYY-MM-DD format, and
because there's no ambiguity. Even though I write the month name in English, most
people can recognize at least month names in English, even if they're not fluent speakers.

Following is a function to return the local date with a spelled-out month, localized by
the computer, even though I don't know the month names in any language but my own:

```
function getDateLocalLongMonth(d, lang) {
    if (!lang)
        lang = navigator.language;
    var month = d.toLocaleString(lang, {month: "long"});
```

```
      return d.getDate().toString() + "-" + month + "-" + d.getFullYear();
}

var d = new Date("2014-06-12T12:00:00-00:00");
console.log("Local date, DD-MMM-YYYY:", getDateLocalLongMonth(d));
console.log("Local date, German, DD-MMM-YYYY:", getDateLocalLongMonth(d, "de"));
```

Figure 6-25 depicts the resulting output.

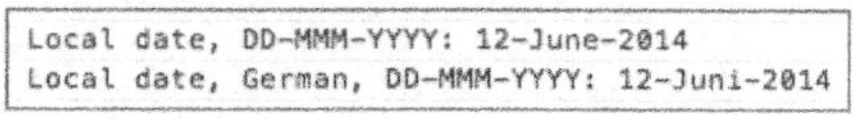

```
Local date, DD-MMM-YYYY: 12-June-2014
Local date, German, DD-MMM-YYYY: 12-Juni-2014
```

Figure 6-25. A date with month localized for English and German

Chapter Summary

This final chapter included a bunch of miscellaneous APIs for alarms, context menus, location, text-to-speech, system queries, the camera, hardware interfaces (Bluetooth, USB, and serial), and internationalization.

Modal Dialogs

As is pointed out in Chapter 1, you can't call the usual JavaScript `alert` and `confirm` dialogs in a Chrome App (they're undefined). But, with the new HTML5 `<dialog>` tag, it's easy to build modal dialogs using only standard HTML, CSS, and JavaScript.

Before Chrome 37 introduced the `<dialog>` tag, the way to implement a dialog was to define a `<div>` element in HTML that completely covered the window, both disabling all user-interface components in the window (making the dialog modal) and partially obscuring the window, making it look disabled. Then, the dialog itself was shown in front with any user-interface components it needed. Now, this complexity is unnecessary. Figure A-1 shows the example app we'll use in this appendix.

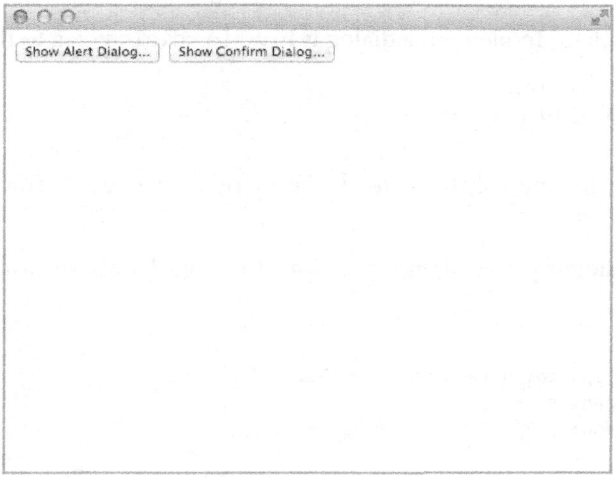

Figure A-1. The app's initial window with two buttons

Clicking the button on the left displays an alert dialog, as illustrated in Figure A-2.

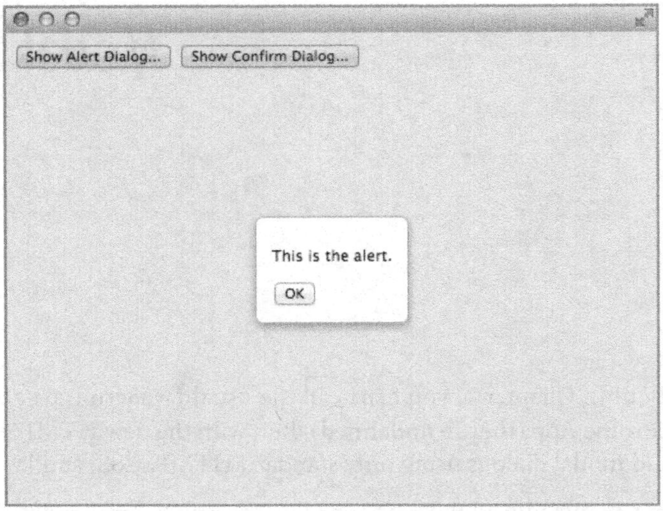

Figure A-2. An alert dialog

Clicking anywhere outside the dialog does nothing. Clicking the OK button dismisses the dialog and restores the original screen. Then, clicking the right button at the top pops up the confirm dialog in Figure A-3.

Clicking Yes shows the alert in Figure A-4. Clicking No shows an analogous alert.

All you need to do to implement a dialog is to add a `<dialog>` tag to the body:

```
<dialog id="dlg-dialog">
    <!-- dialog UI goes here -->
</dialog>
```

You show the dialog modally by using the JavaScript `showModal` method and dismiss it with `close`.

By default, a dialog is pretty plain. The more attractive dialogs shown in the examples use this CSS:

```
#dlg-dialog {
    border: 1px solid rgba(0, 0, 0, 0.3);
    border-radius: 6px;
    box-shadow: 0 3px 7px rgba(0, 0, 0, 0.3);
}
```

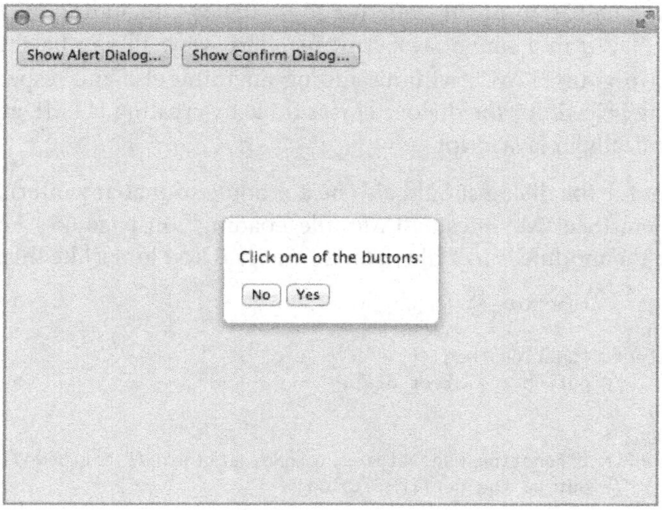

Figure A-3. The confirm dialog

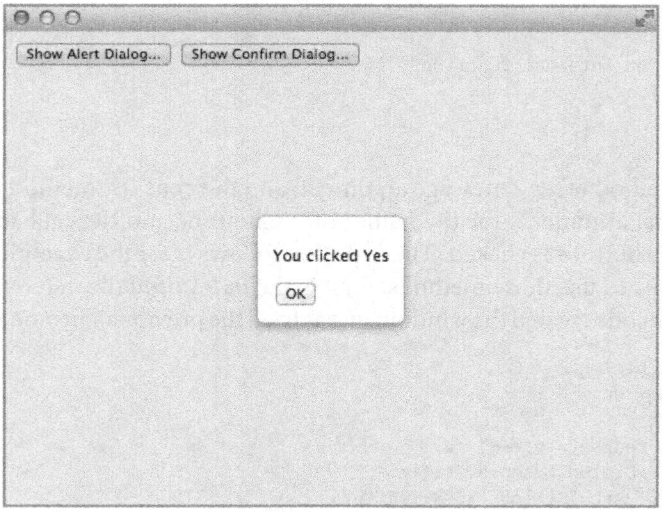

Figure A-4. Alert dialog after clicking the Yes button

The method that's called to show the dialog adds additional HTML within the <dia
log> element, which is what displayed the messages and buttons in the previous examples. We're going to see that soon.

It's most convenient if all of the code for these dialogs, including HTML, CSS, and JavaScript, is placed in a single JavaScript file. That way, all you have to do is add a `<script>` tag to your HTML, without adding anything else and, especially, without actually adding HTML for the dialog. This is done by creating HTML and CSS for the dialogs dynamically in JavaScript.

The JavaScript for the dialog should also be a module so that any internal functions it uses are hidden. (See "Modules and Module Loading" on page 86.) For dialogs, the JavaScript for the module is in a file named *Dialogs.js* and looks like this:

```
var Dialogs = (function () {
    return {
        alert: function (msg) {
            // put up the alert dialog
        },

        confirm: function(msg, btnYes, btnNo, actionYes, actionNo) {
            // put up the confirm dialog
        }
    }

    function internal_function1() {
        // ...
    }

    function internal_function2() {
        // ...
    }
})();
```

The `alert` method takes a message argument, and the `confirm` method takes that and four additional arguments for the names of the buttons and the callback functions if either of those buttons is clicked. The code that follows is for the example program and shows you how to use those methods. First is the *index.html* file, referenced when the *background.js* code created the window, just as in all the previous Chrome App examples:

```
<!DOCTYPE html>
<html lang="en">
<head>
    <meta charset="utf-8" />
    <title>Dialog Example</title>
    <script src="Dialogs.js"></script>
    <script src="DialogExample.js"></script>
</head>
<body>
    <button id="alert">Show Alert Dialog...</button>
    <button id="confirm">Show Confirm Dialog...</button>
</body>
</html>
```

Observe the `<script>` reference to *Dialogs.js*, which contains the `Dialogs` module. We'll get to that shortly.

Here's the example program in *DialogExample.js*:

```
window.onload = function () {
    document.querySelector("#alert").addEventListener("click",
        function () {
            Dialogs.alert("This is the alert.");
        }
    );
    document.querySelector("#confirm").addEventListener("click",
        function () {
            Dialogs.confirm("Click one of the buttons:", "Yes", "No",
                function () {
                    Dialogs.alert("You clicked Yes");
                },
                function () {
                    Dialogs.alert("You clicked No");
                }
            );
        }
    );
};
```

Of interest here are the calls to the two methods, `Dialogs.alert` and `Dialogs.confirm`, and the two callbacks for the latter, which also call `Dialogs.alert`.

Now, going back to the module in *Dialogs.js*, it has an internal function that adds the needed HTML and CSS to the body:

```
function setup() {
    if (!document.querySelector("#dlg-dialog")) {
        dlg = document.createElement("dialog");
        dlg.id = 'dlg-dialog';
        document.body.appendChild(dlg);
        var css = document.createElement("style");
        css.type = "text/css";
        css.innerHTML =
            "#dlg-dialog {" +
            "    border: 1px solid rgba(0, 0, 0, 0.3);" +
            "    border-radius: 6px;" +
            "    box-shadow: 0 3px 7px rgba(0, 0, 0, 0.3);" +
            "}";
        document.body.appendChild(css);
    }
}
```

The code is a little hard to follow, but if you study it, you'll see that all it does is add the HTML and CSS we saw previously to the `document`. It first tests to see if it's already added, so it's set up only once.

Here is the method for `alert`, which was sketched in the preceding module example:

```
alert: function (msg) {
    dialog("<p>" + msg + "</p><button id='dlg-close'>OK</button>",
        [
            {
                id: 'dlg-close'
            }
        ]
    );
},
```

This method calls the internal `dialog` function with two arguments:

- HTML for the dialog, which in this case is the message with a button underneath it

- An array with an element for each button, each of which consists of the `id` for that button and an action, the default being to simply close the dialog

The method for `confirm` is a little more involved because it has two buttons and actions:

```
confirm: function(msg, btnYes, btnNo, actionYes, actionNo) {
    dialog(
        "<p>" + msg + "</p><button id='dlg-no'>" + btnNo + "</button>" +
        "<button id='dlg-yes'>" + btnYes + "</button>",
        [
            {
                id: "dlg-no",
                action: actionNo
            },
            {
                id: "dlg-yes",
                action: actionYes
            }
        ]
    );
}
```

Here's the internal `dialog` function that does most of the work:

```
function dialog(html, actions) {
    setup();
    dlg.innerHTML = html;
    dlg.showModal();
    var funcs = [];
    for (var i = 0; i < actions.length; i++) {
        funcs[i] = (function(index) {
            return function() { // index bound here instead to function dialog
                dlg.close();
                if (actions[index].action)
                    actions[index].action();
            }
```

```
        })(i);
        document.getElementById(actions[i].id).addEventListener("click", funcs[i]);
    }
}
```

The first three lines are straightforward: they call setup to add the HTML and CSS if they're not already added, set the supplied HTML (the first argument to dialog) as the inner HTML for the dialog, and then show it modally.

The tricky part is setting up handlers for the buttons, each handler stored as an element of the funcs array. The obvious way to do that is like this:

```
for (var i = 0; i < actions.length; i++) {
    document.getElementById(actions[i].id).addEventListener("click",
        function () {
            dlg.close();
            if (actions[i].action) // i is bound to function dialog
                actions[i].action();
        }
    );
}
```

But, this won't work because (as the comment indicates) the variable i is bound to the dialog function, not to the event-handling function. Its value when the event handler is called will be whatever the for loop set it to when it terminated (perhaps 3). To fix this problem, you must call a function to set each element of func to the event-handler function, which gets the index bound to that intermediate function, unique to each button, instead of to the outer dialog function. That's what's done in the dialog function. (This is a trick you'll want to use whenever you're having this sort of function-closure problem.)

After dialog is implemented, you can add any number of customized methods in addition to alert and confirm.

Registering Chrome Apps with Google

Before a Chrome App can access Google APIs, you must register it with Google. Registration is documented by Google (*http://bit.ly/app_identity*) (read the "User Authentication" section), but as of October 2014, the Google Developers Console user interface has been updated, and the step-by-step instructions are out whack with what the website does. What follows here works as of this writing, but be warned that it might change again by the time you read it.

Registering a Chrome App and Getting a Client ID

To register your Chrome App and obtain a client ID, you need to do the following:

1. Go to the Google Developers Console (*http://bit.ly/developers_console*).
2. Click the Create Project button. In the New Project window that opens, type the project name and then click the Create button, as shown in Figure B-1.

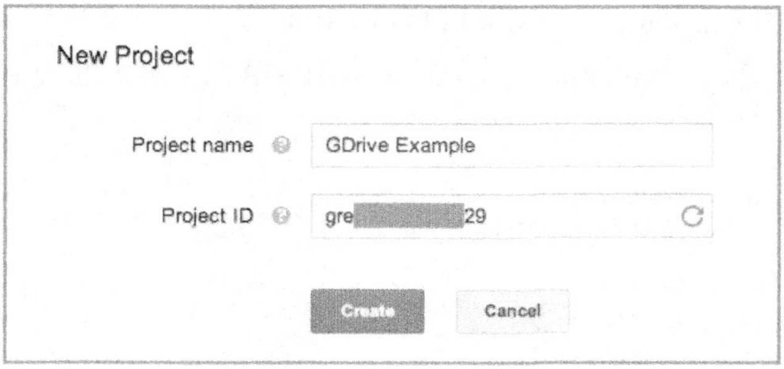

Figure B-1. Creating a new project

3. In the Developers Console, in the "APIs & auth" section, click APIs and turn on any APIs your app needs. For the example in "Accessing Google APIs" on page 106, this would be Drive API, as shown in Figure B-2. (A few others are also enabled by default.)

Figure B-2. Enabling the Drive API

4. Again, in the "APIs & auth" section, click Credentials and then click CREATE NEW CLIENT ID under OAuth. In the dialog box that opens, click the "Installed application" radio button and then Chrome Application. Enter the app ID and click Create Client ID, as shown in Figure B-3. (See "Fixing the App ID" on page 230 to see how to establish a fixed app ID.)

5. The client ID displays, as shown in Figure B-4.

6. Copy the client ID and update your manifest with OAuth2 client ID and scopes:

```
{
    "app": {
        "background": {
            "scripts": [ "background.js" ]
        }
    },
    "manifest_version": 2,
    "name": "GDrive",
    "version": "1.0.0",
    "permissions": [
        "identity"
    ],
```

```
        "key": "MIIBIjANB...yyltEwIDAQAB",
        "oauth2": {
            "client_id": "2546277...3kj.apps.googleusercontent.com",
            "scopes": [
                "https://www.googleapis.com/auth/drive"
            ]
        }
    }
```

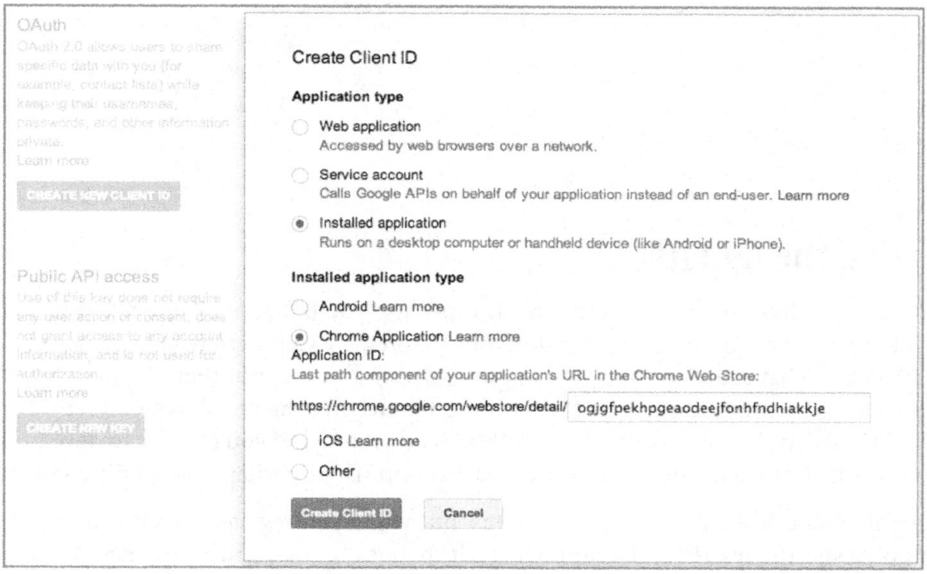

Figure B-3. Creating a client ID

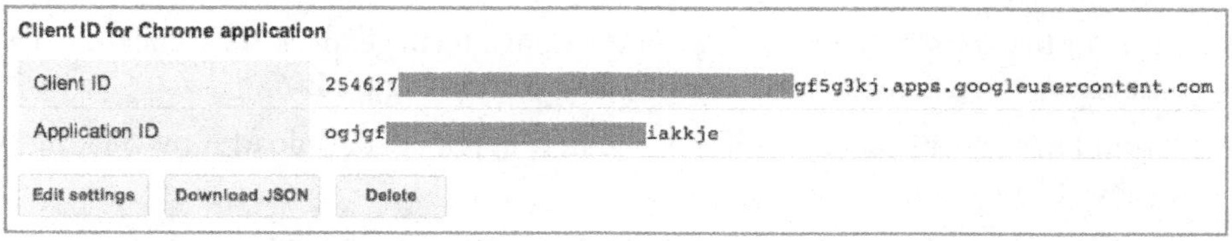

Figure B-4. New client ID is displayed

7. On the first call to `chrome.identity.getAuthToken` (see "Accessing Google APIs" on page 106), you are asked to confirm the permissions, as shown in Figure B-5.

Figure B-5. Authorizing the app

Fixing the App ID

Generally, while you're developing a Chrome App you'll load it in unpacked form by clicking the "Load unpacked extension" button on the Extensions page, as described in Chapter 1. That causes an app ID to be assigned to the app, but then if you install the app, either by dropping a .crx file onto the Extensions page or downloading it from the Chrome Web Store, a different app ID will be assigned. If you go back to developing the app as unpacked, you might get the earlier app ID, or perhaps even a different one.

Usually you don't care what the app ID is, but when you register an app, you need to supply a specific app ID, and it's annoying if it changes because you have to keep updating the app's registration and getting a new client ID. It's much easier to fix the app ID so that it never changes during development.

Here's what you do:

1. Early in the app's development, on the Extensions page, pack it by clicking "Pack extension," which generates a .crx file, as shown in Figure B-6.

2. If you have an unpacked version of the new app loaded, unload it by clicking the trashcan icon.

3. Install the packed extension by dragging the .crx file to the Extensions page. Verify that the app is installed and runs by clicking its "launch" link on the Extensions page. (It may no longer be at the top of the page, so scroll down until you find it.)

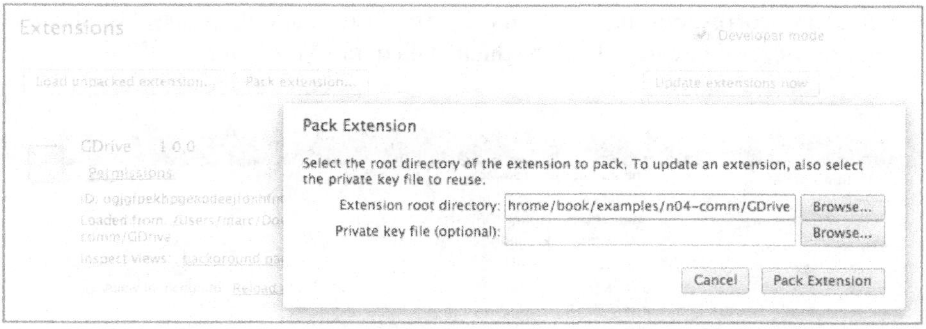

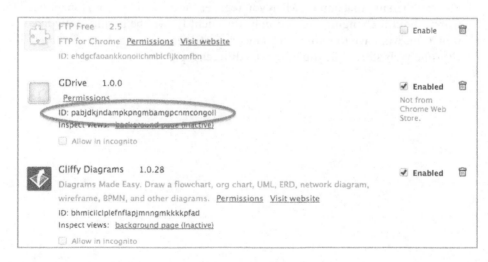

Figure B-6. Packing a Chrome App

4. Find the *manifest.json* file stored inside Chrome (not the one you used for development). Begin by using the Mac Finder, Windows Explorer, or whatever your system offers to navigate to the user data directory. Instructions for finding it are at the Chromium Project's User Data Directory page (*http://bit.ly/user_data_directory*). For example, on Mac OS X it's at *~/Library/Application Support/Google/Chrome/Default*, and on Windows Vista, 7, or 8 it's at *C:\Users\<user>\AppData\Local\Google\Chrome\User Data\Default*, where *<user>* is your username.

5. On the Extensions page, find the app ID, as shown in Figure B-7.

Figure B-7. Getting the app ID from the Extensions page

6. Find the corresponding directory in the user data directory, as shown in Figure B-8, and navigate down to the installed *manifest.json* file.

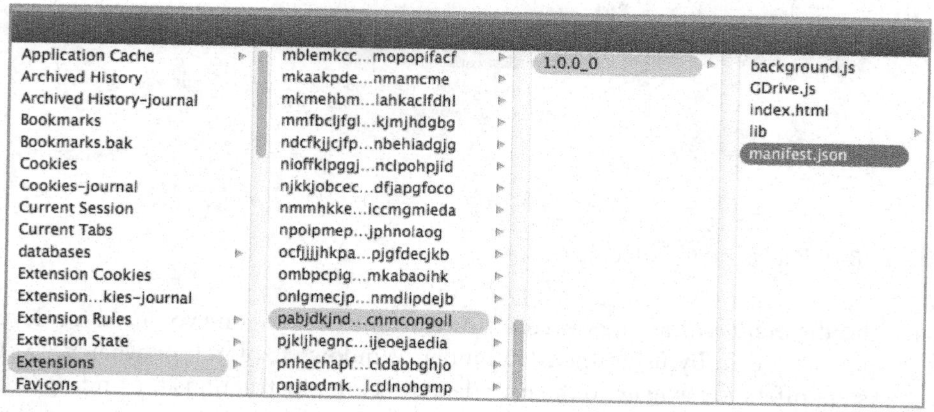

Figure B-8. Finding the manifest.json file in the installed App folder

7. Copy the key property from the installed manifest and paste it into the *manifest.json* file in your development source. With the key in place there, Chrome will always use the same app ID, whether the app is loaded as unpacked or installed. You can then use that app ID when you register the app, and you no longer need to worry about it changing. Accordingly, the client ID will be permanently fixed, as well. (You will have to remove the key property before you upload the app to the Chrome Web Store, and you may get a different app ID then.)

Using Google Cloud Messaging

"Google Cloud Messaging" on page 114 explains how to code a Chrome App to receive messages from Google Cloud Messaging (GCM). You can see the overall architecture in Figure 4-10. This appendix explains how to set up a GCM project, how to code an example app server to communicate with GCM, and how to send GCM messages from Amazon Simple Notification Service. Nothing here is particular to Chrome Apps; everything would work equally well with Android apps or any other app using GCM.

Setting Up a GCM Project

1. Go to the Google Developers Console (*http://bit.ly/developers_console*). You'll need a Google account if you don't already have one, but as of this writing, you don't need to establish billing.

2. Click the Create Project button. In the New Project window that opens, type the project name and then click the Create button, as shown in Figure C-1.

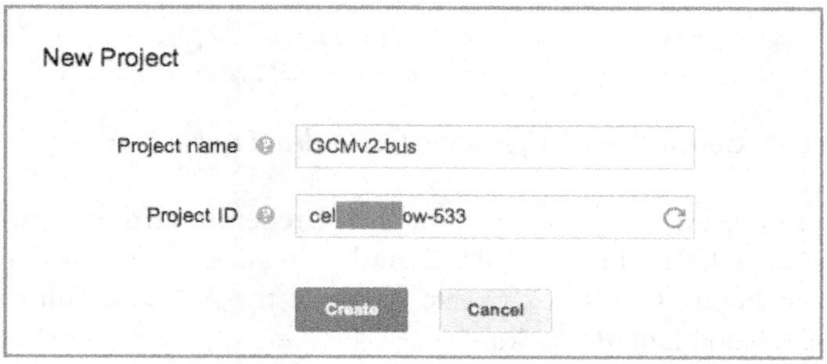

Figure C-1. Creating a new project

3. After a pause, the window will refresh to show the project number (see Figure C-2), which you should copy and paste into the *background.js* file of the Chrome App so that it can be passed to `chrome.gcm.register` as the sender ID (the code is shown in "Example Client" on page 116). (For Android and other apps, you would do things differently, but you'll still need the registration ID.)

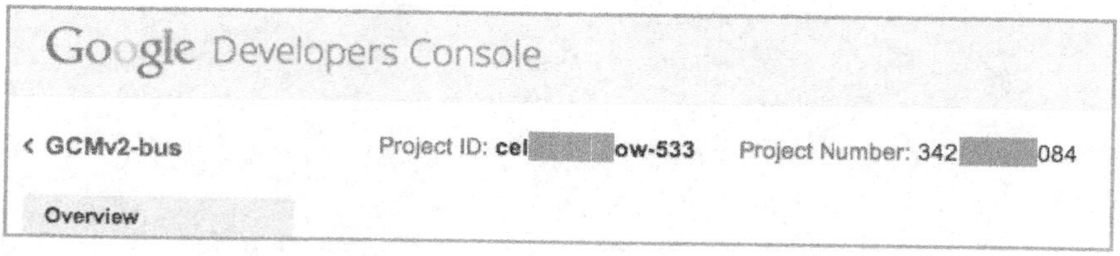

Figure C-2. The project number for the new app

4. In the "APIs & auth" section, click APIs and then turn on Google Cloud Messaging for Android (Figure C-3). *Do not turn on Google Cloud Messaging for Chrome*; that is for the older `chrome.pushMessaging` API. Some other APIs will be turned on, as well, as shown in Figure C-3, but that's OK.

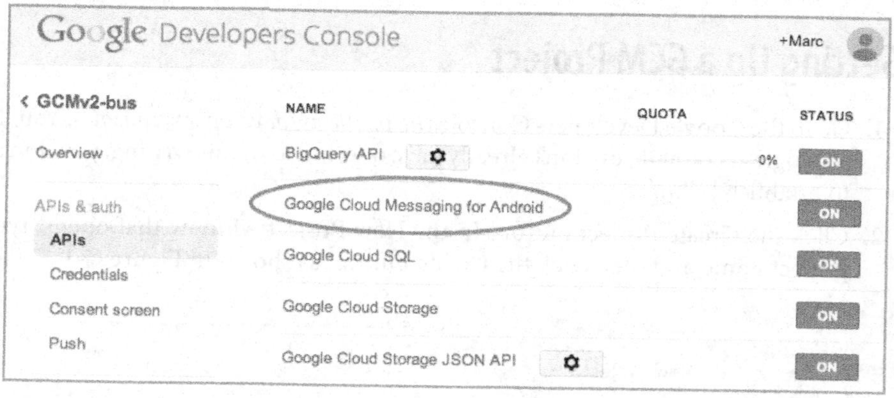

Figure C-3. Google Cloud Messaging for Android turned on

5. Again, in the "APIs & auth" section, click Credentials. In the "Public API access" section, click CREATE NEW PAGE and then click "Server key" to get the dialog shown in Figure C-4. Click Create to create the API key. You can leave the IP-addresses field blank if you want.

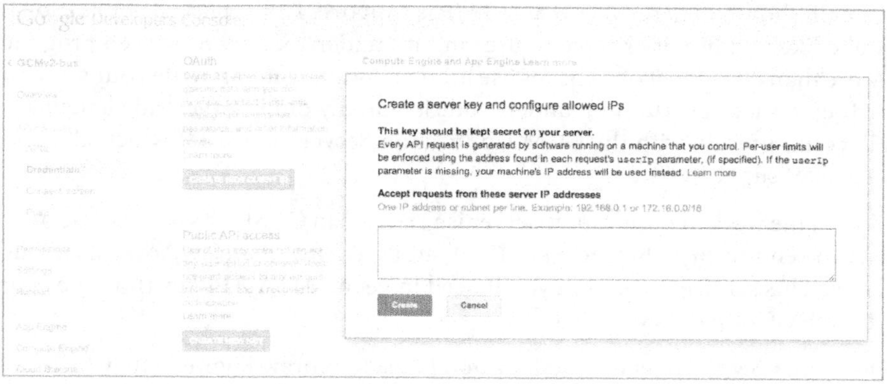

Figure C-4. Creating a server key (API key)

6. Copy the displayed API key (see Figure C-5) and paste it into the server script shown in "Example App Server" on page 235 (or whatever server app you've developed). The app server will need this to communicate with the GCM Connection Server.

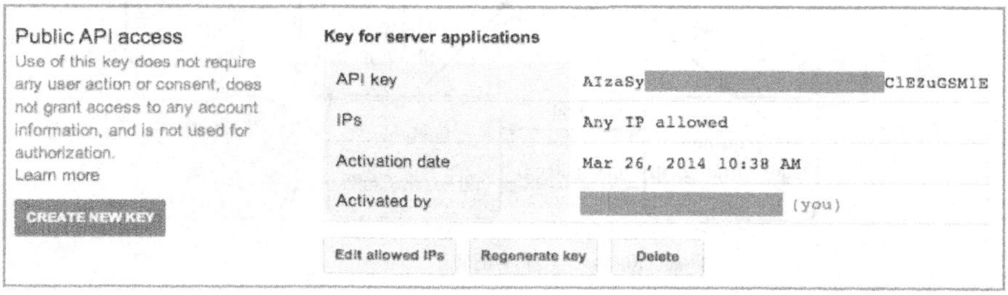

Figure C-5. The API key

This completes the app and project registration with the Google Developers Console, because all you need is the project number (with Google Cloud Messaging for Android turned on) and the API key.

Example App Server

There are several ways to communicate with the GCM Connection Server to send a message, all of them described at *developer.android.com/google/gcm*. (As of March 2014, this page refers only to Android, not to Chrome Apps, but what's said there does apply to the chrome.gcm API discussed in "Google Cloud Messaging" on page 114.)

Here I'll show a PHP script, because PHP is supported by almost all application servers you're likely to use, it's simple to use, and it's understood by most web programmers. (More than 80 percent of websites use it.) If you want, you can write your server in Java, Python, JavaScript (running under Node.js), or any other server-side language. It will still communicate with the GCM Connection Server via HTTP, which all server-side languages support.

Most of the work in the example server isn't related to GCM—it's to get some interesting data to send to the Chrome App. For that, it accesses the New York MTA Bus Time server. This service is free, but you'll need to get an MTA API key (not to be confused with the GCM API key).

There are now *three* servers, so it's a good idea to redraw Figure 4-10, which I've done in Figure C-6, to show that the app server communicates with the MTA Bus Time server to get bus statuses.

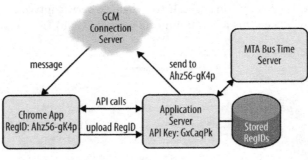

Figure C-6. Our example Application Server communicates with two other servers

I won't go into the MTA Bus Time API, of course, except to say that you can get the status of the bus stop at 5th Avenue and 46/47th Street (stop 400516) by using this HTTP query (spread across two lines for readability):

```
http://api.prod.obanyc.com/api/siri/stop-monitoring.json
?key=<MTA_KEY>&MonitoringRef=400516
```

The result comes back as a complex object (converted from JSON to a PHP object, as we'll see), which you have to study to find the relevant data—in this case, only the buses within one stop of 46/47th Street. (As all New Yorkers know, 5th Avenue is one-way south, so all buses go the same direction.)

After data is extracted from the returned object, a typical status message looks like this:

```
12:45:50 -- M4 at stop; M4 1 stop away@5 AV/WEST 47 - 46 ST
```

That message is then sent to the GCM Connection Server, also via HTTP, as we're about to see.

Recall from "Google Cloud Messaging" on page 114 that a Chrome App that wants to receive GCM messages must send its registration ID to the server. The server, in *gcmv2-bus.php*, checks for the presence of a regID query parameter and, if it's nonempty, saves the registration ID in the *regID-bus.data* file. If the parameter is missing, the server begins broadcasting status messages. Here's the first part of the PHP code:

```php
define('REG_ID_FILE', 'regID-bus.data');
define('API_KEY', 'AIzaSy...CaqPk');
define('MTA_KEY', '91474b6...3f95');

$url = "http://api.prod.obanyc.com/api/siri/stop-monitoring.json?key=" .
  MTA_KEY . "&MonitoringRef=400516";

if (!empty($_REQUEST['regid']))
    store_regID($_REQUEST['regid']);
else
    broadcast();

function get_regIDs() {
    if (file_exists(REG_ID_FILE))
        return unserialize(file_get_contents(REG_ID_FILE));
    return array();
}

function store_regID($regID) {
    $a = get_regIDs();
    $a[$regID] = 1;
    file_put_contents(REG_ID_FILE, serialize($a));
}
```

If you don't know PHP, the details aren't important, but you do need to know that the get_regIDs function returns an array of registration IDs to which messages are to be sent.

The broadcast function queries the MTA Bus Time server every 15 seconds:

```php
function broadcast() {
    $num_sent = 0;
    for ($n = 0; $n < 20; ) {
        $regIDs = '';
        foreach (get_regIDs() as $k => $v)
            $regIDs .= ',"' . $k . '"';
        $regIDs = substr($regIDs, 1);
        if (send_message(API_KEY, $regIDs))
            $n++;
        sleep(15);
    }
}
```

It gets a fresh array of registration IDs each time, too, in case a client registered while it was looping. (Such registration would invoke a different execution of the script, but I didn't bother programming any locks to prevent simultaneous access to the file of registration IDs.) The code at the start of the for loop assembles the registration IDs into a comma-separated list, which is what send_message needs, something like this:

```
"APA91bHSH-NzFPIZvl15B",
"APA91bFxX-lplMoOtpuNw",
"APA91bGNU-yNCMkeK1PQu"
```

 In working out this example server, I somehow got a couple of server instances running on the server computer with no way to kill them because they were running on a shared host on which I have very limited permissions. That's why the app is designed to terminate after 20 statuses are sent; a real server would keep running until it's terminated, perhaps with a separate management utility, but that's overkill for a book example.

Here's the send_message function, which does one query of the MTA Bus Time server and sends the message to the GCM Connection Server, but only if the message is non-empty (there is a bus within one stop) and it's different from the last message sent:

```php
function send_message($apiKey, $regIDs)
{
    global $url;
    global $prev;

    $response = send_request(false, $url,
      array("Content-Type: application/json"));
    $x = json_decode($response);
    $sd = $x->Siri->ServiceDelivery;
    $rt = $sd->ResponseTimestamp;
    $msv = $sd->StopMonitoringDelivery[0]->MonitoredStopVisit;
    $s = '';
    foreach ($msv as $k => $v) {
        $mvj = $v->MonitoredVehicleJourney;
        $dist = $mvj->MonitoredCall->Extensions->Distances->PresentableDistance;
        $stopName = $mvj->MonitoredCall->StopPointName;
        switch ($dist) {
        case 'at stop':
        case 'approaching':
        case '1 stop away':
            $s .= "; {$mvj->PublishedLineName} {$dist}";
        }
    }
    if (!empty($s) && $s != $prev) {
        $prev = $s;
        $msg = substr($rt, 11, 8) . " -- " . substr($s, 2) . "@$stopName";
        echo "<hr>$msg";
```

```
        $data = <<<EOT
            {
                "data": {
                    "message": "$msg"
                },
                "registration_ids": [$regIDs],
                "delay_while_idle": true,
                "time_to_live": 600
            }
    EOT;
        send_request(true, "https://android.googleapis.com/gcm/send",
            array("Content-Type: application/json", "Authorization: key=$apiKey"),
            $data);
    }
}
```

Expressions such as $mvj->MonitoredCall->StopPointName in the code refer to sub-objects within the object returned by the MTA Bus Time server. (It took me an hour or so of playing around to figure out where the data was that I wanted.) If the status is to be sent (!empty($s) && $s != $prev), it's prefixed with the time, suffixed with the stop name, and then sent to the GCM Connection Server as part of a data object that also includes the array of registration IDs.

Finally, send_request uses cURL to send HTTP requests by using GET or POST:

```
function send_request($post, $url, $headers, $postText = null) {
    $ch = curl_init();
    curl_setopt($ch, CURLOPT_HTTPHEADER, $headers);
    curl_setopt($ch, CURLOPT_URL, $url);
    curl_setopt($ch, CURLOPT_POST, $post);
    curl_setopt($ch, CURLOPT_RETURNTRANSFER, true);
    if ($postText)
        curl_setopt($ch, CURLOPT_POSTFIELDS, $postText);
    $response = curl_exec($ch);
    curl_close($ch);
    return $response;
}
```

For uploading registration IDs, this PHP file is executed from the Chrome App's *background.js* page, as we saw in "Example Client" on page 116:

```
function sendRegistrationID(registrationID) {
    // Should use https
    Ajax.ajaxSend("http://basepath.com/servers/gcmv2-bus.php?regid=" +
        registrationID, 'json',
        function (status, response) {
            if (status == 200)
                chrome.storage.local.set(
                    {
                        registered: true
                    }
                );
```

```
        else
            console.log('Error sending registrationID');
    }
  );
}
```

For broadcasting, I just executed the server from a web browser, as shown in Figure C-7. That's OK for an example, but for a real application you'd want to start the app server directly from the web server, perhaps by using cron.

Figure C-7. Starting the app server from a browser

Using Amazon Simple Notification Service

If you just want to test a GCM-receiving Chrome App without going to the trouble of developing an app server, you can send messages directly with Amazon Simple Notification Service (SNS). (Interestingly, as of this writing Google doesn't have a similar feature.) Here's what you do:

1. If you don't already have one, set up an Amazon Web Services (AWS) account at *aws.amazon.com* (*http://aws.amazon.com/*). You might need to establish a billing account, but the cost for sending a few messages is either free or only pennies, so don't worry about it.

2. Go to the SNS console (*http://bit.ly/sns_console*) and click the "Add a New App" menu item. Give the app a name (see Figure C-8), choose GCM as the Push Platform, and enter the GCM API key that you got from the Google Developers Console (not from Amazon).

3. When the app is created, click the Add Endpoints button and enter the registration ID from a Chrome App, as shown in Figure C-9.

 There's probably an API for uploading the registration ID directly from the Chrome App, but I didn't bother. I just copied it from the *regID-bus.data* used by the PHP app server and pasted it into the SNS dialog. Or, you could use console.log to display it from the Chrome App and copy it from there. Note that SNS refers to the registration ID as a Device Token.

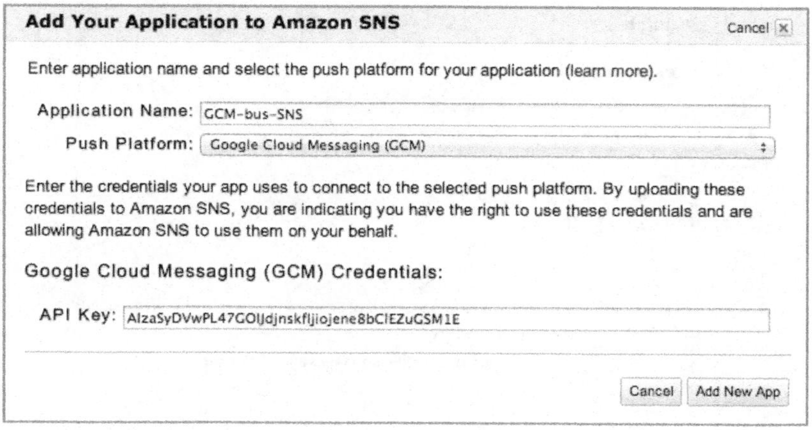

Figure C-8. Creating a new SNS app

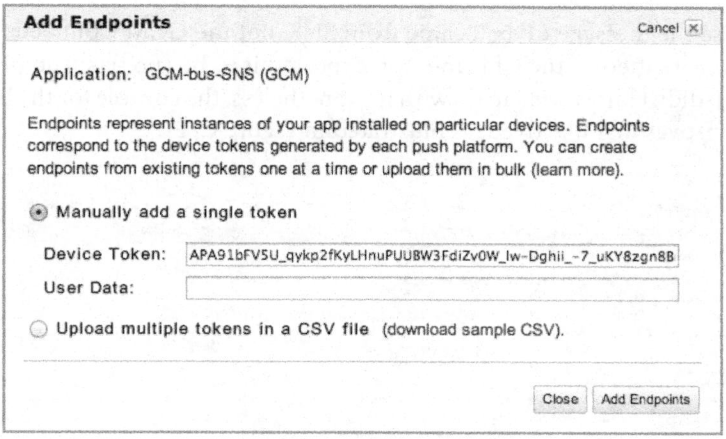

Figure C-9. Creating an SNS endpoint

4. After the endpoint is created, check it and click the Publish under Endpoint Actions menu item. Type a message, as demonstrated in Figure C-10, and click the Publish Message button to send the message.

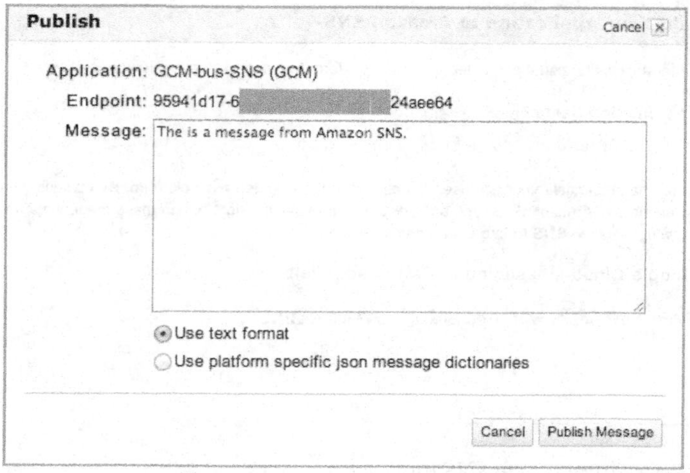

Figure C-10. Publishing a message with SNS

5. Because the message I typed came from SNS, not the GCM Connection Server, it wasn't formatted as the Chrome App expected it to be (no `message` property), so the app didn't know what to do with it. Nonetheless, the console for the background script proves that it arrived, as illustrated in Figure C-11.

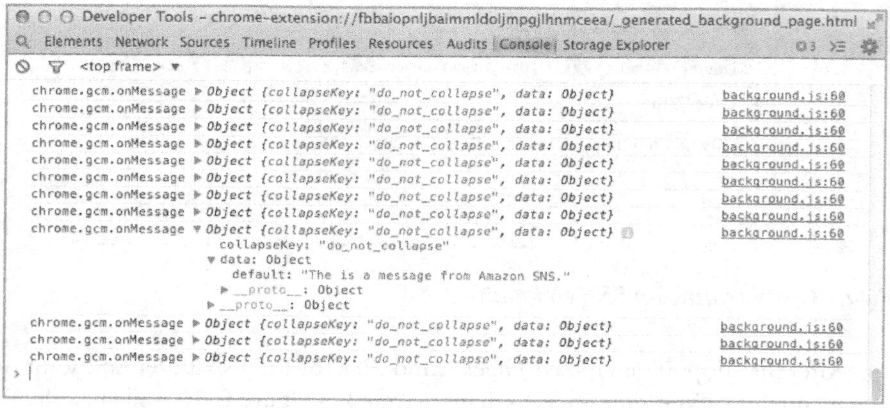

Figure C-11. Console log from Chrome App showing a message

Using Cordova to Build Chrome Apps for Mobile Devices

Apache Cordova is a layer of software that provides HTML and JavaScript support so that an app written using those technologies can run under a native operating system. Of course, any modern browser can do that already, but Cordova provides the wrapping in the form of a native app, so the user who installs and uses it sees it as a native app.

Google's Augmentation of Cordova

Google has added plug-ins to Cordova that implement the Chrome APIs, as shown in Figure D-1.

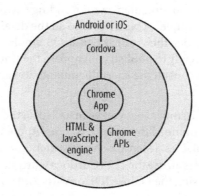

Figure D-1. Cordova layers

Not all APIs are supported, although support is widening as time goes on. To see the current state of affairs, check the Mobile Chrome Apps page (*http://bit.ly/mobile_chrome_apps*) and the list of supported APIs (*http://bit.ly/apis_and_libraries*).

Even though Cordova runs your app on Android or iOS, you can't call any native Android or iOS APIs if you still want your app to run on Chrome—you can use only Chrome and HTML APIs.

Development Tools and Debugging for Cordova

Mobile devices ranging from phones to fairly large tablets have two important differences relative to desktop or laptop computers that will affect your user interface design:

- The screen is usually smaller—for phones, much smaller. You need a layout that works on all screen sizes, or you can use CSS to implement a so-called "responsive" interface that adapts to the screen size. There's lots of information on the web about how to do that; just search for "responsive css" to find it.

- Users usually operate the interface with their relatively large fingertips instead of a precise mouse pointer. So, buttons and other controls must be accordingly bigger. You can handle that with responsive CSS too, if you want, or just make the controls big on all devices.

The other major issue with Cordova is that not all the Chrome APIs are implemented, as I already mentioned.

Creating and Testing Cordova Chrome Apps

Because Google's tools and documentation for building Chrome Apps for Cordova are very new and somewhat complex, I won't go into all the details here, but I will sketch it out in general. Testing under the Android and iOS emulators is easy, but things get complicated when you're ready to publish your app on the stores (Google Play or Apple's App Store), so you should consult the latest documentation at the Mobile Chrome Apps website.

The following discussion assumes that you've installed all the Android and/or iOS Cordova tools, including, if you need them, Java, Xcode (Apple's developer tools), and the Android and/or iOS emulators. (Step-by-step instructions are on the Mobile Chrome Apps website.) My examples all use the cca (Cordova Chrome App) command-line tool. You can also develop by using the Eclipse IDE or with Android Studio, but I won't show examples of those approaches.

To construct a Cordova app, you begin with a Chrome App built to run under Chrome. That is, at a minimum it has a manifest, a background page, an HTML page, and a JavaScript file all in an app folder, as we've already seen in several examples.

Next, you run this command in a terminal window or shell to construct the Cordova app:

```
cca create <mobile-app-folder> --link-to=<app-folder>
```

In this example, *<mobile-app-folder>* is the name of the folder to be created to hold the mobile app, and *<app-folder>* is a path to the existing app folder. The cca command creates a new folder named *<mobile-app-folder>* that contains code for the native app, and also a subfolder named *www* that links to the existing *<app-folder>*. That way Chrome-targeted code and the Cordova-targeted code are shared, and any changes to one are reflected in the other.

For example, suppose that you have an app folder named *Hello* that implements a Chrome App that runs in Chrome. You would change to its parent folder and run cca create, getting something like this:

```
$ cca create Hello-mobile --link-to=Hello
cca v0.0.3
## Checking that tools are installed
Android SDK detected.
Xcode detected.
Searching for Chrome app source in /Users/marc/examples/02-developing/cca/Hello
## Creating Your Application
create Hello-mobile Hello Hello
Writing config.xml
Changing directory to: /Users/marc/examples/02-developing/cca/Hello-mobile
platform add ios
platform add android
plugin add org.apache.cordova.file
plugin add org.apache.cordova.inappbrowser
plugin add org.apache.cordova.network-information
plugin add org.apache.cordova.keyboard
plugin add org.apache.cordova.statusbar
plugin add org.chromium.navigation
plugin add org.chromium.bootstrap
plugin add org.chromium.i18n
plugin add org.chromium.polyfill.CustomEvent
plugin add org.chromium.polyfill.xhr_features
plugin add org.chromium.polyfill.blob_constructor
prepare
Done!

Your project has been created, with the following symlink:
/Users/marc/examples/02-developing/cca/Hello-mobile/www -->
/Users/marc/examples/02-developing/cca/Hello

Remember to run +cca prepare+ after making changes
(full instructions: http://goo.gl/iCaCFG).
$
```

This gets you more than 600 files in dozens of subfolders of *Hello-mobile* that provide Android and iOS native apps for the Chrome App, including lots of Java (for Android) and Objective-C code (for iOS). You don't need to know what those files do or mess with them in any way. Your Chrome App source code is in there, too, but because its folder is linked to the app folder you already have, you can work there, as you've already been doing.

To run the Cordova app on an emulator, you change to the Cordova folder, *Hello-mobile* in this case, and execute either:

    cca emulate android

or:

    cca emulate ios

Either command will open the corresponding emulator in which you can test your app, as shown in Figure D-2.

Figure D-2. An app running on Android and iOS emulators

After you make changes to the app, you update the generated Cordova wrapper with the following:

```
cca prepare
```

You then test it again by using the `cca emulate` command.

Debugging Cordova Apps

Because Cordova doesn't yet have anything as powerful as Developer Tools for Chrome, it's best to do as much debugging as possible under Chrome before you build and test the app for a mobile platform.

You can at least see the console log when you're testing on the Android emulator. With the emulator running, execute the following:

```
adb -e logcat -v time chromium:V *:S
```

The `-v time` part puts the time onto the log, and the `chromium:V *:S` part filters the log so that you see only lines pertaining to Chromium.

I haven't located any instructions for viewing the log when you're using the iOS emulator, but perhaps they'll be available by the time you read this.

Publishing Cordova Chrome Apps

You publish Android-targeted Chrome Apps on Google Play, and iOS-targeted apps on the Apple App Store. Both require that you first create developer accounts. Without getting too much into the details—which are still evolving as I write this—for both platforms you first create a release package with one of these two commands:

```
cca build android --release
cca build ios --release
```

Then, you take the resulting build and submit it to the store using the procedures established by Google and/or Apple.

For an iOS app, you'll probably want your own splash screen, which is shown briefly while the app launches. You can replace the default splash screens with your own. The `cca create` command places them in the *platforms/ios/<app>/Resources/splash* folder, where *<app>* is the name that appeared in the manifest. For example, these are the files that were supplied when I created the Hello app that we saw earlier:

```
Default-568h@2x~iphone.png
Default-Landscape@2x~ipad.png
Default-Landscape~ipad.png
Default-Portrait@2x~ipad.png
Default-Portrait~ipad.png
Default@2x~iphone.png
Default~iphone.png
```

If you're curious, *Default-Landscape~ipad.png* is in Figure D-3.

Figure D-3. The default iPad landscape splash screen

Testing Using the Chrome Dev Editor

The Chrome Dev Editor (introduced in "Using the Chrome Dev Editor" on page 6) makes it especially easy to test mobile apps on Android, because it bypasses all of the tedious cca steps described earlier in this appendix. (It may also support iOS someday.)

First, you need to install the Chrome App Developer Tool for Mobile (CADT) on your Android device. As of this writing, it's not available on Google Play, but you can get it from the CADT repository on GitHub (*http://bit.ly/cadt_repo*). To install it, follow the "Using a Pre-Built Binary" installation instructions on that page. However, if you access the page from your Android device, the APK will install directly; it's not necessary (or possible) to run the adb command as the instructions say.

Connect your Android device to the computer that's running the Chrome Dev Editor (USB is easiest) and start the CADT. Then, from the Chrome Dev Editor menu, choose Deploy to Mobile; you should see your app running on your Android device.

It's not possible to produce an APK file with the Chrome Dev Editor or with the CADT, so they're just for testing. To publish your application, you must create the APK using the steps presented in "Publishing Cordova Chrome Apps" on page 247.

Index

We'd like to hear your suggestions for improving our indexes. Send email to index@oreilly.com.

About the Author

Marc Rochkind has an MS in computer science (Rutgers, 1976) and worked for Bell Labs from 1970 to 1982, much of that time on parts of Unix, especially the Source Code Control System, for which he is well known. His 1985 book, *Advanced UNIX Programming*, was the first book that explained how to program the Unix kernel. Since leaving Bell Labs in 1982, Marc has had several management and nonmanagement positions in various software companies and done lots of consulting. In 1988, he started a venture-capital–backed company, XVT Software, that provided tools to enable programmers to develop portable GUI applications—the first such tool. Later, he was the vice president of software at two venture-capital–backed companies, one that produced an employee-scheduling product, and the other with an online-knowledge-base product.

He has written three computer-related books: *Expert PHP and MySQL: Application Design and Development* (Apress, 2013); *Advanced UNIX Programming, First* and *Second Edition* (Prentice Hall, 1985; Addison-Wesley, 2004); and *Advanced C Programming for Displays* (Prentice-Hall, 1988). He's also written one novel, *Bernie's Bar & Girll*.

Currently, Marc develops iOS, Mac OS, Windows, and Chrome apps (listed at *basepath.com*); does some consulting; and writes books.

Colophon

The animal on the cover of *Programming Chrome Apps* is a crested screamer. The crested screamer or southern screamer (*Chauna torquata*) lives in wetlands, estuaries, and swamps in Peru, Bolivia, Paraguay, Brazil, Uruguay, and Argentina. This big bird weighs up to 11 pounds and can measure up to 3 feet long.

The crested screamer is a nonmigratory bird that flocks in large groups. A couple will be monogamous, either seasonally or, more typically, for life. Both parents build a nest near water where they lay two to seven eggs in a clutch and incubate them together for 43 to 46 days. The fledging period for a young bird lasts 8 to 14 weeks.

The crested screamer's call is reported to be audible from a distance of up to two miles, a quality that gives this bird its name. It has air sacs under its skin that are believed to keep it warm. The birds' unappetizing flavor and texture make them infrequent prey. Bony spurs of up to two inches in length on mature birds are located on the inner side of each wing; single males are known to use them to vie successfully for females, and both sexes use them to protect their territory and win fights with other couples.

Many of the animals on O'Reilly covers are endangered; all of them are important to the world. To learn more about how you can help, go to *animals.oreilly.com*.

The cover image is from Wood's *Illustrated Natural History*. The cover fonts are URW Typewriter and Guardian Sans. The text font is Adobe Minion Pro; the heading font is Adobe Myriad Condensed; and the code font is Dalton Maag's Ubuntu Mono.

Have it your way.

Get even more for your money.

Join the O'Reilly Community, and register the O'Reilly books you own. It's free, and you'll get:

- $4.99 ebook upgrade offer
- 40% upgrade offer on O'Reilly print books
- Membership discounts on books and events
- Free lifetime updates to ebooks and videos
- Multiple ebook formats, DRM FREE
- Participation in the O'Reilly community
- Newsletters
- Account management
- 100% Satisfaction Guarantee

Signing up is easy:

1. Go to: oreilly.com/go/register
2. Create an O'Reilly login.
3. Provide your address.
4. Register your books.

Note: English-language books only

To order books online:
oreilly.com/store

For questions about products or an order:
orders@oreilly.com

To sign up to get topic-specific email announcements and/or news about upcoming books, conferences, special offers, and new technologies:
elists@oreilly.com

For technical questions about book content:
booktech@oreilly.com

To submit new book proposals to our editors:
proposals@oreilly.com

O'Reilly books are available in multiple DRM-free ebook formats. For more information:
oreilly.com/ebooks